Ka Mate
Travels in New Zealand

Dan Coxon

Copyright © 2011 Dan Coxon
All rights reserved.
ISBN: 1466334142
ISBN-13: 978-146633414

For Hannah,
as always

CONTENTS

1.	*Tamaki-makau-rau (Auckland)*	1
2.	*Paihia - Waitangi*	15
3.	*Te Tai Tokerau (Northland)*	32
4.	*Te Ika a Maui (North Island)*	47
5.	*Te Whanganui-a-Tara (Wellington)*	60
6.	*Wairarapa*	85
7.	*Ahuriri (Napier)*	98
8.	*Taupo - Rotorua*	109
9.	*Te Paeroa-o-Toi (Coromandel Peninsula)*	132
10.	*Waitomo*	145
11.	*Otautahi (Christchurch)*	168
12.	*Hakaroa (Akaroa) - Te Whakatakaka O Te Ngarehu O Ahi Tamatea (Hanmer Springs)*	179
13.	*Kaikoura*	197
14.	*Wairau (Blenheim) – Whakatu (Nelson)*	214
15.	*Te Tai Tapu (Abel Tasman)*	227
16.	*Kaiteriteri - Mawhera (Greymouth)*	238
17.	*Ka Roimata o Hine-Hukatere (Franz Josef)*	250
18.	*Tahuna (Queenstown)*	263
19.	*Otepoti (Dunedin)*	272
20.	*Waihopai (Invercargill) – Te Anau*	283
21.	*Moeraki - Otautahi (Christchurch)*	295

A, ka mate! Ka mate!
Ka ora! Ka ora!
Ka mate! Ka mate!
Ka ora! Ka ora!
Tenei te tangata puhuruhuru
Nana nei i tiki mai whakawhiti te ra!
A, hupane! A, kaupane!
A, hupane! A, kaupane!
Whiti te ra!

> **The *Ka Mate!* haka, as performed by the New Zealand All Blacks rugby team**

1
Tamaki-makau-rau *(Auckland)*

'How you doing?'

The queue for passport control at Auckland International Airport was remarkably short, and when I reached the front of the line the girl behind the counter smiled at me, as if she could sense that this was my least favourite part of international travel. Luckily I recognised her greeting from previous trips to this part of the world, and resisted the urge to begin reciting all my problems and petty worries. This was my first visit to New Zealand, but when I'd travelled to Australia it had taken me almost two weeks to realise that the people there didn't actually have a lively interest in their fellow men, and that the question was simply another way of saying hello. Once I'd worked out the correct response it made me feel like a secret agent in a Seventies spy film. I had to reply with the right line of code, or risk being shot in the back down a dark alley.

'I'm good thanks. And you?'

'Yeah, I'm good.'

This password was obviously the main entry requirement for New Zealand, and she barely glanced at my passport before reaching for the rubber stamp.

'You've come here from Fiji then?'

I'd assumed at first glance that she was one of the local Maori people – the Polynesians who had inhabited the land they knew as Aotearoa before it was settled for a second time by Europeans in the eighteenth century – but it occurred to me as she sat with the stamp poised above my little red book that she could just as easily be from one of the Pacific Islands, possibly even Fiji. Having come from Europe myself it was unthinkable that friendliness was a character trait that an immigration official might possess, and it took me a few seconds to formulate a coherent answer.

'I've just had two weeks there. One on Viti Levu, then the last week out in the islands. I have to say I loved it, I might go again sometime.'

'Yeah, it's a special place, eh? And you're staying here for three months?'

'That's right.'

'Well have fun, won't you. You're gonna love it here, New Zealand's really neat. You going to the South Island?'

I explained that my plans were a little hazy, but that I definitely wanted to see both islands.

'You've gotta go to the South Island, it's so cool. You're gonna have a great time.'

She held the passport out to me across the desk, the formalities apparently finished with. It was only as I walked through to the baggage hall that I realised how much information she'd teased out of me during our short conversation, and how well she'd handled the exchange. As a first experience of the country it supported the stories I'd heard about Kiwi hospitality. I'd only been on their soil for five minutes, and already I felt at home.

Like most of us, I had a preconceived idea of New Zealand. When asked to summarise the country in a few simple words I'm sure many of us would mention Australia, as if the two were still linked by their joint history of misguided colonization. It doesn't help that most of us can't

Ka Mate

tell one national flag from the other, or, indeed, that some Australians can't either. The movie fans among us would almost certainly add that most of the *Lord Of The Rings* trilogy was filmed there, with a fleet of sci-fi nerds in the wings ready to back us up. We might mention the game of rugby too, as we know that the nation loves the sport with a passion. Finally, we might also mention the Maori people, that great warrior race who have lent the New Zealand All Blacks rugby team some of their ferocity with the traditional war dance known as the *haka*.

Oh, and sheep. New Zealand has lots of sheep. I think we all have a sneaking suspicion that the Kiwis eat lamb for breakfast, lunch and dinner, then perhaps go and sit in a field full of sheep to watch the sun set. If they're not too busy playing rugby, of course.

My luggage was surprisingly swift to appear on the carousel, another indication that things here might not be quite as European as they seemed, and then it was time for the ritual humiliation of the customs check. My normal experience of customs consisted of a quick scamper through the *Nothing To Declare* lane, my eyes firmly fixed on the trolley in front of me, but I'd bought several souvenirs while I was in Fiji, and the arrival documents stated that I had to declare them.

For once fortune was smiling on me. The *Nothing To Declare* line stretched for a good fifty feet, and then doubled back on itself for a further twenty. The *Goods To Declare* lane, by contrast, was entirely empty. I passed my arrival documents to the bored-looking official, who spared them a brief glance before signalling off to his left. For a fraction of a second I expected armed guards to rush me from both sides, then he handed my documents back.

'Join line two.'

I actually felt rather sorry for this official, encumbered as he was with a job that could easily be replaced by a random number generator, so I offered him what I hoped was a non-suspicious but disarming smile and hurried on my way. Line two consisted solely of an elderly gentleman with a rather battered suitcase, and before I knew it I was standing at the customs desk, facing two ladies wearing skin-tight rubber gloves. The taller of the two smiled at me, which was a rather disconcerting image when combined with the gloves, and she held her hand out for my documents.

'Lets see what you've got then. Just some wooden souvenirs from your travels, is it?'

I had the offending items isolated in a plastic bag, so I upended it over the desk and allowed them to spill out. Somehow the wooden mask, bead necklace and replica cannibal fork looked rather small and pathetic now they were exhibited in the open, and I felt embarrassed about wasting their time.

She lifted the mask and examined the obviously homemade *Treated Wood* stamp on the back, then she held out her other hand for the carrier bag.

'That's all fine. I'll put some tape round your bag for you so the boys know it's been checked. You here for long?'

I said that I was hoping to be in New Zealand for about three months.

'You'll be wanting to go to the South Island then. It's beautiful down there, eh?' She smiled and held out the bag, now sporting a twist of coloured tape across the top. 'Hope you enjoy your stay here. They say the weather's picking up, so you should have a good one.'

I smiled and nodded, struck dumb by the unabashed friendliness and good cheer exuded by the staff at Auckland Airport, and having felt less welcome in expensive hotels in Europe. As I walked through the gate onto New Zealand soil I couldn't help grinning – so far the omens were looking good.

* * *

Ka Mate

Once I'd settled into my hotel room the first job was to buy some food, so I reluctantly walked into the city centre with the mundane task of finding a grocery store. Auckland was subtly different from the cities back home, something that I was to grow used to over the following months as I travelled across New Zealand, although it took me a while to pinpoint the differences. The street racers revving the engines of their customised GM Holdens helped to underscore the change, but everything was slightly skewed, from the three-lane high street to the canopies that overhung every shop front. There was certainly no mistaking it for central London.

Thankfully the nearest grocery store, *New World*, supplied everything I needed to survive for the first few days, and it also managed the impressive feat of having more staff at the registers than people wanting to pay, ensuring that my shopping expedition was not only successful, but also surprisingly fast. I called for a taxi from the complementary phone in the foyer and waited outside in the sunshine for it to arrive.

When it pulled up in front of the store five minutes later I was amused to see from his permit that my driver was called William 48. It seemed that New Zealand was so incredibly progressive that they'd started to clone their taxi drivers. His shirt looked clean and freshly pressed, his moustache was neatly trimmed, and all in all William 48 would have put most other taxi drivers around the world to shame.

Once we'd ascertained that I was from England but that I now lived in the US, and that I'd only arrived in Auckland that afternoon, he quickly moved on to what was obviously the favourite topic of conversation in the North Island.

'So, will you be going down to the South Island while you're here?'

I was beginning to feel that I might as well pack my bags and leave tomorrow, as the Aucklanders obviously rated the other island more highly than their own patch of turf. Was it really that much better than the North Island?

William 48 shrugged. 'Life up here's pretty good, you know? But if we go on vacation in this country we tend to go down to the South Island. The scenery's just awesome, it'll take your breath away. You'll enjoy the North, but make sure you leave yourself plenty of time.'

I asked him where he headed for when he was down there.

'Queenstown, usually. It's not cheap, but it's worth it. You'll spend half your savings there, but you'll have the time of your life. The jetboating's great, and you can go skiing in the winter. Or, of course, there's the bungee.'

Ah, the bungee. I was wondering how long it would take someone to get around to that. New Zealand is now as famous for being the home of bungee as it is for anything else in its brief history. As soon as I'd mentioned that New Zealand was going to be my destination, I was asked one question: would I be going bungee jumping?

When I asked William 48 if the bungee was any good he shook his head. 'You'd never catch me doing anything like that, it'd probably kill me at my age. If you want to do it, though, this is the place to have a go. They'll even let you jump off the Sky Tower here if you want to, and if you've got a couple of hundred bucks to spare. You going to try it then?'

I said that I might I'd check it out first, before I signed my life away for the sake of a good story. Something at the back of my mind kept telling me that throwing yourself from a great height with a piece of elastic tied around your ankles wasn't a very smart idea.

William 48 dropped me off outside my hotel, and I eventually managed to manoeuvre my purchases into the elevator and up to my floor. Once it was all unpacked and in the cupboards I collapsed in a heap on the couch, the excitement of being in a new city failing to prop my eyes open. Sleep came remarkably easy.

* * *

The following morning was bright and warm, and I decided to wander up the hill away from the city centre. My route meandered through the lush greenery of the Auckland Domain, originally the site of a Maori fortified village but now used as a public reserve. Today it's dominated by the Auckland Museum: fronted by striking white columns, and with a wide green lawn stretching out before it, I couldn't help wondering if the White House had temporarily been relocated from D.C. Maybe I'd be shot as soon as I attempted to set foot inside. The signs at the edge of the lawn assured me that it was open to the public, however, so I decided to take my chances and set off across the grass towards the front door.

It was a good job that I did, for the Museum housed an impressive collection of exhibits. Such was the wealth of stone carvings, jade adzes, ceremonial cloaks and entire reconstructed dwellings that I found it surprisingly overwhelming, and very little actually sank in. As soon as I found something of interest I'd catch sight of something else from the corner of my eye, and my attention never settled on any one object for long, instead flitting from one place to another like an overexcited child opening presents on Christmas Day. I wasn't helped by the fact that the Maori words were entirely new to me, and at times they were terribly difficult to remember. Was that club I just looked at a *kotiate*, the same as this one? Or was it a *mehe*, like the one to the left? And what the hell was a *wahaika*?

It was while browsing the overpriced jade necklaces and cuddly sheep on offer in the gift shop that I saw the signs for the museum's Maori cultural performance, and I remembered the traditional *haka* that had drawn me to the country in the first place. As I bought my ticket from the front desk I was told that I would be summoned to the performance by a loud blast on a conch shell. I protested that I didn't know what a conch shell sounded like, but in the end it was remarkably easy to identify – unless, of course, someone had just brought an agitated elephant into the museum foyer. About forty of us gathered at the museum's entrance, in front of the man in the grass skirt who had blown the conch. I could see a few people considering making a comment on his attire, but they took one quick look at his well-muscled forearms and thought better of it.

The skirt-wearing Maori led us through into the main body of the museum, where we received an introductory speech before the performance began. When he mentioned the *haka* a murmur ran through the crowd, and it was clear that this was what we'd all come to see. We were told that we should on no account laugh or smile at the men performing the traditional war dance, as they took it very seriously, and anything other than polite attention was considered a grave insult. I doubted that I'd have much difficulty keeping from laughing, but I made a mental note just in case. With all those Maori weapons lying around it could get rather messy if they took my nervous smile the wrong way.

Before we were allowed to see the *haka*, though, we were treated to a variety of traditional songs, weapon demonstrations, and the occasional moment of vaudevillian humour. I was immediately struck by how similar the songs were to those I'd heard only a few weeks earlier in Fiji. There's a tendency to consider the Polynesians and the Maori as two entirely separate races, but in fact they share a common heritage. There are many different accounts of how and when the Polynesians first arrived in New Zealand, but there's certainly no doubt that they did arrive at some point, and that Maori culture developed from these Pacific roots.

Ka Mate

For some reason I hadn't expected the connection to be so immediately visible, and I began to wonder whether any of my other preconceived notions of the Maori were similarly misguided. I'd always assumed that the New Zealand rugby team's most prominent player, Jonah Lomu, was Maori, but I'd read in the newspaper earlier that morning that he was of Tongan heritage. Before I'd arrived in New Zealand I thought I knew who the Maori were, but it seemed that I actually knew very little.

The one thing that I'd been right about was the importance of the *haka*. The aggressive tribal dance was saved for the climax of their performance, and cameras began to flash as soon as the five warriors stepped forward to the front of the stage, slapping their legs and sticking their tongues out. I certainly felt no inclination to laugh as they chanted and stomped their way through the *Ka Mate haka*, but I was strangely transfixed by the performance. Even within the confines of the Auckland Museum there was something intimidating and aggressive about this ancient challenge, and my backside remained firmly rooted to my seat.

The *haka* was over all too soon, however, with a loud shout and some more foot stomping, and we were quickly ushered back into the museum. I was disappointed to find that I hadn't felt the earth move, either literally or metaphorically. Perhaps I'd been expecting too much of my first *haka* experience, but it didn't rate on the same scale as the rugby team's *hakas* that I'd seen on TV. Strictly speaking the *haka* doesn't have to be a war dance, and it can be performed as a protest, a celebration, or for a variety of other reasons. What it does require is a degree of passion from the performer, however, and the conveyor-belt of visitors seemed to have drained that from our hosts. Technically they were excellent, but it was a rather emotionless exhibition.

A few of the performers hung around for photo opportunities with the gathered tourist mob, but I had no desire to know that the large Maori warrior was actually called Kevin and spoke with a British accent. Before they managed to completely undermine the cultural authenticity of the experience I battled my way back out into the sunshine.

* * *

At 1076 feet high the Sky Tower lived up to its name, dominating the Auckland skyline from all directions. It's often been described as looking like a giant hypodermic syringe, and I could certainly see the similarity as I stood at its base, squinting up into the pale blue sky. There was even an entire website devoted to interpretations of its real purpose, most of which seemed to involve spying on, or blowing up, their Australian neighbours. My favourite entry, unfortunately anonymous, and quite possibly submitted by an aggrieved Aussie, suggested that it might be 'A rectal thermometer for some of the world's biggest assholes'.

My first impression as I shielded my eyes against the glare was that it served as an imposing focus for the city centre, and, while not as impressive as the Sydney Harbour Bridge or the Eiffel Tower, it certainly wasn't for lack of trying. It even held the distinction of being the tallest freestanding structure in the southern hemisphere, which clearly left me no option but to go up it.

Due to a quirky piece of Kiwi architectural planning you had to descend into the basement in order to reach the viewing gallery, the reason for which soon became clear as I followed a meandering path through the gift shop to the ticket desk. I couldn't help wondering whether tourists really were stupid enough to fall for such blatant product placement, and received an immediate answer when I found myself strangely drawn towards a rack of replica rugby shirts. After several minutes marvelling at the fact that they could charge so much for what was essentially a black t-shirt with a silver fern logo on the chest, I finally remembered the reason I was there, and made my way to the ticket booth.

I was swiftly ushered into a waiting elevator, and forty seconds later I emerged in the Sky Tower viewing gallery. A sign in the elevator very helpfully informed me that it would take approximately twenty-nine minutes to walk up to the observation level, presumably in order to justify the extortionate entry fee, but maybe also so we could marvel at the fact that someone had been crazy enough to even try. It was a wonderfully sunny day, and I pushed my way through the crowds to the external windows, keen to get a new perspective on the city.

The view from the Sky Tower was breathtaking. On clear days it was estimated that you could see up to eighty-two kilometres into the distance, effectively laying the entire city of Auckland out like a life-sized map. I spent a few minutes calculating exactly which building my hotel was located in, and then I entertained myself by standing on the plate glass flooring that was dotted around the outside of the platform. It was strangely disconcerting to be able to look down past your feet at the pavement over seven hundred feet below, and after a while I felt rather dizzy and had to stop.

They'd also installed computerised telescopes in the platform, and using a joystick and a couple of buttons you could zoom in on any location within sight. For the hell of it I used this technology to follow a man in a green jacket as he crossed the street, but since he seemed intent on doing nothing even vaguely exciting the novelty quickly wore off. It was slightly unnerving to think that there were people up here spying on us poor pedestrians as we went about our dull lives, and I made a silent promise to try and do something quirky every ten minutes or so, just to keep them entertained.

From ground level the topography of the city wasn't clear, but from this height it was immediately visible.

Auckland is the only city in the world to be built on a large active volcanic site, the wisdom of which any sane person would query. There were forty-eight volcanoes dotted across the city, and after a few minutes I was able to make out about twenty, the distinctive conical hills proving easy to identify once you got the hang of it. The most obvious was Rangitoto Island, sitting just inside the harbour entrance. A sign on the wall helpfully informed me that this was also Auckland's youngest volcano, having burst up from the sea floor about six hundred years ago, and that the local Maori name for it meant 'sky of blood'. All in all it made me rather glad that I was due to leave Auckland in a day or two, although I vowed to keep an eye out for sudden eruptions and streams of molten lava, just in case.

As I was about to return to the elevator a man suddenly fell from the sky, stopping just outside the window to my left and hovering in mid-air. Fortunately I remembered William 48 mentioning that you could jump off the tower, and rather than rushing to call security I joined a gathering crowd of spectators. We pressed our noses to the glass and peered at him as if he was an unusual animal at the zoo, and I could sense that the crowd was trying to memorise the exact characteristics of this strange sub-species of human in order to avoid it in later life. The exhibit himself was quite clearly petrified, presumably having worked out that the yellow overalls and plastic helmet they'd given him to wear wouldn't actually offer much protection should the cable snap. He did his best to smile as a couple of tourists took photos through the glass, but he only managed the strained grimace of a condemned man about to face the firing squad.

Then, without warning, he plummeted down to the ground below. There was a communal intake of breath as we all watched him hurtle towards the pavement, but in the final few feet we saw him slow down and make a controlled landing, accompanied by the sound of fifty people letting out a sigh of relief. I noticed that a digital clock above the

Ka Mate

window had started to count down until the next 'jumper', and a few people were taking a seat to wait for them. There was also a sign telling us that 'you too could jump off the tower *today*', but I decided that I'd already had enough adrenaline rushes for one day, and opted to take the marginally slower, but considerably safer, public elevator. As I exited through the main foyer of the building the jumper was just coming back in, still wearing his overalls and helmet, and trailing a variety of loose cables behind him. I was tempted to point out that it was probably safe to take the helmet off now, but one look at his face told me that he'd be sleeping in it for the next week.

The weather had stayed surprisingly fine, so I decided on a whim to spend the rest of the afternoon in Devonport, apparently the most attractive of Auckland's suburbs. Part of its appeal resides in the fact that you can reach it via ferry from the city centre, and sitting on the top deck of the boat as it pulled away from Queens Wharf I was afforded an unparalleled view of the city from the water. The Ferry Building itself, an imposing but beautiful structure not unlike Melbourne's Flinders Street Station, was worth more than a second glance, but it was also pleasant to escape from the bustle of downtown Auckland for a while and put my feet up. It only took twelve minutes to cross to Devonport, but that was more than enough time to relax and enjoy the sea breeze.

Once we'd disembarked, the atmosphere was immediately and markedly different from the city centre. It reminded me more of a small English village than a suburb, the one main street offering a parade of second-hand bookstores, craft galleries and homely-smelling bakeries. I decided to get moving before I started to use the word 'quaint' and was forcibly ejected from the city, so I took a walk along the shore to North Head, yet another volcanic cone and the former site of a Maori settlement. The black rocks at the water's edge attested to its violent geological past, but the area was so tranquil and picturesque now that it was hard to imagine lava flowing down these slopes, or the sea boiling as the earth opened up. The small stretches of beach were still black with volcanic rock, but that didn't deter several children from building suspiciously grey edifices in the sand.

When I returned to the jetty it was almost half an hour until the next ferry to the city centre, so I stopped at one of the bakeries for a coffee and a fudge brownie. When the waitress brought out a large steaming bowl I initially thought they'd brought me someone's soup by mistake. It came as less of a surprise when she returned with a brownie the size of a baby's arm. By the time I'd finished them both, nudging a few remaining crumbs around my plate with a finger, I'd missed the ferry that I was hoping to catch, and had to wait for the next one.

Devonport was so pleasant, however, that this setback didn't trouble me at all. Until the boat arrived I sat on the pier staring at the Sky Tower in the distance, pulling an occasional strange face or dancing on the spot. After all, you never knew when someone up there might be watching.

Ka Mate

2
Paihia - Waitangi

The next morning, as I travelled in my recently-acquired rental car at seventy kilometres an hour along State Highway One, I couldn't help noticing that I was following the Northern Motorway north into Northland, the northern tip of the North Island. Perhaps there had been some confusion over basic directions in the country's past - they were certainly keen to make up for it now. The skies were a little overcast but it was warm and dry, and while I'd enjoyed my stay in Auckland I was eager to get out of the city. Apparently New Zealand had roughly the population of Kentucky living in an area larger than Wyoming, so there was certainly plenty of countryside out there to see.

After a couple of hours I stopped for lunch at a small village called Waipu, and while I waited for my food to arrive at the Pizza Barn I found myself staring at the wall opposite. To my surprise the 'barn' was decorated with Scottish flags, photographs of castles, and other Highland memorabilia, and a swift consultation with my guidebook revealed that Waipu was founded by a group of Scots fleeing the Highland Clearances in 1853, which I suppose went some way towards explaining this displaced Scottish nationalism. Even so, it seemed remarkable that they should still be pinning pictures of Loch Lomond on the wall a hundred and fifty years after their great-great-great-grandfathers settled here.

After demolishing my pizza and an additional side order of garlic bread I returned to the car, the suspension just managing to cope with the added weight. What had appeared to be a coastal road on my map only occasionally passed within sight of the sea, but it was still a pleasant drive and my spirits were high. I was glad to be leaving the bustle of Auckland behind me.

By the time I arrived at Paihia, my first overnight stopping point, the clouds had thickened and a mist was rolling in off the sea. I was here to see the Bay Of Islands, one of the North Island's main attractions, and apparently some of the most amazing scenery that New Zealand had to offer. Unfortunately all I could see was murky greyness. Rumour had it that on a good day you could see almost all of the hundred and fifty islands in the bay from the seafront at Paihia, but today it was the most I could do to make out an occasional rocky outcrop, or a tuft of grass. I had a couple of days in Paihia, however, so all was not lost. The lady at the information centre informed me that the clouds were due to clear tomorrow, so I parked and wandered into town to arrange a room.

This turned out to be harder than I'd imagined. Despite the fact that every other building along the seafront appeared to be a hotel, motel or holiday apartment block, they were all either fully booked or ridiculously expensive. Eventually I fell back on the last resort of the penniless or socially inept, and tried one of the youth hostels.

When someone eventually answered my frantic bell ringing in the hostel office I immediately assumed that he was one of the guests. His dark hair was long and dishevelled, and his t-shirt had two large visible tears along the seam. It didn't take me long to discover that he was supposed to be manning the admissions desk, however, and had just disappeared out the back to microwave his lunch.

Ka Mate

He seemed sympathetic to my plight, and tutted knowingly when I mentioned the horrendous weather conditions, so I sensed that my luck might be changing.

As soon as I asked for a room, though, he shook his head.

'Sorry mate, we're all booked out. Not a single bed left in the place. I think everyone's hanging around, hoping the weather's gonna change.'

I was about to leave when he called me back.

'You've got your own transport, have you?' I told him that I'd hired a car in Auckland. 'Give me five minutes, I might be able to find you something. It's a couple of minutes drive out of town, but it's probably your best chance.'

It turned out that his girlfriend's parents had a flat they rented to holidaymakers during the tourist season, and after a couple of calls he told me that I could have it for eighty dollars a night. That sounded more than reasonable, so he phoned them again to confirm, and told me to come back in ten minutes for the keys. Feeling happier with life now that I no longer had to consider the back seat of my rental car as a sleeping option, I headed back outside for a stroll.

There really was very little to divert the casual visitor to Paihia, and in the end I struggled to fill my spare ten minutes. There was a hardware store, a grocery store, a bookshop-slash-newsstand, and a fair sprinkling of photo developing outlets, but every other storefront seemed to be selling boat trips to the hundred and fifty invisible islands that were lurking somewhere in the mist. Long ago the community must have decided that the islands were always destined to be their main attraction, and everything else might as well pack up and leave. On days like today it rendered Paihia almost unbearably dull.

Eventually I found a woodcrafts shop where I manage to kill almost five minutes, aimlessly browsing carved wine bottle stoppers and wooden kiwis which seem to serve no function at all, then I walked back to the hostel to see if my keys had arrived. I was quite relieved to discover that they had, and that the young man behind the desk had drawn me a map to get to the flat. The fact that it was out of town was no longer an issue, and on the drive there I stopped to buy some basic food supplies.

The map led me back along the road I had driven in on, then down a side street into a residential area. It was actually rather refreshing to be away from the tourist drag of motels and backpacker hostels, and I felt myself relax as I stepped out of the car, a bag of groceries dangling from each hand. The flat itself was part of the lower floor of a house, presumably owned by the same couple that was letting it. It had its own private entrance down the side of the building, as well as a large area of decking, so all in all I felt that I'd done fairly well for myself. It smelled a little damp, so I propped a few windows open to let the air clear, but I really had very little to complain about. In fact I rapidly began to feel at home, and decided that I'd managed to land on my feet.

As the mist showed no signs of clearing I decided to drive back into town and take the ferry across to the nearby village of Russell. Despite its rather dull name, Russell used to be known as the 'hell hole of the Pacific', an altogether more colourful moniker that they maybe should have stuck with. At the time it was mainly populated by seamen and escaped convicts from Australia, which goes some way towards explaining how it acquired this dubious reputation. The persistent problem with Russell, or Kororareka as it was originally known, was one of the reasons that surveyor James Busby was sent out to New Zealand in 1833. Quite how they thought a civil engineer and viticulturist was going to quell hundreds of drunken sailors and convicts remains unclear, but by 1840 visiting French explorer Dumont D'Urville was able to write that Busby had produced 'a light wine, very sparkling and delicious to taste', so at least it wasn't a wasted trip.

The ferry left the main pier every half hour, and I didn't have to wait long for the next boat. When it arrived it was bobbing around in the swell like a large cork, and after a cursory glance at its metal hull and large exposed rivets I had a sneaking suspicion that it was actually made from an Erector set. It only seated about twenty people, and we all had to stoop to fit under a large plastic awning that thankfully kept the mist away. As I stepped onto the boat from the quay, taking care with my footing since I had no desire to take an impromptu plunge into the cold grey waters, the captain tugged on his waterproof hood and nodded at me.

'Y'all right there, brother?'

Since he seemed to be under the mistaken impression that I was either a blood relative or a member of some secret society I simply nodded back, and made my way swiftly under the cover. I had a sneaking suspicion that he might be one of the original sailors who had earned Russell its bad reputation, presumably still clinging onto life through a secret pact with the devil. I took a seat as far away from the cabin as possible.

Once the engine started it turned out that the ferry was actually a miniature speedboat, and we zipped through the waves on a zigzag course across the bay. It was a surprisingly enjoyable trip, and completely different to my ferry ride across to Devonport. As we hit another wave the boat flew across the top of it, and there was a mass intake of breath; then, as we dipped into a trough on the other side, we all breathed out again as if we were on a roller coaster. To be honest, I was disappointed when we pulled up alongside Russell's short pier and had to step out into the mist, which had been joined in the interim by a steady drizzle.

As a valiant attempt to rewrite its bloody history the village was now marketed as 'romantic Russell', although quite why they thought people were going to be put in the mood for love by a handful of craft shops and a small gift-shop-slash-museum wasn't clear. In an attempt to show an interest I took a stroll along the waterfront and glanced at some of the buildings from the original settlement, none of which were significantly older than the apartment I'd rented in the UK, and all of which had been extensively modernised anyway. After that I walked along the shopping street and stared through some of the windows, but really I was killing time, as I was embarrassed to return to the ferry so soon. Eventually I came to the conclusion that the most exciting thing to do in Russell was to catch the ferry back to Paihia, so I took the quickest route back to the pier.

The captain called me 'brother' again as I clambered on board, but this time I was prepared for him, returning his greeting with a 'Nice to see you again, boss' as I lifted the edge of the awning. I'd been intending to sound like an extra from *The Sopranos*, or at least *Starsky & Hutch*, but unfortunately it came out more like *Top Cat*, and I quickly scuttled to the front before he had the chance to ask me exactly what I'd meant by it.

Our high-speed return left a trail of swirling greyness behind us that occasionally afforded glimpses of scattered rocks or a forlorn island beach, but the mist hadn't cleared at all by the time we pulled up at Paihia quay, and there seemed to be little chance of seeing the islands today. Instead I walked back to my car, and drove north to Waitangi and the Treaty House.

Waitangi was where the surveyor James Busby had first settled when he'd arrived in Bay Of Islands, in a two-bedroom house not far from the cliff top. This original house was built around a timber frame, constructed from blue gum trees in Sydney, Australia, then shipped across to New Zealand, and quite remarkably it was still standing today. The house had been widely extended since Busby's time, but

Ka Mate

had recently been renovated to something like its original state.

Busby was born in Edinburgh, Scotland, but in 1824 his parents moved to Sydney – of their own volition, apparently – and he is widely attributed with being the first person to grow grape vines in the world-renowned Hunter Valley. His post in New Zealand was an awkward one, as he was an ordinary citizen on foreign soil and held no official powers or benefits. The house was simply known as the 'British Residence' during Busby's time, and in March 1834 he called the local Maori chiefs to his home to choose a national flag. With a typically British sense of organization he intended to unite the tribes together as a single nation.

The chiefs of 25 tribes attended, and eventually voted by a narrow majority for a St George's Cross with a smaller white and blue cross in the upper left-hand quadrant, a flag already used by the Church Missionary Society. This flag was recognised by the Admiralty as the flag of New Zealand, and was used in following years to identify all ships built in the fledgling country.

A year and a half later Busby called a second meeting at which thirty-four chiefs signed a Treaty of Independence, a figure that was later increased to a total of fifty-two signatures. It declared New Zealand as an independent Maori state and called upon the British Crown for protection. Apparently Busby was aware of the poor treatment of the Aborigines in Australia, and wanted to do the right thing by the Maori people. Their flag became known as the Flag of the United Tribes of New Zealand and could be seen flying at locations across the north of the island, as well as on ships trading with Sydney.

All of this changed in January 1840 with the arrival of Captain William Hobson. Hobson had been sent as the new Lieutenant-Governor of New Zealand, replacing Busby and establishing the first official rule of a British governor on New Zealand soil. There had been rumours of a French interest in the country and, as always, the British were keen to frustrate their Gallic cousins. Within a week of Hobson's landing the Treaty of Waitangi had been thrown together, and it was translated into Maori overnight by Henry Williams, leader of the Church Missionary Society. On 6 February the local Maori chiefs gathered at Waitangi and signed the Treaty, then it was duly sent around the country for other chiefs to add their names to. The Flag of the United Tribes of New Zealand came down, to be replaced by the British Union Jack.

The Treaty is still an item of some discussion and controversy today. For such an important document it is remarkably short, perhaps so that Henry Williams wouldn't have to tax himself too much when translating it. After a preamble of only about two hundred words it launches into its three main articles, then succinctly winds up in less that a hundred words. It looks more like a school assignment than an official document, especially given its lasting importance in New Zealand politics. Apparently Williams' son helped him with the translation, so this might not be entirely a coincidence.

There are many books devoted to the wording of the Treaty and its various points of mistranslation or open interpretation, so I will keep this summary brief. Essentially the first article ceded the rights and powers of sovereignty to the British monarch. The second article, probably the most contentious of the three, guaranteed the Maori chiefs exclusive possession of their land as long as they wanted it, but gave the Crown an exclusive right to purchase these lands should they wish to sell. The third and final article extended to the Maori all the rights and privileges of British subjects, and this article is generally considered to have been fairly well translated – Williams was obviously getting into his stride by that point. The first two articles were poorly translated in areas, however, and thanks to the substandard translation efforts of a British missionary, and the hurrying effect of the French interest, a document was produced that is still argued over to this day. Add to this the fact that many prominent Maori chiefs did not sign the Treaty at all, and that others weren't even shown it, and you can see why it has remained so contentious.

The Treaty itself wasn't signed in the house, this formality having taken place on the lawns between the building and the sea. A marquee was erected there from spare spars and sails that Hobson had brought with him on board the HMS Herald, and as I walked across the close-cropped grass I tried to imagine the makeshift construction that had stood there over a hundred and fifty years ago, billowing in the sea winds. A tall and impressive flagstaff marked the point on the lawn where the historic event took place, but the area was now populated by several clusters of tourists, carefully unpacking sandwiches from their backpacks. In the end the leap proved too much for my imagination, and I had to remain content with the artist's impression of the signing that hung in the Treaty House. Today's picnickers were far removed from the gathering of proud Maori chiefs that once occupied these lawns.

The house itself, having grown organically around James Busby's first unimpressive dwelling, was purchased by Lord and Lady Bledisloe in 1932 and gifted to the nation. It was renamed the Treaty House at their request, in memory of the great events that had unfolded there, and after extensive renovations it opened to the public in 1934. There was considerable support from the local Maori community for the project, and they had performed a traditional *hui* as part of the opening ceremony. Six years later, in 1940, the local Maori community also built a traditional ceremonial house in the Treaty House grounds as part of the double centenary celebrations. Named *Te Whare Runanga,* it stands alongside the Treaty House as a symbol of Maori involvement, and I made a point of spending some time there before I left.

The view of the building from the lawns was certainly impressive, the *whare*'s sloping wooden roof reaching down almost to the ground on either side. The terracotta paint applied to the wooden carvings was typically Maori too, and many of the eyes in the carved faces gleamed with polished shells. A single post stood upright in the centre, topped by a life-sized figure holding a canoe paddle in his well-muscled arms, his seashell eyes staring menacingly at the path up to the doorway. This was Kupe, the Polynesian explorer who was said to have discovered New Zealand while crossing the ocean in a canoe with his wife. One can only assume that he developed such enormous biceps from all that paddling.

Kupe is also credited with giving the country its Maori name, Aotearoa, usually translated as 'Land Of The Long White Cloud'. More recently the name has been retranslated as 'Land Of The Lingering Twilight', which may prove to be the more accurate rendering: the Polynesians who first settled here would have been used to conditions closer to the equator, and in the summer months the daylight would have lingered much longer than they'd expected. Whether the name derived from Kupe's poeticism or from the seasonal changes, it has lasted through the centuries, and now adorns much of New Zealand's official literature. Aotearoa, the Maori homeland, is ascending once again.

I stopped for a moment to try and take in the many detailed carvings that adorned the front of the building. As I drew closer I was able to read the sign outside, explaining that it was customary to remove your shoes when entering the *whare*, accompanied by a sea of discarded footwear that extended at least five feet out on either side. Not wishing to ignore local custom I removed my shoes clumsily and kicked them into a clear corner, desperately hoping that I'd be able to find them again. The front porch looked more like an end-of-season sale at a shoe store than an important cultural and historical site.

As I stepped carefully into the building I hoped that the rummage sale outside wasn't indicative of conditions within, but of course all those shoes had to come from somewhere. The crowds inside were trying to maintain a sense of decorum, but with so many cameras flashing and people sliding around the polished floor in their socks the mystique was somehow lost. Having avoided a tour group on their way back out of the building, and sidestepping a few screaming children, I was finally able to look at the carvings. Traditionally a meeting house such as this would have displayed carvings of the ancestors of the local tribe, but since it was intended as a national meeting house *Te Whare Runanga* contained carvings representing the various tribes from across the country. The figures themselves were crafted by the men of the tribe, while the woven panels to either side were produced by the women. Each carving told a particular story from the tribe's history or mythology, most of which seemed to involve someone sticking their tongue out and holding their belly – which, of course, all the best stories do.

The carefully carved spirals on the faces and bodies of the figures were amazingly intricate and held my attention for some time, as did the similar spiral patterns painted on the ceiling beams. When another large group arrived at the entrance, however, I decided that it might be the best time to make my exit, and I emerged again into the daylight. It took me a few minutes to find a pair of shoes I liked, which coincidentally were also the ones that I'd arrived in, then I set off across the lawn to find another of the sights at Waitangi: the 115 foot long war canoe.

This was also built for the 1940 double centenary, from three huge trees. It required a minimum of seventy-six paddlers to handle safely, and it occasionally still took to the water for events or celebrations. Its official title was *Ngatoki Matawhaorua*, after the explorer Kupe's canoe, and I was impressed that this traditionally made boat was still seaworthy, especially given its enormous size. There were carved figures along either side, as well as large carved pieces at both bow and stern. These looked wonderfully organic in design, their interwoven spirals and curves bringing to mind the thick, dense fern bracken that flourished in parts of New Zealand. It was spectacular to see the boat in its entirety, but I suspected that it looked even more impressive on the water, especially once the paddlers worked up some speed. One of these bearing down on you in the heat of battle would be a fearsome sight.

I wandered back to my parked car filled with newfound respect for the Maori people, both as craftsmen and as warriors. In their heyday they must have made formidable opponents, especially if the size of Kupe's biceps were anything to go by.

* * *

I awoke the following morning with high expectations for the day. It took only a glance between the faded curtains to bring me crashing back down to earth. The skies were grey and threatening rain, and even this far inland I could see tendrils of mist working their way up the street. I had no time in my schedule to wait for the weather to change, so if I wanted to see the islands it would have to be today. Assuming that the boat could get within a few feet of them, of course.

The booking centre for the cruises marketed itself as an information point, and when I stepped inside I was bombarded with information. There were at least four different companies operating out of the one building, and each displayed an array of posters, flyers, timetables and pricing charts. You could zip on a high-speed jetboat through the marine park, or choose the more sedate Swimming With Dolphins cruise. I opted for Kings Cruises, simply because I'd seen their name around town, and as I bought my ticket I asked the lady behind the counter how the morning's forecast was looking.

'Ah yeah, this mist is gonna clear, you're gonna have a beautiful morning by about ten o'clock.'

This sounded suspiciously like the line I was told yesterday at the *actual* information centre, but I was feeling generous, so I decided that the citizens of Paihia were a naturally optimistic bunch. As I waited at the end of the pier there was certainly no suggestion that the sun was coming out, the mist having been joined yet again by a nagging drizzle. Visibility was so poor that I kept my eye on the end of the jetty for fear of wandering over the edge by mistake.

When the boat arrived it looked fairly modern, and considerably larger than the Russell ferry. At least I'd be able to peer out into the mists in comfort. I found myself a seat by the window and slung my jacket onto it by way of a reservation while I bought a cup of coffee from the bar. As I trickled its sugary warmth down my throat I began to feel a little more positive about the trip, although that might just have been the caffeine at work.

The boat chugged slowly across the bay, allowing me plenty of time to finish my drink while there was only grey murk to peer out at. Our first stop was Cook's Bay on Roberton Island, which was just visible through the mist. It was named after Captain James Cook, who'd first landed there in 1769 and had spent a total of ten days in the Bay Of Islands. Given the length of his stay I assumed that the weather was slightly better than today.

After this we stopped at Moturua Island, although this simply offered more of the same. There was a Department of Conservation hut on the island that it was possible to stay in overnight, but since it ran on solar power I suspected that it would be a little cold and dark at the moment. Today it sounded about as appealing as snorkelling in mud.

It was after Moturua Island that we encountered our first real excitement of the morning. The boat suddenly stopped in open water, and for a brief second I wondered if we'd broken down. The captain quickly came on the P.A. system and told us that we'd happened across a pod of bottlenose dolphins, however, and that we'd be stopping for a few minutes to watch them.

The bottlenose is the largest dolphin species to be found in the Bay Of Islands, and once one of the crew had opened the doors to the front deck we all clambered outside into the damp air to get a better view. I'd initially assumed that we'd be peering at hazy specks on the horizon, but I was pleasantly surprised to see that the dolphins had come to us. A few of them were swimming right up to the boat, circling around us and passing several times over. Some tilted slightly to the side and watched us with one eye, and I wasn't entirely sure who was more intrigued by this chance meeting, us or them. It's widely known that dolphins are one of the most intelligent species on the planet, but I was surprised at how immediately obvious this was, even in such a fleeting encounter. One flipped out of the water alongside the boat and somersaulted through the air, a piece of impromptu acrobatics that made me wish I'd had my camera ready. It was no wonder that marine theme parks were so attracted to these born performers.

After a few minutes they realised that we were just another bunch of dull tourists in waterproof jackets, and the pod began to drift away. Once I was back inside I noticed another boat approaching them, and after wiping the condensation from the window I saw that it was the Swimming With Dolphins group. The dolphins circled around the boat and there was a flurry of activity on deck as everyone hurriedly tugged on their wetsuits and snorkels. Then they all climbed into a large net that was dangling off the side - looking for one surreal moment like the catch of the day - and were lowered into the water. The dolphins took one look at them, sidling up alongside the net filled with this strange new species of fish, then decided that this was all a bit silly really, and rapidly vanished back into the waves. Left behind were several peeved tourists in wetsuits, desperately treading water and looking colder with each passing second. I liked this disappearing act even more than the somersaults, and I chuckled in my seat for several minutes as we pulled away.

Standing outside had numbed my cheeks and the end of my nose, so I was forced to buy another cup of coffee. While I watched the barman wrestling with the espresso machine I let him know how impressed I was with the dolphins.

'They're so playful, they're just like little kids,' he told me, ducking dramatically out of the way of a cloud of steam. 'I've worked on cruises like this in heaps of other places, and these are the friendliest I've seen. The others never used to come up to the boat so often, but these do it every time. It's like they want us to play with them.'

I considered mentioning the disappearing act I'd witnessed when the Swimming With Dolphins group entered the water, but decided against it in case that was one of his previous jobs. Instead I made a general comment about the weather as I passed him a handful of coins.

'You guys have been keeping me busy,' he joked as I turned back to my seat, cradling the warm cup between my hands. 'It's certainly a good day for selling coffee.'

Our next stop was Urupukapuka Island, the largest in the Bay and the only one that you were allowed to camp on, but the mist was heavy again and we weren't able to see much. After that our final destination was Piercy Island, also known as Motukokako. It was named after a Maori chief who had landed there and climbed the 487 feet to the top, and the land was still owned by one of the local tribes. Within New Zealand it was famous for the 'Hole in the Rock', although the title was a typical case of Kiwi understatement and didn't really do justice to its magnificent natural arch.

In Auckland I'd been warned that cruises used to go through the 'Hole', but since an accident when a jetboat clipped the rocks a couple of years ago they didn't attempt it any more. Our captain was clearly either unaware of this or completely insane, however, as he began telling us over the P.A. system that he usually took his boat through the archway. I peered through the window at the waves crashing against the inside of the arch, sending curtains of spray over ten feet into the air, and I began to feel a little queasy. Fortunately I wasn't so panicked that I switched off entirely, and I also heard him say that the weather was too bad to attempt it today. The image of passing through that violent maelstrom was still imprinted on my mind as we headed back to Paihia, though, and I was looking forward to being back on dry land.

As I disembarked I asked the barman about the accident at the 'Hole in the Rock', and he seemed blissfully unaware of it. Apparently most of the boats still steered through it, the jetboat taking you through at over forty miles an hour, and I considered myself to have had a lucky escape. It seemed the Kiwis weren't happy unless they were jumping off buildings or hurtling towards rocks at high speed. I was rather glad to be standing on solid ground again.

* * *

From Paihia I drove northwest, following the coast around as far as the Karikari Peninsula and then heading inland to Kaitaia. The roads here were small and winding, and often narrowed down to one-lane bridges as they crossed streams and rivers. Some of these bridges looked as if they'd been there for decades, the original wood reinforced in places and coated with a new layer of pavement, which was slowly crumbling away at the edges. Right of way was clearly marked at the entrance to each bridge, but I still paused at each one just to make sure.

As I headed north the scenery gradually changed. There were still occasional stands of the pine trees I'd seen further south, but they were slowly joined by tall ferns and spindly cabbage trees, a type of palm so named because the heart of the fronds apparently tastes like cabbage. It was a strange mix of temperate and tropical plant life, and as I entered Kaitaia I noticed that the weather here reflected that same mix. It was warm and slightly stifling as I followed the main road to my hostel, but on the horizon charcoal-grey storm clouds loomed.

As I drove into town I passed a sign that appeared to say 'Welcome' in three different languages: the English was followed by the Maori greeting *Haere Mai*, and then another in an unidentified language, *Dobro Dosli*. After my difficulties finding a room in Paihia I'd phoned ahead and booked in at Mainstreet Lodge, a hostel that also offered *en suite* rooms, and as I checked in I asked about this third language. It turned out that it was Dalmatian, or Yugoslav as it's known now, and that the settlement was originally founded by Dalmatian immigrants. The Dalmatians had retained a great deal of their national identity in their new home, just as the Scots had in Waipu, and they were still an active sector of the community. It was surprising to see so many nationalities settled in New Zealand, but I couldn't help feeling that I'd yet to see anything of Kiwi culture.

The evening remained hot and humid, the storm finally hitting at four o'clock in the morning and waking me as the rain rattled off the metal roof. I battened down the hatches and sealed myself in, slowly falling back to sleep to the sound of torrential gunfire.

3
Te Tai Tokerau *(Northland)*

I woke to a high-pitched buzzing by my ear. The rain from last night had withdrawn and sunlight was glowing behind the thin curtains of my room. The buzzing turned to a whining drone as something passed by my other ear, so I sat up and turned the light on.

It didn't take me long to find the culprit, a large swollen mosquito that had fed so hungrily on me during the night that she was struggling to get more than a few feet off the floor. As she flew past the light bulb her body glowed bright red, the busy night having turned her into a flying sac of blood. Eventually I caught her when she was near the centre of the room, her flight trajectory taking her so close to the floor that I managed to drop a book on top of her. When I peeled it away from the tiles there was a brilliant splat of blood the size of an old half penny coin beneath. The fact that it was mostly my blood made it seem even gorier, but despite my best efforts I couldn't seem to remove it. I stepped around it as I got ready for the day.

My schedule was a fairly busy one, as I'd decided to take one of the many tours up to the very north of the island. It was possible to drive there yourself, but the tour provided lunch and I was hungry for some human interaction again. Besides, with the discount I received for staying in the hostel it was only marginally more expensive than buying lunch out.

The coach was actually an old beaten-up bus, and as I climbed onboard I decided that the dents and scrapes gave it some character. Most of the exit signs and other notices were in Japanese and English, and our driver, who introduced himself as Robin, explained that the company bought the buses second-hand in Japan and shipped them over to New Zealand. Once they'd run them into the ground they repainted them and sold them on to students.

I wasn't entirely sure whether he was joking or not, a feeling that would be repeated throughout the day. Robin was from one of the three Maori tribes that populated the top end of the island. He was unusually tall and slim and didn't fit the short, muscular image of Maori men that I'd formed so far. He was also constantly smiling and joking as he steered the bus around the bends in the tiny country roads, occasionally breaking into a high-pitched laugh that peppered our trip. It was hard to imagine a better host for our journey, and he brought a smile to everyone's faces within minutes of leaving town.

As we passed a farm to our left he pointed out a bush turkey skittering out of the road into some high grass. 'You see that turkey?' he asked over the P.A. system. 'Us Maori, we've found the best way to eat these turkeys. First you shoot it and you pluck it, then you put it on the fire in a big pot. You boil it up in the pot with a gumboot for a good few hours, then you throw away the turkey and eat the gumboot. Huhuhuh huh huh.'

He finished with a distinctive chuckle, the joke obviously still amusing him no matter how often he told it to coaches full of tourists. It wasn't a great joke, but it was hard not to laugh along with him, and looking around I saw that everyone had been infected by his good humour. The round trip up to Cape Reinga and back was about a hundred and fifty miles, but at least we would have a few giggles along the way.

The tour drove part of the way up to the Cape via Ninety Mile Beach. The beach had been granted main highway status and any vehicle was allowed to drive along it, but it quite specifically stated in my car rental agreement that it was out of bounds. When I asked Robin about this he explained that there were only five exits from the beach that took you back to the access roads, and tourist drivers often miscalculated the incoming tides and ended up getting stranded. They tended to abandon their cars, only to return at low tide to discover them buried in the sand. The coach company offices were apparently wallpapered with pictures of half-submerged rental cars, a fact which started him chuckling again.

As we left the road we passed a large sign declaring the speed limit, and then we were on the beach. The sand by the entrance was very soft, and even as a passenger I could feel the tires struggling to get a grip. Once Robin had charged through this first patch, however, the beach was wet and packed down, and the driving seemed flat and easy. After a few miles we stopped for a photo opportunity, the ripples of the waves on the sand creating a wonderful backdrop for holiday snaps.

There was a large mound in the sand nearby with several gulls pecking at it, and Robin told us that this was the carcass of a juvenile sperm whale that had collided with a ship offshore. It had washed up on the beach about eight weeks ago. There were many sperm whales in the waters near here, and in the winter the locals often rode up and down the beach on quad bikes looking for ambergris. This waxy substance is produced by the digestive system of the whales, possibly as a defence against the hard beaks of the giant squid they feed on, and it sometimes washes up onto the beaches. It's still used as a fixative in expensive perfumes, and the locals received seven dollars per gram for what they found, a good price for something that might just be lying on your doorstep.

Once we were back on the bus Robin revealed that the beach wasn't ninety miles long at all, and was actually closer to sixty-four miles. The distance was originally calculated according to the number of days it took local farmers to drive their cattle along the beach, but they forgot to bear in mind that the cows walked more slowly over sand. The name stuck because it sounded impressive, but I have to confess that I was disappointed – I felt as if I'd been cheated out of twenty-four miles of sand, although I wasn't sure quite what I'd been intending to do with it.

He also told us over the P.A. system that they held a fishing competition annually along this stretch of coast, offering $3000 prize money for the largest snapper. A friend of his had entered a few years ago and caught a tiny snapper, hardly big enough to keep. It was the only thing he caught all morning, so at lunchtime he took the fish back home and cooked it on the barbecue. He was still curious to know who won the competition so he went to the final weigh-in that evening, only to find that no one else had caught anything all day, and the snapper he'd eaten for lunch would have been worth $3000. I wasn't sure whether this was another of Robin's jokes or an actual occurrence, but he told us that they now called his friend 'snapperguts', so it seemed as if it might be true. With a laugh like his it didn't really matter.

Our next stop was beside a rocky outcrop known as 'the Bluff': this was still Maori owned, and at high tide it became an island. It was particularly popular among the local tribes as a snapper fishing spot, and it was also possible to pick Green Lipped mussels off the rocks at low tide. The tour bus used to stop by the rock so that people could help themselves to the shellfish: a few years ago, however, one of the tourists ventured onto the lower rocks, slipped, and was swept away by the sea. Being a tourist here was a dangerous pastime, what with the jetboat accidents, unpredictable tides, and slippery rocks. It was remarkable that bungee jumping ever developed - travelling from one place to another was starting to feel like an adrenaline sport in itself.

I'd never eaten New Zealand Green Lipped mussels, but I'd heard enough about them to know that they were considered to be the largest and best mussels in the world. I asked Robin how it was that such desirable shellfish were living here free for anyone to collect.

'Well, most of the mussels you buy in the shops come from the mussel farms further south. But these waters here,' he gestured with his arm, 'are where they come from originally, you see? The mussels spawn off the coast, they lay their young on the seaweed out there. Then when the tide's right the seaweed washes in with all the young mussels attached to it, and the companies come up here and collect them for their farms. So you see, if you eat a New Zealand Green Lipped mussel, there's a good chance it's come from this beach. We're pretty lucky here, what with the snapper and all.'

Once we were back on the bus we drove a few more miles along the beach before turning off along a streambed, complete with about a foot of fast-running water. The bus ploughed through this easily, sending wings of water spraying out to either side, and it made me glad that I'd decided against driving up here in my rental car. I was even happier with my decision once Robin pointed out that we had to keep moving as the water turned the streambed into quicksand – many tourists had stopped here to take a photo, only to find themselves slowly being swallowed up by the ground. If Robin was to be believed there were still some cars down there, many feet below the surface and probably still sinking. I was pretty sure that the insurance companies wouldn't have paid out for those.

When we reached drier ground the bus pulled over and parked, and we all filed out to look at the sand dunes. From some angles it was easy to believe that we were in the middle of the Sahara, as a few of the dunes rose over four hundred feet high. Robin opened a hatch in the side of the bus and pulled out what appeared to be large red and blue plastic trays.

'Okay, so who's going sand tobogganing then?'

I asked if he was going to go first and show us how it was done.

'No, you won't get me doing something stupid like that. But you guys have fun!'

I doubted I'd get another opportunity to toboggan down a sand dune in the near future, so I slipped my shoes and socks off and joined the straggling line of children and terrified adults winding their way slowly up the side of the closest dune. It didn't look too steep, but for every step forward my foot slipped about six inches back, and long before I reached the top my thigh muscles were burning from the effort. I wasn't the only one, and we all stood around at the summit gasping air back into our lungs.

'Who's going first then?' Robin shouted up from the foot of the dune, his hands cupped around his mouth. 'Just put your feet inside the toboggan and lean back with your hands on the sand. When you want to brake, dig your hands in. If you can't brake fast enough the stream will always catch you. Huhuhuh huh huh.'

A couple of the children went first, putting the rest of us to shame as they managed a controlled stop not far from the bus. The lady in front me careened down the slope however, alternately screaming and laughing as she went, and wound up landing with a splash in the stream at the bottom. By the time she'd managed to get herself upright the sand had stuck to her wet clothes, her forearms and most of her face. She was still smiling, though, so I gritted my teeth, closed my eyes, and pushed myself off.

The main benefit of tobogganing on snow is that any flakes which find their way onto you melt away within seconds. By the time I reached the bottom of the dune, having dug my hands in firmly from about halfway down to avoid a wet and unhappy ending, sand had found its way into every uncovered pocket, nostril, ear, mouth and fingernail. As I stood up I felt several pounds heavier, and I pulled my pockets out to allow the sand that had lodged in them to pour back into the dune. An exploratory finger in my ear felt like it was being pushed through sandpaper.

Despite all that, however, it was enormous fun, and I found myself joining the considerably shorter line of people heading back up the dune for a second attempt. I figured that the damage had already been done, so I might as well get properly coated in sand, although my legs struggled to get me back up to the summit. This time I landed unceremoniously in a large clump of grass about three quarters of the way down, but it was much easier and cleaner than trying to brake again so I didn't worry too much. Robin seemed to enjoy it all immensely, and he grinned at me as I handed my sled back.

'You not going for a third time?'

I shook my head. I figured it was time to quit, before all the skin was sandblasted off my palms.

As we drove inland towards the Cape several of us set about emptying our pockets and a few suitable orifices, and before long there were piles of sand across the aisle and some of the seats. I found myself looking out the window with a smile on my face, even as I teased a small sandcastle out of my hair. This was my first taste of New Zealand's extreme sports, and it had proved to be hugely enjoyable. Bring on the bungee.

We passed through an area of burnt out forest, and Robin came on the P.A. to tell us that this was the site of a car wreck the previous week. It came as no surprise to hear that it was two sightseers who had careered off the road into the trees, and it was a wonder that any tourists managed to leave New Zealand alive. Fortunately they had both scrambled out of the car, but the rented BMW had caught fire and ignited several of the nearby trees. The Department of Conservation - or DoC, to give it its more commonly used title - became involved as there were a large number of rare trees and animals in the area, including a very rare snail, which I'd imagine had little chance of outrunning a forest fire. The fire jumped the road at one point, and the trees on either side had been reduced to blackened stumps. I could tell from his tone that Robin blamed the tourists for their reckless driving, but I could sympathise with their predicament – they were probably preoccupied with all the stories of quicksand and jetboating accidents. Even so, the damage was extensive and a major environmental worry, and the forest wouldn't recover for many years to come.

Cape Reinga itself sat right at the top of the North Island, and although it was often assumed to be the northernmost point of mainland New Zealand that honour actually lay with one of the headlands further round the coast. Just off the Cape the Tasman Sea and the Pacific Ocean met in the Columbia Bank maelstrom, and in bad weather the waves could reach thirty feet high, causing ships to travel many miles out of their way to avoid the area.

It was a fairly wild and desolate place, and when the original lighthouse was built offshore on Motuopao Island, with a lens shipped across from England, a family had moved up here in order to operate and service it. Crossing from the mainland to the island by boat wasn't easy, so they had developed a system whereby they travelled from one landmass to another in a basket suspended from a cable. After a year and a half - during which time the basket got stuck halfway across the water on two occasions and the occupants had to be rescued - they finally came to their senses and moved back to the mainland. In 1941 the light was moved to its new location on the Cape, where it still stood today.

Today's lighthouse was fairly small and functional, having run on electricity since the move in 1941, but what impressed me most about it was its isolation. Apart from the parking lot with a few coaches and cars stopped in it there was nothing much of anything for miles in every direction, and even the parking lot was situated a fair walk from the lighthouse itself. As I stood on the headland and looked out to sea, a solitary seagull crying overhead, I felt as if I was on the edge of the world. The weather was calm today but a white line stretching to the horizon marked the meeting point of the Tasman and the Pacific, the waves on either side of it running in slightly different directions. A signpost told me that I was 10,499 nautical miles from London, but it felt like more.

While some of the other people from the coach posed for photos in front of the signpost, I wandered back to the parking lot and asked Robin about the significance of this area to the Maori. I'd heard that it was an important site, not just for the local tribes, but for all New Zealand Maori.

He nodded as I mentioned this, and looked about him as if he was imparting secret information.

'That's right. *Reinga* means "place of leaping", and we believe that this is where our spirits travel after we die. Out on the rocks out there, by the ocean, there's a single pohutukawa tree. Our spirits travel the length of Ninety Mile Beach, the way we came today, and when they reach this tree at the northern end of the country they travel down through the roots and across to Three Kings Islands. There they bid farewell to Aotearoa before heading back to the home of our ancestors, Hawaiki.' He leaned towards me as if he was about to reveal something that was for my ears only. 'I tell you what though, when I go I'll be flying Air New Zealand.'

Once the chuckling was over I walked out to the cliff edge to try and see the spirit tree. Eventually I found it, growing from the side of a rocky headland, and I realised that the true cultural significance of this site had been overlooked. The lighthouse was far less interesting than the beliefs and stories surrounding this lone tree growing on the rocks, and yet there was nothing here to point out its significance or even its existence. As far as I could see I was the only one even looking at it. It seemed a shame, but perhaps that was the way the local Maori wanted it. As I'd seen at Waitangi, there was nothing like a crowd of tourists for tainting a cultural icon. I felt privileged to have seen it, and was glad to return to the bus leaving it untouched.

Our last stop of the day was at the Ancient Kauri Kingdom, which despite its tacky name provided at least a degree of interest. Kauri trees provide the oldest workable timber in the world, and some of the timber used in the store here had been carbon dated at fifty thousand years old. It seemed rather tragic that after fifty thousand years it had ended up as a picture frame or a pair of salad spoons, but it certainly lent these souvenirs an extra novelty value.

Kauri trees still grew in the area, but all the craft items on display were carved from logs dug up in the surrounding swampland. This had become a lucrative sideline for many of the local farmers whose land covered ancient forest remains. Once these logs had been allowed to dry, and the rotten exterior was sawn off, the core was still perfectly workable. Due to the effort involved, and the fact that it took up to two years for the logs to dry out, the timber was disproportionately expensive, and the goods on sale were certainly on the pricey side. I felt that I had to buy something, though, if only so that I could drag out my fifty thousand year old souvenir at dinner parties, and I opted for a cheese board and knife in the hope that they might at least be functional.

Robin was busy spraying the sand off the outside and inside of the bus, but once we'd all finished buying pointless wooden trinkets he drove us back to Kaitaia. He dropped me back at the hostel just in time for an early dinner, and he waved goodbye through the open window as he drove back to the company depot. It had been a long day for all of us, and it amazed me that he found the energy to do this every day, still laughing and joking as if he was enjoying it as much as us. Hopefully the tourism class held at the nearby Tuku Wairua Centre would produce even more gems like Robin.

* * *

The following morning I checked out of the hostel, having remembered to close all the windows overnight to keep the mosquitoes out. It was another mixed day, overcast but strangely warm, and I decided to drive back down the west coast towards Auckland, to see how much it differed from the east. It was referred to in all the tourist literature as the Kauri Coast, and it was certainly more heavily wooded than its eastern counterpart. Apparently the climate here was particularly suited to the kauri, but further south they struggled, and they weren't seen at all south of Hamilton. It was only five or six degrees warmer, but that small change in temperature seemed to make all the difference.

After a few hours driving I stopped at the Waipoua Forest Sanctuary to see one of the oldest living kauri. Only a few minutes walk from the parking lot through a peaceful slice of woodland stood Tane Mahuta, generally considered to be the largest of New Zealand's kauri trees. Named after the God of the Forests from Maori legend, the tree was almost 168 feet high and over 45 feet around. The plaque at its base also told me that forty-seven different species of fern, orchid and flowering plant lived in the canopy, including the native olive tree, and *Bulbophyllum Pygmalum*, the world's smallest orchid.

The tree was undoubtedly large, but I found myself underwhelmed by the experience. Not only was it smaller than I'd expected, dwarfed by the large and crowded viewing area at its base, but it was also far too easy to reach. I'd have enjoyed it a lot more if I'd had to struggle for an hour through dense forest, rather than take a casual stroll a few minutes from the parking lot. Apart from anything else, it might have been a little less busy, and it would certainly have felt less commercial.

After a few minutes wandering around the base, dodging to keep out of the path of the amateur photographers, I retraced the short trail to the parking lot. There was another coach full of tourists just turning up, so it seemed that there was no hope for poor old Tane Mahuta – it was quite a demotion from God of the Forests to tourist freakshow.

About a mile down the road there was another parking place and a signposted forest walk, and since it looked a lot quieter I decided to chance it. A notice at the entrance stated that this was a high-risk car theft area. A charge of two dollars was levied for the secure parking, payable directly to the watchman on duty. The only person I could see was sitting in a car by the start of the forest walk with his door open, so I headed in his direction. I thought I might have the wrong car at first, as it had so many dents and rust patches that it looked as if it might fall apart at any moment, but then I noticed a sign like the other one propped by the open door. As I drew closer I could see the guard through the dusty windshield - a vastly overweight Maori who'd surely struggle to see off any prospective car thieves - and I waved a greeting. He waved back but made no effort to stand up, and I had to walk around the door to reach him.

'Do I pay you for the parking?'

He grunted and scratched at his domed stomach, pulling his t-shirt up so that it sat between the rolls of his chest and his belly.

'Yeah, that's two dollars, bro.'

I handed the money over and he dropped it into a little tin at his side.

'Thanks very much. The walk starts over there, just follow the path.'

I doubted that he'd ever been further than the edge of the parking lot, but he seemed friendly and polite so I waved goodbye to this unusual Maori Buddha and headed for the gap in the trees.

The walk was certainly more rewarding than the Tane Mahuta stop, and offered a wide variety of kauri trees, including a cluster of four growing within a few feet of each other, their roots entwined. The hardened resin, or 'gum', of the trees used to be put to good use by the local Maori, as a tattooing pigment and a fire starter. They also mixed it with plant juices to produce a primitive chewing gum, and when the European settlers grew wise to this they began collecting it for their own uses, which ranged from an ingredient in paint and sealing wax to a base for perfumes. These settlers became known as New Zealand Gumdiggers, and they often dug up to three hundred feet into the forest floor to uncover fallen nuggets; as these balls of resin became harder to find they even began to bleed the trees themselves, climbing the trunks using a rope and spiked shoes, cutting an incision in the wood, then returning six months later once the resin had hardened to harvest it. It was no surprise to discover that this practice was banned in 1905 due to the damage it was causing.

After about half an hour I reached Te Matua Ngahere, yet another enormous kauri, and this time I was truly blown away by the spectacle. It might just have been the lack of crowds, but I found myself overawed by it, and I spent a few minutes simply staring up at the broad canopy. Tane Mahuta was the largest kauri, but officially Te Matua Ngahere was the older of the two trees, current estimates placing it at around two thousand years old, an incredible statistic that made it more or less contemporary with Christ. As I returned to the parking lot I imagined the changes and events that must be recorded between the rings of its mammoth trunk.

Ka Mate

When I reached my car the overweight guard looked up briefly from his newspaper and waved in my direction. I suddenly realised that he was the only person I'd seen in the hour or so that I'd been there, the crowds at the other stop not having made it this far. Perhaps it was the two dollar parking fee that dissuaded them, and it occurred to me that maybe that was the whole point of it. I liked this interpretation of the Maori Buddha's job, a kind of guardian against the swarms of tour buses, and I gave him a long and heartfelt wave in return. A more cynical side of me knew that it was probably just a moneymaking scheme by one of the local tribes, but if two dollars was enough to keep the hordes at bay then I was more than happy to pay.

In order to travel south I needed to pass through Auckland again, as all the main roads seemed to divert via the city, and I worked out that I would have just about enough time to reach it before nightfall. In the end I decided that I'd rather take my overnight stop a little further north, however, having enjoyed my few days away from the bustle and hyperactivity of city life. After almost an hour of driving I stopped at Orewa, encouraged by the pleasant-looking motels and lodges that lined the main road through town.

For some strange reason I opted for a hostel called *Pillows* which advertised itself with a large pink neon sign on the highway, making it look as if it might actually be a brothel. As I checked in I noticed a sign on the office wall advertising the fact that 'day rooms' were available, which only reinforced this impression. In actual fact it seemed to be a very neat, privately owned little hostel, with its rooms arranged around a pleasant open courtyard. It was by no means luxurious, but for an overnight stop it had everything I needed.

I spent the rest of the evening trying to plan my route over the next few days and waiting for a potato to bake in the communal oven. After much deliberation I decided to head southwest from Auckland towards Waitomo, famous for its glowworm caves. Hopefully I would reach it by tomorrow evening, and could book a tour for the following morning.

Little did I realise that tomorrow would bring some new information and a surprise change of direction, and that Waitomo would have to wait. New Zealand's favourite pastime beckoned.

Ka Mate

4
Te Ika a Maui *(North Island)*

I still planned to drive down to Waitomo the following morning, and as I packed my belongings back into the car beneath the neon *Pillows* sign I traced the day's route in my head. Once I was underway the road south took me through the town centre, so I stopped at the large *New World* grocery store and topped up on food. There was also an internet café nearby and I decided that I ought to check my inbox, just in case there was anything important awaiting my attention.

My final week in Fiji before travelling on to New Zealand had been spent on Nacula, one of the outer islands of the Yasawa Group. While there I'd become friendly with Ian and Heather, a couple from Wellington. They were slightly older than me and already had two children, Olivia and Kate, but we immediately hit it off and spent most of our waking hours exploring the local village and nearby islands together. Under sustained pressure from them I'd promised to visit during my New Zealand tour. They were lovely people, but being British to the core I felt slightly embarrassed about forcing my way into the home of a family I hardly even knew. Promises and email addresses were exchanged before I caught the ferry back to the mainland, and I fully intended to meet up with them once I reached Wellington. Beyond that I'd thought no more of it.

I was surprised, therefore, when I saw an email from my new friends, and even more surprised when I discovered that it was more than the usual gossip and family news that peppered my inbox. Not only were they repeating their invitation to visit, but they were also reminding me that the Wellington Rugby Sevens started on Friday.

We'd discussed the international rugby tournament when we were in Fiji, as both Ian and Heather had been to see it several times and were full of praise for the competition. The Hong Kong tournament used to be the highlight of the Sevens rugby calendar, but recently the Wellington competition had threatened to steal pole position. The event was as much about drinking beer and spotting the various costumes in the crowd as it was about what happened on the field, but the final rounds were always hotly contested. Many of New Zealand's star players had come through the seven-player version of the game first. Perhaps the best known, and the player of most interest to me, was a certain Jonah Lomu.

There are many things to like about Lomu. Although his face adorns adverts across the world, and he's well known for his high-visibility sponsorship deal with *adidas*, he still comes across as softly spoken and humble in interviews. Not since Mohammed Ali's heyday has sport had such a gentle giant among its heroes, and he represented a refreshing change from the gossip column antics of the Beckhams. Everyone in New Zealand simply called him Jonah, as if they were actually close friends, and he was exactly the sort of person you'd invite round for tea with your parents. Assuming that you were wealthy enough to pay the food bill, of course.

Even when it came to the more physical side of rugby Jonah had always acted like a gentleman. There was a famous brawl with former England captain Lawrence Dallaglio during the pool stages of the 1999 Rugby World Cup, when Dallaglio landed an elbow on Jonah's head seconds after he scored. Insults were hurled and a few blows exchanged. When the match was over Jonah spoke to Dallaglio about it, and when he discovered that he'd been pushed from behind and had fallen awkwardly they both said their apologies and cleared the air. You got the feeling that if Lomu seriously injured you during a tackle he'd probably come off the field and drive you to the hospital himself.

Despite being New Zealand's best-known rugby player, however, Lomu had been struggling with his health for most of his life. He attended the Rugby World Cup in Australia in 2003, but only to be awarded the Investec Special Merit Award for services to the sport. The same year he played only five matches for his team, the Wellington Hurricanes, and on May 31 2003 the kidney condition he'd suffered from all his life forced him to start using a dialysis machine. Within two months of starting dialysis he also began to suffer from neuropathy, which causes pins and needles in the extremities, loss of balance, and can even lead to paralysis. It might sound unlikely, but the world has never seen Jonah Lomu operating at a hundred percent.

Jonah was such a fan of the seven-player version of the game that he'd had it written into his New Zealand Rugby contract that he would always be available to play Sevens tournaments, however, as long as it didn't clash with his All Blacks commitments. His illness would keep him out of this year's competition, but ever since he'd joined the Wellington team he'd had his own hospitality box at Westpac Stadium. There was a good chance that he might be there for the Sevens.

Having been on the road for over a week I actually had no idea of what day it was, and when I glanced at my watch I was rather shocked to discover that the Sevens tournament started tomorrow. Wellington was eight hours' drive away, but this was too good an opportunity to miss. If I could get a ticket then I might just take the detour.

When I visited the tournament's website my hopes sank. Not only did the ticket vendor list the event as sold out, but there was even a news item proudly announcing that it was a sell-out before Christmas. I noticed that you could also buy tickets from local Post Offices, so I quickly closed down my inbox and headed back outside, hoping that they might have a few tickets left over. It took me almost fifteen minutes to locate the Post Office, as Orewa had a remarkably confusing layout for such a small town, and I queued for another five minutes before I was called forward to the counter, by which time my hopes had dropped and reality had reasserted itself. The chances of getting a ticket this late in the day were minimal.

'How can I help you dear?'

The lady behind the counter smiled at me, and I felt rather ridiculous as I blurted out what I knew about the Sevens tournament, including the fact that it was sold out but that I was hoping they might still have some tickets put aside.

She consulted her computer and shook her head at me. 'I'm sorry, there's no tickets showing on here. We just sell them from the ticket agents you see. Have you tried their phone number?'

I hadn't, so she wrote it down on a slip of paper for me and passed it under the window.

'There you go, they might be able to help you. Good luck.'

I told myself that I'd need more than luck as I slouched back to my car. It had always been optimistic to assume that I'd be able to get a seat so late in the day, especially given Wellington's improving status in the Sevens circuit. I threw the slip of paper she'd given me onto the dashboard, and I was about to drive out of town on the first leg to Waitomo when I decided that I might as well give it a try. After all, I'd already abandoned any hope of finding a ticket - what was the worst that could happen?

Ka Mate

The number rang for a while, then I was put on hold as a recorded voice told me that I was in a queuing system. I nearly hung up there and then, but I decided to give it a couple of minutes. In fact it took only a few seconds for my call to come out of the queue, and a tinny voice at the other end asked which event I wanted tickets for.

'The Wellington Sevens, please,' I muttered, expecting her to laugh into the mouthpiece.

'And where would you like to sit?'

Somewhere within spitting distance of the Westpac Stadium would be nice, although I'd take anything within sight of Wellington. 'I don't mind really, where do you recommend?'

'How many tickets were you looking for?'

'Just the one.'

'I can give you a seat on Aisle Eighteen, that's more or less behind the goal posts. Would that be okay?'

I was so shocked that it took me a few seconds to rediscover my voice. 'This is for the *Wellington* Sevens, isn't it? *This* year's Wellington Sevens? The one starting tomorrow?'

'That's right yes. You can collect your ticket from the box office at the stadium at any point tomorrow morning, but you'll need to take ID with you. Would you like me to book that for you?'

I managed to murmur a stunned yes and gave her my credit card details, then I hung up. It was unbelievable that I'd succeeded in securing a ticket to a sold out event less than twenty-four hours before it started, but unless this was a very elaborate prank it seemed that I was now heading down to Wellington. A glance at my watch told me it was half past ten already, and a quick calculation revealed that I'd better get on the road if I hoped to arrive at a reasonable hour. I tried calling Ian and Heather to tell them that I'd like to accept their kind offer of a bed over the weekend, but all I got was their answer machine. I left as polite and gracious a message as I could manage, in the hope that they'd not gone away at short notice, and after some minor bodily contortions I managed to dig the directions to their house out from the corner of my bag. Then I propped it on the dashboard where I wouldn't lose it and placed my mobile phone where I could reach it quickly if they called back.

It was time to start the long drive to Wellington.

Although I didn't have to travel the entire length of the North Island - I'd already moved some way south of Cape Reinga - it was still a longer trip than most people would attempt in one day, a proper road trip of epic proportions. On the plus side it would give me a good overview of the North Island. On the minus side, it was a bloody long way.

I managed to sketch out a rough route using the main highways, but I was surprised to see that there wasn't one road running straight from Auckland to Wellington. Given that these were the only two cities of any size in the North Island, I'd expected there to be a direct route between them. State Highway One did link the two, but it wound a strange looping course through the centre of the island, as if the planners were playing dot-to-dot with the major settlements when they really should have gone in with a ruler. I could only imagine that most people weren't stupid enough to attempt to drive from one city to the other, at least not on a regular basis, and that once again I'd managed to distinguish myself.

It was only a short stretch back down to Auckland, although I was dreading the city traffic. My route didn't deviate from the main roads, however, and I sped through the city with relative ease. It probably helped that I'd been this way already and was familiar with the layout, but from here onwards it was all new territory, and I was careful to keep my map open on the passenger seat.

I intended to follow State Highway One all the way down, although I'd pencilled in a few short cuts that would hopefully avoid the loopier stretches. Once I was out of Auckland's suburbs I drove almost due south towards Hamilton, a place that I'd been warned was a little light on character, something that made it stand out in an otherwise intriguing country.

It was more or less lunchtime by the time I arrived on the outskirts, so I pulled over for some fast food, opting for the quickest and easiest option. In Jonah Lomu's autobiography he recounted a McDonalds lunch he ate during the 1999 Rugby World Cup that consisted of two Big Macs, two Quarter Pounders, two Fillet-O-Fish, two McChicken Sandwiches, fries and twenty Chicken McNuggets. I figured that if Jonah could justify it, so could I. I only managed a paltry single chicken burger and fries, but since I wasn't likely to spend several hours running and weight training that afternoon it was probably for the best.

Having reached the outskirts of Hamilton I'd assumed that it wouldn't be long before I emerged from the other side, but in fact the city seemed to sprawl for miles in every direction. The highway followed a confusing, winding course through the centre, and I started to wonder if the road engineer had suffered from a bad case of the shakes on the day he drew up the plans, presumably after several years of heavy drinking. I was sure that I'd passed the same grocery store three times, and I appeared to have done a full circuit of the centre before the buildings finally started to thin out. I checked my map again to make sure that the city had finally spat me out in roughly the right direction, then I got back to the serious business of driving.

From Hamilton my route sent me eastwards and inland, and the scenery started to undergo noticeable changes. The kauri didn't grow this far south, and although there were still a few cabbage trees around their presence was less visible. Instead the terrain became significantly hillier and was punctuated by small pine forests: it would have reminded me of areas of lowland Scotland, if it weren't for the occasional patches of pampas grass swaying gently by the roadside. The pine forests must have formed part of the country's timber industry, as every few minutes a large logging truck rumbled past in the opposite direction, taking the timber up to Hamilton or Auckland. This was the first sign I'd seen of a thriving industry other than tourism, but I was still surprised by the lack of sheep.

It was another couple of hours before I reached the shores of Lake Taupo, and the magnificent scenery there helped to reenergize my tired mind. The lake itself was enormous, stretching far into the distance, where mountains suddenly rose from the waters and towered majestically on the horizon. The weather was so clear that I could see individual streams and outcrops on those distant peaks, and I promised myself that I'd return here before my trip was over. The town itself had a strong tourist infrastructure, with motels and resorts lining the road as it skirted the lake edge - as well as water-skiing and kayaking companies in abundance - but despite this commercial aspect the scenery spoke for itself. I remembered that the South Island was supposed to be even more impressive than the North, and my hopes for my trip rose.

As I drove out of Taupo I passed a large sign, stating quite clearly in white on black that 'The Coroner thanks you for driving safely'. I liked this tongue-in-cheek approach to road safety, and found it quite typical of the New Zealand character: there was an underlying seriousness to the message, but it was delivered with a smile and a wink. I like to think that we all drove a little more carefully as we left Taupo, if only to keep their temperamental Coroner happy.

When I'd checked the map that morning I'd noticed that this stretch of highway was called the Desert Road, and it immediately brought to mind America's long stretches of desert highway. In reality I was disappointed by the rather dull scrubland that gradually asserted itself as I drove further south. I couldn't help feeling that if they were going to call it the Desert Road they should at least have shipped in a few tons of sand to dump by the roadside, so that tourists like myself could enjoy the ride - it reminded me of the Australian bush more than a traditional desert. I suspected that the name had arisen because the Scrub Road would have sounded somewhat pathetic, and I was reminded of the Ninety Mile Beach debacle once again. The New Zealand government really should invest in some more sand.

My confusion increased as I passed a 'Slippery When Frosty' sign by the roadside. What kind of desert was this? Peering at the mountains in the background I could now see a dusting of snow on their peaks, and presumably the cold weather reached as far down as the road during winter. Did the Kiwis even know what a desert was? Or had those road planners been on the bottle again?

After a few more miles, and in a moment of rare generosity, I conceded that there were certainly very few farms or other buildings in the area, and there were at least some desert-like sandstone formations at points along the road. Even the highway itself eventually stopped winding drunkenly from side to side and settled into a single straight line, and if I'd been reckless enough to screw my eyes half closed I could probably have imagined that I was driving through a desert.

Just as I thought this an unusually large raindrop landed on the windscreen, followed by another two, and then a slow pattering on the car roof. Within seconds I was caught in one of the largest downpours I've ever experienced, the water pouring from the sky in one unending stream. It was as if I'd accidentally driven under a waterfall, and the visibility was so poor that I considered pulling over to the side of the road for a few minutes. If I stopped I might be washed away, however, so I decided to slow down instead. After a few tweaks of the radio I managed to find a news station, and their weather report informed me that these showers usually appeared over the centre of the North Island during the summer months. Apparently the extra heat caused more water to evaporate from the lake, and it ended up getting dumped over the plains to the south and east. Given my limited knowledge of New Zealand's climate this seemed to make some kind of sense, although privately I suspected that it might be God laughing at whoever named the Desert Road. Even England's Lake District didn't get rain like this.

Eventually, just south of Taihape, the rain dried up and I was greeted by blue skies again. I was about two thirds of the way down the North Island, and making fairly good time. I still hadn't heard anything from Ian or Heather, but by now I'd figured out that they were probably at work, so I didn't expect a phone call until six at the earliest. By then I would almost be in Wellington.

The scenery this far south was of the green, hilly variety again, having left the scrubland and torrential rain of the Desert Road behind me. There were also a number of striking white cliffs among the hills, which looked as if they might be chalk but were more probably sandstone. After a few million years of erosion they might end up with a desert after all.

From here the highway swung slightly west, probably when the planner's pen slipped as he reached for his bottle of vodka, and as I passed through Hunterville I noticed that someone had changed the town sign to 'Hooterville'. Given that the driving fatigue had numbed my brain I found this enormously funny, and chuckled at it all the way through town. Unfortunately Hooterville didn't really live up to its title, although it did seem to have an unusually large number of farms, and I finally got to see some sheep. They often occupied the same fields as the cows, possibly for ease of access when the farmer fancied a mixed grill, but their numbers still weren't terribly impressive and I wondered if we'd all developed a slightly lopsided view of New Zealand. After Hunterville I passed through Bulls, whose sign had miraculously avoided the pens of the graffiti artists. Quite why Hunterville should be a more obvious target than Bulls I wasn't sure, although perhaps the culprit had decided that Bulls had a pretty stupid name to begin with and didn't require his intervention.

It was as I left Bulls that my mobile finally rang, and I pulled over to the side of the road. It was Ian calling me back to say that they'd love to have me stay with them, and marvelling at the fact that I'd managed to get myself a ticket for the Sevens. I gave him the abbreviated version of my story and thanked them again for their hospitality, which he brushed off in typical Kiwi fashion. Having given my location we estimated my arrival at about nine o'clock, and he said that they'd make sure they had some food for me, along with a bottle of wine or two. Obviously it would be rude not to accept such a kind offer, and in return I offered him the most sincere thanks that my British upbringing could muster before hanging up. I was actually a little nervous about seeing the family, having only known them for four days on a remote island in the Pacific. I was sure that a glass of wine or two would help smooth over any awkwardness, however, and I pulled out onto the road again before the nearby sheep started getting restless.

In the end I arrived in Wellington close to eight-thirty, having sailed down the west coast and into the city with ease. The mountains to the east of the highway were quite spectacular with the late afternoon sun shining directly on them, and for the first time I was reminded that the *Lord Of The Rings* movies were shot here. I'd read somewhere that most of the films' locations were in the South Island, but these awe-inspiring mountains could easily have been used as a backdrop for some of the scenes.

It was fairly easy to follow the map that Ian and Heather had drawn me in Fiji, and before long I was driving through the suburbs searching for their house. When I found it I was impressed by the size of the two-story home, and once again I found myself happy to be staying in a residential area. I had nothing to give them by way of a gift, but after a quick rummage through my bags I found the remnants of some macadamia brittle I'd bought *en route*. I decided to take it with me to the front door as a paltry offering. It wasn't much, but it felt better than turning up empty-handed.

As it turned out, they were simply amazed that I'd driven almost the entire length of the North Island in one day. Ian and Heather were both slim and athletic, as were their children Kate and Olivia, so I was surprised when they opened a large wedge of cheese and a bottle of wine while we discussed the various places that I'd passed on my drive down. I could see Ian's background as a teacher coming through when he sent the girls off to get ready for bed, but then he settled back in his chair and took a long sip from his glass of wine. The Kiwi mentality might be geared towards an active, outdoor life, but they certainly had no problem unwinding.

Ian was a keen rugby fan and taught the sport at his school, so as soon as the subject cropped up I asked him who the Maoris were in the current national squad. I knew that Jonah Lomu was actually Tongan rather than Maori, but I wasn't sure about any of the other players.

'There's not many, to be honest. Carlos Spencer's part Maori, but when it comes to the others I'm not certain. There's lots of part-Maori players, but probably not the ones you'd think. When the Maori team plays touring sides it's usually full of blonde and ginger guys, which tells you all you need to know. Most of the coloured guys in the All Blacks are Poly boys.'

Poly boys?

'Polynesians - Tongans and Samoans generally, but sometimes the Fijians too. Joe Rokocoko's Fijian, Tana Umaga's Samoan. There's not really any full-blood Maoris in the team.'

Ka Mate

Our conversation unravelled as the evening went on, helped by a few bottles of wine, and by the time we finally staggered to bed it was past midnight. As we said goodnight I thanked Ian and Heather again for their generosity in opening their home to me. Most people liked to think of themselves as excellent hosts, but the New Zealanders prided themselves on it, welcoming visitors with open arms. I was starting to realise what a remarkable nation the Kiwis were.

5
Te Whanganui-a-Tara *(Wellington)*

Unfortunately my hosts were both working the next day, but they'd kindly left me instructions on how to reach the Westpac Stadium from their house. It was only a short stroll to the nearest station, and from there the train took me straight to the stadium – there was even a large concrete walkway leading me directly from the platform to the box office. It really couldn't have been much simpler, and I found myself wishing that all sports venues were so accessible.

The Westpac Stadium is affectionately known as the Cake-Tin, and given its circular shape and steep sides it was easy to see why. As I approached the ticket office I became nervous again, and almost convinced myself that I'd been the victim of a malicious prank: there were already hundreds of people queuing up outside the main gates, most of whom must have booked their tickets in October or November of last year. It seemed infeasible that I should be able to walk up to the counter and collect a ticket I'd paid for yesterday.

In contrast to the masses gathering outside the stadium gates there was hardly any queue at the ticket office, however, and after the couple of people in front of me had moved on I was ushered forward to the grille. When I said that I had tickets to pick up for today and tomorrow the girl in the window bravely quelled the urge to laugh in my face, and instead asked if I had some ID with me. I'd brought my passport just in case a credit card wasn't enough, and I slid it through the gap in the window.

She rifled through a box filled with envelopes several times for dramatic effect before turning back to me.

'Here you are Mr. Coxon, these are your tickets. This one is for today, the other's for tomorrow. You're in Aisle Eighteen, so that's straight through the main gates over there, then to your left. We've already taken payment on your credit card, so that's you. Okay?'

She slid my passport back through the slot along with a white envelope, and I looked at them in quiet disbelief: against all the odds I was now holding a pair of tickets to the Wellington Rugby Sevens. I hurried to the gates as quickly as possible before someone tried to steal them off me. Having come this far I felt sure that catastrophe was lurking around a corner.

The queues for the gates hadn't subsided while I was at the ticket office, but at least it was a sunny day and it gave me some time to stare at the weird and wonderful costumes on display. Even though it was still early in the morning the temperature was rising, and I suspected that the man who'd come in a suit made out of bubble wrap would regret his decision by the afternoon. I was equally concerned that the group of four boys in nothing but boxer shorts and black body paint would be shivering in those very shorts once the sun went down. There were nurses and cowboys, a Fred Flintstone and an Austin Powers, and even a few mad fools wearing England rugby tops. It made me wish that I had something more interesting to wear. In the end I made do with a black and red Edinburgh Rugby cap, which in this part of the world almost counted as fancy dress.

Once I'd made it through the gates I found my seat easily enough. The ground was already shimmering slightly in the heat, and I seemed doomed to blacken and melt like a plastic figure under a magnifying glass. Fortunately I remembered Ian telling me at some point last night that everyone swapped seats throughout the competition, so I moved a few rows back into the shade. Hopefully by the time anyone claimed this space my own seat would be a bit more sheltered. The lady at the ticket office had been right, however – these were excellent seats. I was positioned almost directly behind one of the sets of goal posts, skewed just slightly to one side to allow a better view of the pitch. I'd arrived just in time for the first match and some of the players were warming up directly in front of me, although I didn't recognise their nationality from the strip. Checking my watch it appeared that things would be underway in a couple of minutes.

The structure of the competition seemed remarkably simple at first glance, but this impression proved to be deceptive and it slowly became more and more complex as the tournament progressed. You might have to read the next two paragraphs a few times over before you fully understand them – I know I certainly did.

There were four Pools of teams in the competition, and the first day was taken up with the matches from each of these Pools. Each Pool contained four teams, and each team played the other three once during the Pool Round. So far, so simple. On the second day it grew more complicated. From day two it became a knockout competition, at least in principle. The top two teams from each Pool qualified for the Cup Round, in which the winner of one Pool played the Runner-up from another. The losers of these matches got knocked out of the Cup Championship, but then competed against each other in the Plate Championship. Meanwhile the winners continued to compete for the Cup.

Still with me? Excellent. The third and fourth ranked teams from each Pool also competed against each other, this time in the Bowl Championship. In a similar manner to the Cup Championship, the third team from one Pool played the fourth from another Pool, with the losers of those matches getting knocked out of the Bowl competition. While the winners continued to compete for the Bowl, the losers then competed in the Shield Championship. All of this happened more or less simultaneously throughout the final day, eventually ending up with four winning teams: the Cup winners, the Plate winners, the Bowl winners and the Shield winners. By then everyone would be so confused that we'd all go off and have another beer to try and forget about it. Assuming that we hadn't already drunk the bar dry, of course.

To the uninitiated it was a strange and complex system, but there was a kind of logic behind it. The Pool stages finished on the first day, but all the teams continued playing throughout the second day, and everyone had a chance of winning a trophy. The Cup was the only one that really mattered, but the other competitions kept the fans involved and ensured that the teams still had something to play for. Presumably over a number of years you could manage to win the Bowl, the Plate *and* the Cup, hence creating an entire dinner set. The Shield was rather useless in this respect, probably explaining why it was the least valued prize. I'm sure the Shield winners went home feeling that they'd really missed out on the kitchenware.

Each team fielded seven players, and each half lasted seven minutes. There was a two minute interval between halves, and players shown the yellow card had to leave the field for two minutes. This numerical symmetry suggested that the game's officials sensed they'd already bamboozled most of us with the competition's structure, and were determined to keep the rest of it simple. Other than that it was pretty much the same as the standard Rugby Union rules, for Sevens was in essence a simpler, faster version of the traditional game. Sevens rugby was played at speed with the emphasis firmly on attack, and it was surprising how high a score some teams could accumulate in fourteen minutes of play.

The first match of the day was Argentina versus Tonga, by no means a crowd-puller but tightly contested nonetheless. I used this opportunity to slip off to the bar, and returned to my seat ten minutes later with a couple of plastic bottles of beer. I was used to the alcohol-free policies at British rugby grounds, and these bottles of Lion Red lager felt like a luxury. As my first taste of New Zealand beer, though, it failed to blow me away: the slightly warm lager that I swilled around my mouth could just as easily have been any number of familiar generic brews, and even then it would have sat at the cheaper end of the scale. I knew that Lion Red was one of the more commercial brands, however, so I wasn't too disheartened. Today I intended to enjoy the rugby – beer appreciation could wait until later.

I had no real interest in the day's matches until Scotland played South Africa at 2.15, so I spent my time quietly sipping my beer and observing the swelling crowds. When I first entered the stadium it was less than a quarter full, but the numbers were growing rapidly as the day progressed. To the right of me was a group of Polynesians dressed in blue doctors' gowns, with the word 'Doctours' emblazoned across the front. It soon became clear that they would be one of the main attractions for the day, as a couple of them walked between the rows offering free sun block to all the spectators. One balding fan even had it rubbed into his scalp for him, but it was all done in such good humour that he simply laughed as his head was slathered with white cream. I got the feeling that this wouldn't be the last we saw of the Doctours.

Most of the nations represented in the competition were familiar to me, with the exception of somewhere called Niue, pronounced 'New-ay' by the announcer when he came on the P.A. system. I discovered later that this was a small coral island near the Cook Islands, covering only just over a hundred square miles. For an island with a population of less than two thousand they did remarkably well in the opening stages, even if they did lose all their matches, and I could sense the crowd starting to get behind them. Apparently their name meant 'behold the coconut', which was such an excellent name for a country that it was no wonder we all warmed to them so quickly. When England beat them 41-7 I wasn't sure whether I wanted to cheer, laugh or cry.

Before long a few inflatable balls appeared in the crowd and were bounced at random around the gathered masses, occasionally straying onto the pitch and being collected by stern-faced officials. For every one that was confiscated another two appeared, and from time to time the officials realised they were fighting a losing battle and simply threw them back.

True to my expectations the Doctours didn't stay silent for long, and accompanied by loud clapping from his medical team one of them disappeared out of the Aisle Eighteen exit. He reappeared at the next aisle along a few seconds later, and when the people there were clapping in time too he disappeared once again – only to pop up one aisle further round. There were thirty-six aisles in total, and when he reached the seats directly opposite ours he received a big cheer from the Doctours, and from me. For the last six or seven aisles we clapped him home again, and when he finally arrived back at his seat a round of applause burst out across the stadium. I was sure all the clapping and cheering must have confused the players and referees, but South Africa still managed to beat Japan by fifty points to nothing, so it hadn't done too much harm. I secretly suspected that a few of the South African players might have been more interested in watching him than in playing the obviously mismatched game.

In the interval after the South Africa game I heard a whisper behind me that Jonah Lomu was in his hospitality box, and in my excitement I managed to knock over my bottle of beer. Fortunately they provided you with screw-on caps, so nothing was spilt and I silently thanked those forward-thinking fellows at Lion Red.

It didn't take me long to spot the great dome of Jonah's head over the balcony railing, and I was pleased to see that he was sitting on the level immediately above mine. The Doctours started a slow chant of 'Jo-nah, Jo-nah' that gradually rose to his ears and prompted a rather shy wave over the balcony edge. There was an audible buzz of excitement in our area over the fact that the big man was here with us, and I couldn't help feeling sorry for the players on the pitch. New Zealand achieved a resounding win over Kenya and no one even noticed.

When one of the inflatable balls eventually came to us the Doctours quickly secured it and started a chant of 'to the top, to the top', pointing up to where Jonah was sitting. They knocked it behind them and attempted to get as much height on it as possible, but the next person in the chain mistimed his shot and the ball went sailing off to our left. The Doctours heckled this pathetic effort, then began a new chant of 'burst their ball, burst their ball'. It took a few minutes for the ball to find its way back to them, but once they had it again one of them removed the plug and pushed down on it, the air escaping with a loud hiss. After a minute almost all the air had been expelled, and the deflated ball drooped across his lap like an empty bag.

The Doctour who'd run the circuit of the ground half an hour earlier stood up again and began to clap his hands.

'To the top, to the top, to the top...'

A couple of them pointed up at Jonah, and amidst laughter from the rest of us they attempted to throw the empty husk of the inflatable ball up to the balcony. It took three or four throws to get it back far enough in the crowd, and then someone stood up with it and slung it as high as they could. As it reached the apex of its trajectory Jonah stood up in his hospitality box, and leaning over the railing he plucked the screwed up piece of plastic from the air.

Ka Mate

A cheer erupted around us, and a couple of the Doctours smiled and waved at Lomu. Then they turned to us and start clapping in time again.

'Jo-nah, Jo-nah, Jo-nah...'

Eventually the excitement died down and Jonah disappeared back onto his balcony, but it had been an amusing diversion that brightened up the Pool stages of the competition. Most of the early games were severely mismatched anyway, and there were no real surprises on the scoreboard.

During one of the intervals between games a muscular New Zealand fan sitting two seats along from me leant over the empty spaces and tapped my arm.

'Those Doctours fellas, they're funny guys, hey?'

I agreed with him – they'd certainly kept me amused.

'I think they're here most years, I've seen them here before anyway. They're pretty funny guys.'

'You've been to the Sevens before then?'

'Every year since it started. I live up in Hamilton, but I drive down here just for this. It's fantastic the Sevens, such a good atmosphere. You here for both days?'

I said that I was, and he held out his hand.

'I'm Jeff by the way. I'll be here tomorrow too, so you'll see me both days. Got the same seats for both of them.'

I assumed from his looks that Jeff had some Maori blood in him, although I was less sure of this than I might have been a few months ago. His stomach hung over the top of his jeans a little, although he wasn't as overweight as the security guard I'd seen at the kauri forest walk, and he sported a slightly greying moustache. He also had the well-muscled arms that I'd seen on the carving of Kupe in Waitangi – which made me wonder if he'd rowed all the way here – and he displayed a large tattoo across one forearm. He would have looked threatening in a dark alley, but his smile made him less imposing in the daylight.

'I've been looking forward to the next match,' I said, rescuing my hand from his grip. 'I lived in Edinburgh for a while you see, and Scotland are playing France.'

'You've got no chance then. I'm half French, and our guys are gonna walk all over you. You wait and see.'

'Probably, but you never know. We've played pretty well so far.'

He smiled at me as a thought occurred to him. 'Tell you what, I'm nearly out of beer. I bet you that France beat Scotland – the loser has to buy the next round. Deal?'

Given the favourable exchange rate the beers here were fairly cheap for me, so I took him up on his offer. Jeff grinned to himself as we shook hands on it, his grip tight enough to make my fingers ache. 'You ain't got a hope mate.'

France got off to a good start, and they led all the way through the match. The Scottish defence was fairly solid, though, and they managed to keep the scores low and the victory still within touching distance. Jeff looked comfortable with his position, getting to his feet from time to time to cheer his French compatriots or to applaud an impressive piece of play. He finished his bottle of beer and gestured towards it with a knowing look.

Just as the match was drawing to a close, however, the Scots seemed to find a burst of energy, and the French were caught off guard. Their defence crumbled like a stale French loaf, and before anyone quite knew how it had happened the referee was blowing his whistle to indicate that the Scots had scored. The whistle also marked the end of the match, with the final scoreboard showing a 10-7 victory to the Scots.

I turned to Jeff, prepared to point out as tactfully as possible that mine was a Lion Red, but he was already up out of his seat.

Ka Mate

'You wanting another bottle of the same?'

I nodded.

'I thought we had that one in the bag there, but you guys stole that away from us. Well played mate, I didn't think Scotland were gonna manage that. I'll just be a minute with the beers. I'll leave my coat and bag here so you know I've not done a runner.'

He laughed and sidled past some of the other spectators on his way to the bar. I couldn't quite believe the final score myself. I was used to supporting a losing Scottish team, but I had to admit that it was a gutsy and positive win – for once they hadn't given up in the final quarter, and the last minute offensive was wonderfully executed. The French team was warming down in front of us, and a few of them looked as if they might burst into tears at any moment. To lose was bad enough, but to lose to Scotland? That had to sting.

With an easy victory later in the day against Japan, it looked as if Scotland would be through to the Cup Championship. They'd lost their first match of the day to South Africa, but with victories in both their other games they should qualify second in the pool. It would all rest on France's final match against South Africa, one of four games that had been held back to finish the day off in style. The main sides in contention for the Cup played a match each at the very end of the day: Australia against Argentina, South Africa against France, England against Samoa, and New Zealand against Fiji. At the start of the tournament you'd have expected those eight teams to qualify for the Cup, but with Scotland's surprise win it looked as if France might be struggling. England had scored easy wins against Canada and Niue, already guaranteeing their place in the Cup competition.

Before the closing games, however, there was a parade of the participating nations. It came as little surprise to see Jonah Lomu leading the parade out onto the pitch:

since he'd moved to Wellington he'd become a local hero as well as an international superstar, and following his recent recovery from debilitating illness the crowd gave him a rousing reception. He was wearing a hideous white *adidas* tracksuit that made him look as if he was in his pyjamas, but he was paid several million dollars a year for wearing it, so I was almost prepared to forgive him. In 2004 *adidas* renewed his sponsorship contract despite his kidney disease, showing a confidence in him that reflected Jonah's celebrity status even when he wasn't active on the playing field.

The players themselves didn't participate in the parade, presumably preparing themselves for the forthcoming matches, and instead we were treated to a stream of cheerleaders and dance groups. The Canadians were rather predictably dressed as Mounties, although I wasn't convinced that black hotpants were officially part of the uniform; the Japanese wore karate outfits; while the Australians looked rather dull in green and gold. My personal favourites were the English dancers, who come out onto the pitch dressed as characters from *Dad's Army*, complete with 'Who Do You Think You Are Kidding, Mr. Hitler?' playing over the P.A. system. It was still a cliché, but an entertaining one.

On his way back to the hospitality boxes Jonah walked through the crowd, signing autographs and posing for photos. Even from a distance his height and bulk were obvious, his distinctive bald head weaving a slow trail back up to the balcony. Some of the Doctours fought their way to the front to have their photo taken with him, and he greeted them as if they were old friends. He might have undergone major surgery and spent hours on dialysis, but none of his charisma had deserted him.

Jeff was looking for France to conjure up a surprise win against South Africa after the parade, but they lost in the end by a slim two point margin and were out of contention for the Cup. A slightly unconvincing English win over

Samoa meant that both Scotland and England were through, so I celebrated with another bottle of Lion Red. The final match of the day was between New Zealand and Fiji, and the drunken crowd rallied behind their home team – in the end they won by a nineteen point margin despite Fiji's current good form, and the local boys seemed to be the team to beat on the second day. Fiji qualified for the Cup competition too, having won both their other matches, but their heads went down after the defeat. England and New Zealand emerged from the first day as the two teams that were in form and really in contention.

I said goodbye to Jeff, having promised to see him again tomorrow, and followed the surging crowd back to the train station. The transport network was obviously used to coping with large events, as they'd laid on extra services and there was a train waiting for me when I finally struggled through to the correct platform. In the dark I almost missed the stop where I was due to get off, but fortunately an elderly couple pointed it out to me and I slipped through the doors just in time.

Ian and Heather had given me their spare key, and when I pushed open the front door the lights were out and the house was in silence, so I snuck through the darkness to my room. The roar of the crowd was still ringing in my ears as I drifted off to sleep, that final bottle of Lion Red taking its toll.

* * *

The following day things were noticeably muted. It was a Saturday, so Ian and Heather were already in the kitchen when I staggered out of bed, nursing a small but insistent hangover. They made me a cup of coffee, put some toast on for me, and generally mothered me until the point when I stumbled out through their front door. The train almost lulled me to sleep with its hissing rhythms as it carried me back to the Westpac Stadium for the second day of the competition.

The Doctours were nowhere to be seen, presumably nursing hangovers worse than mine. Jeff was already there, though, heartily tucking in to several triangles of sandwich that he'd brought with him in his bag. I nodded a greeting and tried to settle into a comfortable position on the hard plastic seat. A glance around the ground showed me that it was less than a quarter full, populated only by the hardcore rugby nerds and a few poor souls like myself, nursing hangovers from one bottle too many of Lion Red. The rugby got underway with a minimum of noise and bustle. They were probably worried about waking the spectators.

The authorities were obviously used to this slow start on the second day. They opened proceedings with the quarterfinals for the Bowl Championship, the competition played between the losing two teams from each pool. Both France and Tonga had slipped down to this second division due to bad performances yesterday, but otherwise it was left to the minor teams. USA lost to Canada in the opener, then Tonga beat Japan without difficulty in the second match. France similarly waltzed to a win over the Cook Islands, and before we even really knew it we were through to the last quarter final in the Bowl round. This was between Kenya and Niue, and for the first time there was a murmur of excitement from the crowd. We'd all warmed to both these sides yesterday, due in part to a wonderfully theatrical dancing warm-down that the Kenyans performed after every match, and there was a buzz of interest in the outcome.

In the end it was Kenya who won over the Niueans despite the impressive number of vowels in their name, and the cheer that erupted from the crowd suggested they were a popular winner. We had a chance to see their warm-down exercises again too, so everybody was happy.

At 2.30 the quarterfinals for the Cup Championship began, and I noticed that there was a sudden surge in the crowd numbers. The Doctours started to reappear in ones and twos, still dressed in their outfits but definitely subdued compared with yesterday.

Jeff leant across and tapped me on the arm again.

'Your English boys are playing next. You gonna support them again?'

Earlier this morning I'd had a trawl through my bag for any kind of costume I could wear to the Sevens, as I'd felt strangely underdressed yesterday. There were some truly terrible fashion choices to be found, but nothing I could call a costume. Fortunately, before my hangover forced me to sit back down on the bed, I did manage to find something of interest. As Jeff watched I plunged my hand into my backpack and slowly withdrew a large St. George's Cross, like a magician pulling scarves from his sleeve. It measured about five feet across, and I slid a plastic rod that Ian had lent me into one end to act as a pole. Jeff grinned at me.

'See, now you look like a proper supporter. Tell you what, I'll cheer for England too since you've got the flag. Just don't tell my family, okay?'

Due to New Zealand's resounding victory last night we were playing Fiji in the quarterfinal, so I suspected that Jeff was Maori rather than Polynesian after all. Even so it was rare for anyone to offer to support England, and I gladly passed him the flag to wave above his head as the game began.

Jeff yelled 'Come on England' until he was hoarse, but no matter how much he waved my flag the Fijians had come out fighting, and they ended up beating us 24-19. Fiji had struggled through a bad first day of the competition, but in typical fashion they'd raised their game when it came to playing the English. Since England captain Martin Johnson had lifted the Rugby World Cup in 2003 we'd definitely become the team everyone loved to beat.

I still had some hope left as Scotland were due to play next, but any dreams of a Scottish resurgence were quashed by a solid Argentinean performance. It meant that both my teams were now out of the Cup Championship, but because of the draw they would now play each other for the Plate. The old rivalry between Scotland and England always lends an extra edge to these confrontations, and a few excited whispers went around the ground as people realised the draw for this afternoon. I was disappointed to no longer have a team in contention for the Cup, but the Plate match would at least be some consolation.

The last two Cup quarterfinals ended with close victories for South Africa and New Zealand, and then we switched back to the Shield semi-finals. You'll recall that these were played out between the losing teams from the Bowl Championship, so we saw USA versus Japan, followed by the Cook Islands playing Niue. Both matches were fairly one-sided - strangely so considering that these were the four least successful teams of the tournament - and the final was to be played between Japan and Niue. There was some interest in the crowd as we all appeared to have adopted Niue as our spiritual home, but the time was generally used for bathroom breaks and visits to the bar.

The Bowl semi-finals followed, and Tonga won a resounding although not unexpected victory over Canada. The second semi-final was between France and Kenya, and although France were the most highly regarded team competing for the Bowl they looked lacklustre when they took to the field, as if yesterday's defeats had destroyed their confidence and self-belief. In contrast Kenya were not a naturally gifted side, but with the crowd behind them and a few moments of magic from their players they managed to scrape a 12-7 win. The crowd surged to its feet as the final whistle went, and the Kenyans left the field to a hard-earned round of applause. The French slowly skulked off in a manner that seemed entirely in keeping with their uninspired performance, and Jeff remained unusually silent. I offered

Ka Mate

him one of my beers as a consolation. Today's matches weren't going well for either of us.

By this stage the Doctours had finally woken up, and one of them started handing out blue hairnets for everyone to wear. I pulled mine unwillingly over the top of my cap, knowing that I looked ridiculous, but safe in the knowledge that everybody else looked at least as ridiculous as me. Eventually our entire area of the stand was kitted out with them, visible proof of the power of peer pressure, especially when combined with large quantities of beer. They also handed around homemade sandwiches to anyone who wanted them, and I gratefully accepted a chicken salad roll. As least there was no chance of anyone's hair falling into my food.

As I finished eating Jeff stood up to let someone through, and he introduced me to his brother, who'd been sitting elsewhere in the stadium but had come to join us for a while. He was quite clearly drunk and appeared to have no teeth, and I couldn't help leaping to the assumption that he'd lost them in a beer-fuelled brawl. Compared with Jeff his frame was thin and wiry, but there was a slightly insane gleam in his eyes that made me uncomfortable. Jeff seemed relaxed beside him, though, so I convinced myself that it was just my imagination working overtime. Even so, I concentrated on the rugby for the next half hour, my eyes glued to the pitch.

The Plate semi-finals were next, which meant that Scotland and England were taking to the field. In typical fashion the Scots played their best game of the tournament, while the English were facing similar problems to the French, their heads dropping after their last defeat. It was a desperately close game in the closing minutes, each team trying to secure the victory with a few moments of brilliance, but in the end it was Scotland who won through, beating England by a narrow two-point margin. I hurriedly concealed my England flag beneath my seat and waved my

Edinburgh Rugby cap above my head. I figured it was about time I enjoyed a celebration, even if it did require a sudden change of allegiance.

The other Plate semi-final was a similarly close affair between Australia and Samoa, with Australia battling through to win by another two-point margin. After these close matches the Cup semi-finals were a disappointment, Argentina easily beating a Fijian side that seemed to have spent all its energy on defeating England earlier in the day, and New Zealand proving their excellent form against an outclassed South Africa. The home crowd was understandably exuberant in its support of New Zealand, but in the end it was a disappointingly easy win.

After this there were only the finals still to play, and I made a quick trip to the bar before the matches began. Jeff had disappeared off with his toothless brother, so I was able to immerse myself in the action on the pitch.

First up was the Shield final between Japan and Niue. In truth it was only a consolation prize, and throughout the competition both teams had struggled to equal the ability and professionalism of the better-known sides. The players were eager to leave Wellington with a prize in their cabin baggage, however, and the crowds were drunk enough to get caught up in the moment. When the final whistle went and Niue were declared winners we all leapt to our feet, applauding and cheering as if they'd won the entire tournament. They did a lap of honour, stopping halfway along each side of the pitch to do their traditional *haka*, and I made sure my camera was ready by the time they reached our stand.

Strictly speaking the word '*haka*' should only be applied to traditional Maori dances, but people commonly used the term for dances from the Pacific Islands too: to most observers Niue's war dance looked remarkably similar to a Maori *haka*, undoubtedly due to their shared Polynesian heritage. I'd already seen a *haka* performed at the Auckland

Ka Mate

Museum, but the passion and exhilaration evident after Niue's win lent them an intensity that the cultural performance had lacked. They stripped off their shirts and launched into it bare-chested, some of them displaying intricate tattoos on their upper arms. Being such a minor team in the sport they weren't as physically imposing as the New Zealand professionals, but the experience was still thrilling for the crowd, earning a spontaneous round of applause when they finished. For a nation of only two and a half thousand people they'd shown a lot of heart in this competition, and we were all keen to acknowledge it.

Next up was the Bowl Championship final between Kenya and Tonga. At the start of the day we'd all expected to see France facing off against the Tongans for this prize, and while the crowd support for Kenya had been admirable, none of us really expected them to have much chance of winning. The Pacific Islands – especially Samoa, Tonga and Fiji – had a tendency to under perform at times, but they still played rugby with a passion and intensity that most other countries envied. If they had one weakness it was that their confidence could drop if they fell too far behind their opponents, but that was unlikely to happen against the Kenyans. As long as they managed to play for the full fourteen minutes, the Tongans should walk away with the Bowl.

Kenya played a solid match, however, and by the time the referee's whistle blew at full time the scores were level at 12-12. This sent a few of us flicking through our programs trying to find the procedures for a tie, but fortunately the announcer came on the P.A. to explain that they would play an extra five minutes each way, but that from this point onwards the golden goal rule applied. The first team to score points would be declared the winner, and there was a buzz of excitement in the stadium as the referee blew his whistle for play to restart.

From the first second of overtime the result never looked in doubt. The Kenyans had seen their chance for glory and they were determined to clasp it with both hands, drawing on every scrap of energy left in their bodies as they threw everything they had at the Tongans. When they finally scored the whole of the Westpac stadium surged to its feet – apart from a handful of sulking Tongans. Following Niue's lead the Kenyans entertained us all with a victory lap, stopping on each side of the pitch to do their dancing warm-down exercises. It was no *haka*, but the novelty value combined with the ear-to-ear smiles that never left their faces more than compensated for the *haka*'s ferocity. They might have only won the Bowl, the prize for the best losing team from the Pool rounds, but you would be forgiven for thinking that they'd just won the World Cup. No one wanted to deny them their hard earned moment of victory, and even the Tongans rose to their feet as they left the field.

The final of the Plate championship followed, having been slightly delayed due to the extra time taken for the previous match, but Scotland never looked like beating an in-form Australian side. Yet again a competitive team had exhausted all their energy and spirit on beating England. It was an embarrassment that they didn't even manage to score a single point before the whistle blew, but no great surprise to those of us who were familiar with Scotland's ability to let their supporters down. Australia won the Plate Championship final 32-0, and deserved every single point.

The Aussies weren't popular in New Zealand – perhaps even less so than the English – and their team was booed before and after every match, so they understandably decided against doing a lap of honour. If they'd attempted it a few empty bottles might have been lobbed out of the crowd. They did their warm-down exercises at our end of the pitch, however, and I noticed that Eddie Jones, the coach for the national Rugby Union side that lost to England in the 2003 World Cup finals, was wandering among the players.

Ka Mate

These would definitely be the guys to look out for in years to come, and I made a note of some of their names.

Eventually the pitch was cleared and the Argentineans emerged, closely followed by the home team. AC/DC's 'Back In Black' was played over the P.A. system as the New Zealand players sprinted onto the grass, but it was drowned out by the roar of excitement from the Wellington crowd. I even found myself rising to my feet to cheer them out, if only so that I could see over the heads of the fans in front of me.

A New Zealand victory never really seemed to be in doubt, but for the culmination of two days of competition the Cup final was something of a disappointment. I certainly couldn't convince the largely Kiwi crowd of this, with Jeff now back alongside me and looking as if he might burst a major artery every time New Zealand won a point, but from the perspective of a neutral observer it was a disappointingly one-sided match. By half time the home team were the only ones to have scored, and Argentina looked to be out of contention. They came back briefly at the start of the second half, but then one of their players was shown the red card for biting and sent off the pitch. With their numbers reduced to six men there was no hope of a recovery, and New Zealand secured a comfortable 31-7 victory. I joined Jeff in his victory celebrations, but the win left me with a hollow feeling. I'd hoped to see some inspirational rugby, and instead I was greeted with a whitewash.

The crowd was still on its feet as the New Zealand team started their lap of honour, stopping on each side of the stadium as the Niueans had done to perform a celebratory *haka*. At least I'd have this spectacle to make up for the disappointment of the final, and I scrambled through my bag to get my camera ready. They seemed to take forever to complete the circuit of the pitch, however, and they stopped every few yards to do yet another *haka*. After fifteen minutes of this the team began to get bored, and a few of them drifted away, chatting with friends and officials. The *haka* broke up and it looked as if the entertainment for the evening was over. They never made it to our side of the pitch, and after a few hopeful minutes I eventually packed my camera away again and joined the disappointed stream of stragglers making their way out of the stadium. Not only had they failed to deliver a thrilling final, but they'd also denied me the chance to see a true New Zealand victory *haka* at close quarters. Instead of being carried away by the euphoria of a win for the home side, I felt deflated and empty.

As my train pulled away from the station I looked around me, and I suddenly realised that I seemed to have unwittingly crashed a costume party. To my right sat Mel Gibson straight from the set of *Braveheart*, his kilt flapping in the breeze from the open window. Opposite sat a man dressed like a Police officer from the waist up, sporting only a pair of black boots and some tight swimming trunks on his bottom half. The badge on his hat read 'Speedo Cop'.

In any other situation I'd have questioned my sanity, or at least my safety, but my two days at the rugby tournament had made this kind of thing commonplace. When Braveheart started handing out lollipops to everyone in the carriage I accepted mine gratefully, and smiled to myself as he opened the door to the driver's compartment and offered him one too. It came as little surprise when the driver accepted, or when he handed out a spare piece of machinery for Braveheart to fool around with in the carriage. At least, we all *assumed* that it was spare...

When I finally reached Ian and Heather's house the lights were out again, and I let myself in as quietly as I could manage. After all the evening's disappointments my spirits had been raised again by a character from a historical movie, some lollipops, and an obscene Policeman. Maybe that made me shallow, but at least the day had ended on a high. It was only as I brushed my teeth that I realised I was still wearing my blue hairnet.

Ka Mate

* * *

After I'd wasted the following morning recovering from a second hangover we drove across the city to see one of Ian's friends. Dave worked as a teacher at the same school as Ian, yet somehow he owned a spectacular house perched on the hillside overlooking Wellington Harbour. We climbed eighty steps from street level to the front door, and as he greeted us with a smile and a beer I marvelled at the view from his lounge window. Apparently there were quite a few houses in Wellington with sweeping views of the harbour, as the hills rose around it on all sides. Even so, I was sure that Dave's panorama must rank among the best – I couldn't imagine a teacher in London owning a house with a view of Tower Bridge.

Lunch was a very pleasant buffet, and we sat outside on the lawn to eat. Several of Ian's colleagues were also there, and it was nice to spend some time among the people of Wellington. After a while, however, I noticed that almost all of them had spent a few months, or even years, in the UK: maybe I wasn't so far from home after all.

I wasn't sure if it was my presence that caused it, but after half an hour they started to talk about their favourite places to visit in the South Island. I'd already had enough recommendations to fill half a year, but I politely listened and nodded my head as they gave me a new hotlist for my trip. In general their views were more critical than the opinions I'd encountered in Auckland, and I wondered if this was a Wellington phenomenon, or if it was due to the fact that most of them were teachers. They were all in agreement that I might as well avoid Invercargill, as its only real attraction was its proximity to the southernmost point of the South Island. Having already seen the top end of the North Island I suspected that this would be enough to draw me there, but I didn't mention it for fear of opening myself up to ridicule. Us Brits had a hard enough time as it was in this part of the world.

Surprisingly Dave also said that Christchurch was worth avoiding, despite the fact that I'd only heard good things about it until now.

'No, trust me,' he said, swigging from a bottle of beer, 'the place is a dump. It's got two good streets in the centre and that's it. I lived there for a while so you can take my word for it. It's a complete shithole.'

I wondered what terrible and unspeakable things the people of Christchurch had done to him to provoke such an extreme reaction, but I decided against probing any further. Christchurch is often said to be the most anglicised of New Zealand's cities, so I wondered if Dave was trying to wind me up. Anyway, I'd decided a long time ago that the so-called Garden City would be one of my stops on the South Island.: before long I'd be able to see for myself if his assessment was a fair one.

After lunch we made our way back into town, and Ian drove us to the city centre. Today was Waitangi Day, the official anniversary of the signing of the Waitangi Treaty, and there was an organised celebration and open-air concert close to the waterfront. Three bands took to the stage at various points during the afternoon, although they had several band members in common and it was hard to tell the difference between them – by chance it was also Bob Marley's birthday, so we were treated to numerous renditions of his greatest hits. It was a relaxed affair, despite a few girls at the front getting overexcited when the winner of New Zealand 's *Pop Idol* TV show came on stage. We lay back in the sun with a small picnic hamper, surreptitiously pouring beer into our plastic beakers when no one was looking.

The sparse attendance at the event surprised me, but there was a strong Maori presence at the festivities – including souvenir stalls with Maori designs on the fringes of the park – and it was encouraging to see this cultural intermingling. Many of the performers also seemed to be Maori or Pacific Islanders, and Ian told me that reggae and rap music were particularly strong in their communities. They certainly had a natural flair for it.

That evening we were joined by Jacob and Maria, another couple that we'd met in Fiji. They were Danish, and Jacob had an amusing habit of raising his eyebrows as he spoke that never failed to make me smile. Ian and Heather's house was rapidly starting to look like a hostel, albeit a remarkably pleasant one, but they still remained as cheerful and relaxed as when I'd first met them at the resort bar. In fact they seemed quite excited that they had so many guests staying, and they opened a bottle of sparkling wine to celebrate.

After a few glasses too many we all ended up in the spa pool that occupied the back corner of their garden, and the conversation turned to politics. I'd noticed several petitions on my travels for the national flag to be changed, and I asked Ian about them as we lounged in the water, my reserved British brain trying to ensure that none of my extremities were touching anyone else.

'If they're going to change it at all, it should be something Maori, something to show that we're living in a Maori country. The silver fern's a strong image for us too, so maybe something with that in it.'

I wondered if there might be some opposition to an explicitly Maori design from the more right wing elements of society. I'd yet to see any racial tension here, but I'd heard that it did exist.

'There's not much racism or anti-Maori feeling here, to be honest. I've certainly not heard any remarks. Having said that, it might be to do with the social circle we move in – most of our friends are intelligent, decent people, so they're not the type to have a problem with it. It probably does happen in other social groups, especially some of the older generation.

'At the end of the day, though, the biggest problem the Maori have is each other. There's lots of fighting between the various tribes, and because they don't present a united front they weaken their cause. The turnout of Maori voters was really low at the last elections too. If they're going to improve conditions for themselves they've got to get their act together - once they do, they'll be a much stronger force in local politics.'

I felt that I'd opened a possible can of worms with my questioning, so before it all got too serious I poured another drink. It was odd to be sitting outside on a cold night, looking up at the stars with a rum and coke in my hand as a stream of bubbles massaged the back of my thighs, but it was a feeling I could get used to. By the time we finally retired to bed, dripping half the spa bath through the house on our way, it long past midnight and I was struggling to keep my eyes open. It had been an enlightening day and had offered some real insights into New Zealand family life, but my feet were getting itchy, and it didn't have anything to do with the communal spa. It was about time I hit the road again.

6
Wairarapa

In 1883 an Englishman by the name of William Beetham decided to plant grape vines on a plot of land he owned near Masterton, a town sixty miles northeast of Wellington. The area had been used as sheep pasture by the first European settlers, but in the preceding years the industry had moved to the South Island where there were fewer land rights issues. By 1895 Beetham was producing bottles of wine of a surprisingly good quality from his Lansdowne vineyard, and visiting Italian Romeo Bragato came to the conclusion that the surrounding Wairarapa Valley was an ideal vine-growing site. It seemed that the area's destiny had been written.

In 1908, however, the New Zealand Prohibition movement began, spurred on by public concern over a per capita alcohol consumption that outstripped even the Australians. Prohibition never became law thanks to the votes cast from overseas by members of the armed forces, but several districts opted for their own 'no-license' agreements. The Wairarapa was one of the first to enforce this, and before long the fledgling wineries went out of business. Beetham's Lansdowne vineyard did not survive.

Until 1967 the bars across New Zealand closed at six o'clock every evening, and the shadow of Prohibition could still be seen. Gradually the social climate began to change, however, and in 1978 Alister Taylor, a publisher and wine enthusiast, planted grapes once again in the Wairarapa, on the outskirts of Martinborough in a vineyard that was to become known as Te Kairanga. By 1980 another five vineyards had been established in the area as Taylor's success became apparent and others followed his example. By 2000 there were over fifty vineyards in the valley, covering a total area of almost two thousand acres, making it one of the youngest and fastest-growing wine regions in the world. Today the region still only accounts for around three percent of New Zealand's wine production, but their star is certainly on the rise. Over a hundred and twenty years on, Beetham's experiment can finally be deemed a success.

Having entered Wellington from the west coast I was keen to exit via the east, and the opportunity to visit Martinborough was too good to miss. It was only a couple of hours away, so once I'd fought off yet another hangover with several cups of coffee and a sausage sandwich I said my farewells and dragged my baggage back out to the car. This was the third consecutive morning that I'd woken with a splitting headache, and it seemed that my route was taking me to a wine region next. Prohibition had well and truly been consigned to the history books.

I'd entered Wellington on State Highway One and I found myself leaving it on State Highway Two, a satisfying symmetry that was almost entirely lost on my hungover brain. Once I was out of the city the road wound up a steep hillside, the occasional gaps in the trees allowing breathtaking views of the valley below – even the logging trucks gave me some time to enjoy the lush green scenery and weren't too much of a nuisance. One truck driver pulled over into a lay-by to allow the queue behind him to pass, a display of basic civility that I couldn't recall seeing from lorry drivers back home. It seemed that we could learn a few things from the Kiwis, and not just when it came to rugby.

Martinborough itself sat on the other side of the hills, on a large plain that formed part of the fertile valley floor. I'd booked a room online in advance, having had a recommendation from Heather last night, and once I arrived in town I stopped at the *Taste Of Martinborough* deli to pick up my keys. Their range of gourmet cheeses and local breads woke me up from my hangover and set my mouth watering. I was keen to get to my room.

    I had to drive through the centre of town first to get there. Martinborough itself was founded in the late 1880s by John Martin, a British settler who must have harboured strong nationalistic sentiments. In an inspired piece of town planning he'd had the central square and the streets radiating out from it laid out in the shape of the British flag. This bizarre formation had lasted over a hundred years and could still be seen. There were eight roads in total leading off the central square, four in each corner forming the diagonal cross, and one in the centre of each side, forming the Cross of St George. I came into town on the bottom edge of the St George's Cross, drove to the centre of the Union Jack, and then exited via the left side of the flag. Road planning in New Zealand was certainly a more creative process than I was used to seeing elsewhere.

    I was staying in a studio apartment known as The Straw House for the night, a name that derived from the way in which the walls were filled with bales of straw and finished with plaster, leaving the wall surfaces looking rough and rustic. The straw also effectively insulated against all outside influences, including noise. Not only was the room attractively furnished in a pseudo-Tuscan style, but they'd also left a rustic feast from the deli in the fridge for me: a quick inventory revealed a loaf of fresh bread, fresh bagels, smoked salmon, soft cheese, eggs, milk and jam. It was more than ample for my needs, and I decided that tonight's dinner could consist of a simple platter.

    Since it was only mid-afternoon, and since the platter would taste considerably better with something to help wash it down, I headed out again in search of a winery.

I'd read that the wineries in the area tended to be of the smaller, boutique variety, and several of them were within walking distance of the town. The owners had kindly left an information folder in my room, so I dug out a map and took it with me for a stroll. If Martinborough's reputation was to be believed then I should stumble across a cellar door easily enough.

There's something very civilised about tasting wine straight from the cellar door. In this era of big business it's highly probable that the wine you taste at the vineyard has travelled the length of the country, either for bottling or due to customs regulations, but there remains something magical about drinking it alongside the vines where it was conceived. Some of the larger wineries have several vineyards and will provide tastings from all of these in their shops, but somehow the wines from the local area always taste more vibrant, more exciting, and more in tune with their surroundings. Perhaps the vines take in some of the characteristics from the local soil through their roots, and it's this that provides the sense of harmony between wine and landscape. Whatever the cause, I'm always a sucker for local produce.

I managed to stroll through town and out the other side before I finally encountered a winery that was open to the public. The name Palliser sounded vaguely familiar, and the lady behind the counter smiled at me as I wandered in, her beefy forearms and rosy cheeks suggesting that she might have just walked in from picking the grapes herself.

'Are you here to taste some of our wines? Would you like to try the whole range?'

I nodded a little too enthusiastically, and she began to dribble depressingly small measures into the glasses arranged on the countertop.

'I'll fill you in on the background a bit then, as I pour. We had our first vintage here at Palliser in 1989, and our name comes from Cape Palliser, at the southern tip of

Ka Mate

the North Island. That's a painting of the Cape on all the labels. Cape Palliser itself was named by Captain Cook after his friend and mentor Sir Hugh Palliser.'

I smiled and nodded as if I was listening, but actually I was distracted by the taste explosion that my tongue was enjoying. These were beautiful wines, and I had to force myself to swirl, sniff and taste them properly.

'We also have a second label, Pencarrow, which is made from the second choice fruit and is of a lesser quality. It's still very nice mind you, but the price is a little bit cheaper. That's named after Pencarrow Heads, just east of Cape Palliser at the entrance to Wellington Harbour.'

I was pretty sure it was the Pencarrow Sauvignon Blanc that I recognised, maybe from the few alcohol-blurred days I'd spent with Ian and Heather. I told her that I'd drunk this before.

'Oh that's good. And did you like it?'

I struggled to find anything more meaningful to say than 'It tasted very nice', but I failed and blurted something out about not really being able to remember. She started to look at me a little differently, and I realised that I'd just knocked back their premium Pinot Noir without even bothering to look at it first.

'Mmm, that's nice. It's very...'

Very what? Very grapey? I'd always been slightly mystified when it came to wine tasting. Despite my best efforts I'd never really felt at home around those people who could take one sniff of a new wine and proclaim that it was very lemony, with a buttery finish and undertones of cigar smoke. I wasn't completely uneducated when it came to viticulture, but somehow my palate seemed to lack the subtle nuances required to detect a hint of burnt rubber, or a slight suggestion of elderflower. The art of wine tasting employed a different language to everyday English, and it was not a language at which I was fluent.

'...it's very drinkable,' I eventually finished, deciding that honesty was probably the best course of action. 'I notice that most of these bottles have screw caps, is that the way you're moving now?'

I seemed to have bluffed my way out of an awkward situation, as she smiled back at me and handed a leaflet across the counter.

'We've used Stelvin caps since 2001, and several of the other New Zealand wineries are now following suit. Up to five percent of our wine used to suffer from cork taint, and they think that as much as fifteen percent might have been affected by less obvious reactions. That's a pretty high percentage of our output, as you can imagine, and that's even if you're using the highest quality corks. This way we can guarantee that the wine inside is exactly as our winemaker intended it, and you're getting a quality bottle every time.'

The screw caps suited me better anyway since I was travelling, and despite the debaucheries of the last few days I was unlikely to finish a bottle at one sitting. After much deliberation I bought a bottle of their Palliser Riesling. My choice surprised me a little, as I used to associate Riesling with the cheap European imports that we suffered in the UK, but the Riesling here was an entirely different drink. Fresh, fruity and fairly dry, it would go well with my smoked salmon and cheese this evening.

Having embarrassed myself at Palliser I walked back to The Straw House and stood my new bottle of wine in the fridge to chill. After a brief consultation with my map I discovered that there were a few more wineries just around the corner, in the opposite direction to the way my nose had led me. It was still early enough for them to be open, so I headed out again with a vow to taste the wines properly this time.

To my surprise there were no footpaths leading from the centre of town to the wineries on the outskirts, and I was forced to walk along overgrown grass verges. The sun was still high in a clear sky, though, and after the tastings at Palliser I was remarkably content with life. To either side of the road vineyards stretched out in the heat, stopping short of the hazy range of hills in the distance. It was easy to see why winemaking would be an appealing career choice.

Muirlea Rise was much smaller than Palliser, covering only five and a half acres, and as I wandered up the front path I worried that I'd misread the signs and was strolling through someone's garden. Fortunately I saw a small shed off to one side that acted as the cellar door, and altered my course accordingly before I ended up in their lounge.

The winery was founded in 1987, and since they were such a small vineyard they'd decided to produce only red wines. When it came to New Zealand wines I tended to think of whites, but I was impressed by the richness and depth of flavour of the reds at Muirlea Rise. These were big wines, more like Australian Shirazes than anything produced in my part of the world, and the berry-like flavours gave them a pleasantly smooth finish. In the end I only bought their cheapest wine, a blend of grapes amusingly marketed as *Justa Red*, but that had more to do with my budget than anything else. If I'd had the money I would probably have bought the lot, and by the case rather than by the bottle. Considering the price tag even the *Justa Red* was an amazingly good wine. Their decision to specialise had obviously paid off.

As I bought my bottle I noticed that the label warned that it might contain egg whites. I was so astonished that I asked the lady at the counter why this was.

'Haven't you heard of egg white fining?' she replied, clearly amazed that someone so ignorant of winemaking techniques had blundered through their boutique cellar door. Once we'd clearly established that I was indeed woefully uneducated, she explained the process for me, making sure to keep everything simple for this wine-guzzling novice.

'Basically it's a technique used by red wine makers to clear the sediment from the wine. Large quantities of egg whites are added to it, and as they sink to the bottom they take most of the impurities and sediment with them. The wine can then be drained off the top, leaving the impurities behind in the egg whites. There can be a risk of allergies, which is why we have to declare it on our labels. You won't taste any of the egg in the wine, though.'

This dashed my hopes of being able to claim that I detected an eggy bouquet at my next wine tasting, but I gratefully collected my purchase and retreated out of the shed. It seemed that I still had a lot to learn.

A little further along the road was Ata Rangi, and I remembered reading somewhere that Jamie Oliver's London restaurant stocked their Pinot Noir. My taste buds began to tingle with anticipation, although that might just have been the after effects of the *Justa Red*. If Muirlea Rise was an indication of the grape quality in the area, then Ata Rangi should be a revelation.

Ata Rangi translates as something like 'dawn sky' or 'new beginning', and when their vineyards were first planted here in 1980 they covered only twelve acres. Today that had expanded to a more impressive ninety acres, and the winery was renowned for its experienced winemakers and high quality wines. As I walked up their main driveway I was intrigued to see vines bearing fruit on both sides of the road, and I stopped to look. These were the first grapes I'd seen since I arrived in Martinborough, and although they were very small and green, not much larger than peas, I was still excited to see the fruit. Who could tell, in a few years' time I might be recovering from a hangover caused by these very grapes.

They'd made an effort at Ata Rangi to design an attractive and welcoming tasting room, incorporating modern features into what was essentially a large barn. There were also oil paintings along the interior walls, many of them of the vineyard and the winemakers who worked on the premises, lending a homely feel to the surroundings. As I started to sample their wines, taking special care to perform my tasting duties in a professional manner, I asked about the grapes I'd seen along the drive.

'Those are actually red grapes,' explained the young man behind the counter, carefully pouring me another small glass to taste, 'although they're still fairly young at the moment so they look green. I think they're merlot and pinot grapes along there. They'll get darker as they ripen and develop that distinctive red look – although that's only in the skins of course, the flesh still stays clear in appearance.'

This was actually one of the few things that I already knew about the winemaking process, and I was keen to show off my knowledge. 'They reintroduce the skins back to the juice don't they, that's where the red colour comes from?'

He nodded as if acknowledging a promising student. 'That's right. That's where you get the tannins in red wine from, the skins, and that's also why you don't get them in white wines. It's the tannins that mature more with age, which is why red wine benefits from cellaring more than white. If you can resist drinking it long enough, of course.'

It was almost as if he'd heard of my poor etiquette at Palliser via the local grapevine (a pun that's surely too good to resist), and I hurried to change the subject.

'I like the paintings, they give the place a lot of character. Are they all of this vineyard?'

He smiled, and for once I seemed to have said the right thing. 'Actually I painted them all myself. I work here as a guide and sales assistant because my wife's the assistant winemaker, but painting's my first love. The one on the left over there's the dinner table at the winery, and lots of the others are of the farmland around the area. I've recently been accepted as a member of the Academy of Fine Arts, so I'm hoping that painting will start to be my main career soon.'

I was tempted to buy one of his works, if only to remind me of the wonderful scenery in this part of the world, but in the end I was seduced once again by the wine. All their wines were spectacular, but I opted for the Rosé and the Sauvignon Blanc as they had slightly lower price tags. The Rosé was another revelation, very dry and surprisingly complex compared with the sweet, floral Portuguese Rosés I'd tried before. Every preconception I'd had was being challenged.

As I walked back up the driveway from Ata Rangi, weighed down by the three bottles of wine I'd purchased, I realised that I was starting to feel rather tipsy. I wasn't exactly drunk – the small tastings they poured weren't generous enough to induce full intoxication – but I'd tasted around twenty wines in one afternoon, and they were beginning to take their toll. I still had an hour before the wineries shut, though, and according to my map there was another cellar door further along the road. I staggered off to investigate.

The Winslow Vineyard was established in 1985 by Steve and Jennifer Tarring, and I was lucky to have Steve himself serve me. I immediately warmed to him as he poured me a very generous tasting of the first wine, and when I started to show some interest in his business he was keen to share its history with me.

'I used to be a microbiologist, at least that's what I trained in. I ended up selling filtration equipment, and a lot of my clients were out this way, at the larger vineyards. They were only too willing to share their secrets with me, so over the years I got to know a lot about the winemaking industry. Eventually I figured the time was right to go into business myself.'

The Chardonnay he'd poured me was unlike any of the others I'd tasted. I was used to Chardonnays tasting sweet and buttery, but this had a cleaner, crisper taste, more like that of a Granny Smith apple.

'Yes, you get that buttery taste from the oaking process, which turns the acid in the fruit into lactic acid. That's the same as the lactose you get in dairy products, which is why it tastes buttery. When it's fermenting in the oak it smells like off milk. I've done something a bit different here: I only oak it for a short period, then I follow it up with further filtration. It keeps that buttery taste away, and gives you a much lighter wine.'

The Riesling he gave me to try next was also markedly different from those I'd had before, the sweetness being nicely balanced by a strong acidic finish. I remarked on the fact that his wines seemed to be untypical of those I'd tasted in the region, and the observation brought a smile to his face.

'I do that on purpose, to try and keep them distinctive. We only produce a few wines each year, and they only total about one and a half thousand cases, so we can't compete with the larger wineries when it comes to volume or price. But what I think we can do is try slightly different things, create some distinctive wines that are different from the other bottles on the shelf. As far as I'm concerned that's the whole point of boutique wineries, to offer something different from the big labels.'

I told him that I thought he'd succeeded, as each wine was a surprise and a delight. I tasted their Rosé next, and even before I took a sip I noticed that it was much darker than the others I'd had, edging towards a purple tone. It was very dry but wonderful drinking, and Steve informed me that it was made from pinot grapes, the same grapes as were used for their Pinot Noir. The skins were reintroduced to the wine just briefly in order to get the distinctive Rosé colour, then it was finished like a white wine.

'I'm afraid we've not got many reds for you try today, but we've had some real success with them at the competitions. In 2000 our Turakirae Reserve won Gold Medal at the International Wine and Spirit Competition in London. Nowadays every other bottle of wine on the shelves seems to have won a prize for something, but the London competition's one of the top awards in the business. We were pretty excited about it, I can tell you.'

It was a shame that I couldn't taste their reds – if the whites were anything to go by, they would have been spectacular – but it was good to hear that this small boutique business was winning international recognition. Steve had an obvious passion for what he did, as well as a willingness to experiment and develop new techniques. He was right in thinking that this distinguished his wines from the output of the larger vineyards, and it also made him an ideal host.

'I actually travelled across to London to pick the prize up myself,' he told me as he rinsed my glass, 'I was that excited about it. The whole thing turned into a disaster though, because when I arrived in London there was a terrible storm, and the city was practically deserted. All the railways were closed down, and when I finally got to the suit rental place to pick up my suit, the bloody shop was shut. Anyway, I spotted someone through the window and managed to persuade them to open the door for me, so I got it in the end. At the awards I was sat with a group of Scotch distillers – they knew nothing about wine, but they gave me a big cheer when I went up to collect the prize. That was a pretty proud day. For our little winery here to have achieved so much.'

I was already struggling to carry all my acquisitions around with me, but I warmed so much to Steve and his passion for what he did that I couldn't leave without buying something. In the end I settled on the Rosé, and having said farewell and good luck I staggered back out into the daylight. The day's tastings added a pleasant fuzziness to the late afternoon sunshine, and I felt content with life as I hauled the four bottles of wine back to my room.

Ka Mate

Once there I unscrewed the cap on my Palliser Riesling and poured myself a glass, piling a plate high with bread, soft cheese and smoked salmon. By the time I'd finished the meal I was full and content. Tomorrow I would leave Martinborough and head north once more, but I now had two Rosés, a Sauvignon Blanc, a bottle of *Justa Red,* and half a bottle of Riesling packed in the trunk. At least a little bit of Martinborough was coming with me.

7
Ahuriri *(Napier)*

I left the Wairarapa Valley the following morning on State Highway Two, this time heading north. My next stop would be Napier, but there was a long drive ahead of me – almost a hundred and fifty miles in total – and my hopes of an early start had been abandoned after yesterday's wine tastings.

Just outside Woodville, a few miles east of Palmerston North, I passed a wind farm perched along the crest of a hill. The tall white windmills turned slowly in the breeze, and I noticed that Woodville itself was proud of them – banners printed with windmill icons hung from all the street lights – but I couldn't help recalling the controversy that had surrounded wind farms in recent years. They were originally chosen for their low environmental impact, but a new campaign fronted by British TV botanist David Bellamy had argued that their impact was catastrophic in terms of violating the natural scenery. I could see his argument, but I rather liked the tall, sleek forms of the windmills. Admittedly they tainted the natural view, but in its place they provided a different, but equally impressive, backdrop. There was something inherently peaceful and calming about the slow, rhythmical turning of the blades, and I found myself hoping that Bellamy's tilt at them failed.

By the time I arrived in Napier it was already afternoon. The lady at the Information Centre kindly pointed me in the right direction to find a room for the night, but the first two hostels I tried were fully booked. Apparently I wasn't the only one to see Napier as an ideal stopover point. I was reminded of the difficulties I'd had finding a room in Paihia, and I promised myself that I'd be more organised in the future.

Fortunately the third hostel had vacancies, so I hurriedly made a booking over the phone and promised to be there to check in within fifteen minutes. In the end it only took me five minutes to drive there. The hostel itself was nestled in the middle of a residential street, and upon closer inspection I saw that it consisted of three houses connected by a series of paths and gates. It all seemed rather rundown and dirty – as many hostels do – but my room was clean and modern, with a separate *en suite* bathroom that looked as if it had only just been installed. They also offered off-street parking, which meant that I could drive right up to my door and unload the bottles of wine with ease.

The one drawback to the hostel was the fact that the shared kitchen was rather small, and in a moment of uncharacteristic extravagance I decided to dine out. A quick flick through the wad of leaflets I'd collected at the Information Centre revealed a restaurant on the seafront that specialised in New Zealand Green Lipped mussels. The opportunity seemed too good to miss. I quickly freshened up from the car journey and changed into a clean shirt, then I headed back outside with a map of the town clasped firmly in my hand.

It was a long walk down Marine Parade to the *Mussel Boys* restaurant, but it was a pleasant evening with a fresh breeze blowing in off the sea, and I was glad to be out of the car. The restaurant was decorated like an upmarket bar, lending it a calm, relaxed atmosphere that I immediately liked. I ordered myself a bowl of mussels in white wine and blue cheese sauce, and a glass of the local lager, then I found a table near the front where I could watch the sun set over the sea.

The walls were decorated with various news clippings about the restaurant and I read them hungrily while I waited for my food to arrive. The original *Mussel Boys* restaurant had been founded in 1997, and there were now three of them across New Zealand. The main farms for Green Lipped mussels were in the Marlborough Sounds, the Coromandel peninsula, Golden Bay and Stewart Island, but the mussels they served here were exclusively from the Marlborough Sounds farms. There were over five thousand acres of marine farms in the Marlborough area, which together produced about fifty thousand tons of Green Lipped mussels each year. Somewhere in the region of eighty percent of New Zealand's mussels were exported, and in 2002 this export market produced a total revenue of one hundred and eighty-five million dollars. That was a huge income from a relatively small area. I could see why the Kiwis were so keen to show off their mussels.

When my bowl arrived I wasn't disappointed. The mussels were enormous, and the flesh that nestled inside the shells was often larger than my thumb. They were amazingly tender too, and I remembered that the mussels served here would be considerably fresher than the ones available at home. The blue cheese sauce was a little milder than I'd hoped, but I could happily have eaten another bowlful without any seasoning at all, so I had no reason to complain. The pint of lager washed the meal down, and by the time I'd finished eating my stomach felt so full that I had to walk gingerly out of the restaurant and back onto the promenade.

Luckily I made it back to the hostel with my meal still nestled uncomfortably inside me, and I settled down to a restless night brought on by overindulgence. I hardly slept a wink until about four in the morning, and even then I was forced to endure strange recurring dreams. But hell, it was worth it.

Ka Mate

* * *

At a little after 11.15 on the morning of February 3, 1931, the ground beneath Napier shifted suddenly. Later studies revealed that it was an earthquake measuring 7.8 on the Richter scale. The centre of the quake was close to the residential areas, and although the tremors were shallow the damage they caused almost demolished the town. The quake lasted for a total of two and a half minutes, but it was many hours before the resulting fires were extinguished and people began to survey the damage. A hundred and sixty-two were dead, and all that remained of the town centre was rubble.

It took only two years for the town to be rebuilt, and by early 1933 Napier was on its feet again. The early Thirties were the low point of the Great Depression, and considering the prevailing economic climate the town's achievement was spectacular. Many of the new buildings were constructed in the predominant styles of the time - Spanish Mission, Stripped Classical, Art Deco – and due to the worldwide slump it was one of the few sites to show such a concentration of bright, modern architecture. Napier had reinvented itself from the ground up, and in doing so had created a town that far outshone the old Napier, on the ashes of which it was built.

In recent years it had become world-renowned for its collection of Art Deco period buildings, and it seemed that the 1931 earthquake might have had a positive influence after all. The next day I decided to walk from my hostel to the Information Centre, the starting point for the Art Deco tour.

By the time I arrived a crowd had already gathered, and they split us into three groups to keep the numbers manageable. My particular group started by walking along the seafront to the Soundshell, a small outdoor stage and dance floor that was built during the reconstruction. Our guide filled us in on some of the background to the rebuilding, then we turned our attention to the stage itself, which displayed an Art Deco 'sunburst' design to spectacular effect: concentric semicircles radiated outwards from the stage centre in a variety of colours, a design that was stunningly effective in its simplicity. The dance floor had originally been used for jazz concerts, and occasionally roller-skating, and as we crossed it on our way into town I tried to imagine what it must have been like in the lively new Napier of the late 1930s. For a while this small coastal town on the North Island of New Zealand had been at the cutting edge of modern culture.

Our next stop was the ASB Bank on the fringes of the main shopping precinct. When the Bank had bought the building in 1992 they'd restored it in the original style, adding some internal offices during the refit, but ensuring that all the traditional features remained visible. The exterior was in the Stripped Classical style, the façade punctuated by a number of flattened columns that lent it a classical appearance, but it was the ceiling panels inside that interested me.

In addition to designs from the Art Deco period the original architects had also incorporated several Maori motifs, which had been restored to their former glory along with the rest of the building. The rafters were painted in traditional red, white and black patterns similar to those I'd seen at *Te Whare Runanga* in Waitangi; in the corners of the panels were representations of the *taiaha*, the Maori fighting staff, and particularly the figure whose head usually adorned its top. It was amazing to see these Maori designs incorporated into Art Deco patterns, and they blended together surprisingly well. Art Deco was often seen as a particularly modern movement, but their reduction of images to simple shapes and patterns owed a lot to ancient art forms, particularly the Egyptians and the Aztecs. There surely couldn't be many Art Deco/Maori combinations, though, and it lent a unique appeal to an already fascinating building. It still radiated the sense of energy and excitement that must have surrounded the town's new beginnings.

As we walked through the streets I noticed that some of the original signs had also been preserved and restored. The new street signs were of a standard kind that I'd seen throughout the North Island – blue arrows mounted on metal poles – but the original signs were picked out in small tiles on the pavements, a basic form of mosaic. I asked our guide about them, and she confirmed that several had been restored. Due to a number of traffic accidents, however, they had gradually been replaced with the new style. Motorists had been unable to read the street names until they were at the street corners, and they had often turned too late, mounting the pavements or clipping the corners of buildings. The old signs looked much more attractive, but I could see the practical appeal of the new ones. A sign was fairly useless if you couldn't read it.

The tour ended at the town's Art Deco centre, where they outlined some of the work done by their volunteers. It was only recently that the local council had come to recognise their wealth of 1930s architecture, a treasure trove that was first pointed out by visiting European and American tourists. Since then the society had overseen all major renovations to Napier's Art Deco buildings, and a height restriction on new buildings was now in place in the centre of town. They also approved all signwriting done by businesses in the centre. The Art Deco tour had rapidly become one of Napier's key attractions, and nothing was allowed to jeopardise its continuing success. It was amazing that a group of concerned locals had achieved so much in such a short space of time – the beauty of the town stood as testament to their hard work.

On my walk back to the Information Centre I managed to spot several more examples of Spanish Mission architecture, as well as the odd ziggurat or sunburst. I even passed a man with a moustache that looked as if it might have been from the 1930s. It seemed that the Art Deco period was still alive and kicking in Napier.

* * *

When the earthquake struck Napier in 1931 it wasn't just the town centre that felt its effects. The land surrounding the town rose with the quake, over five thousand acres of land rising up from the estuaries and swamps. Nearby Marewa took its name from the Maori, meaning 'gift from the sea', and in return for the considerable destruction that the earthquake wreaked in the centre it left plentiful gifts behind. The land it raised proved to be extremely fertile, and the gravely soils were especially well suited to grape vines.

The old streambeds around the area were known as the Gimblett Gravels, a name that was trademarked once the wines started to achieve international success and renown. Trinity Hill, the first stop on the Hawkes Bay wine tour, was typical of the area, and Imogen, my guide, took a few minutes to point out the soil quality to me. Only the smallest pockets of soil could be seen between the gravels that gave the area its name, and even an average handful of dirt contained many stones, both small and large. Because of this the vines had to struggle harder than usual to find a purchase, sending their roots deep into the ground. To the uninitiated it might seem that this would be detrimental to the growing of quality fruit. In fact this shortage of nutrients kept the grapes small and intensely flavoured, and therefore ideal for the production of wine. Einstein once said that in the middle of difficulty lies opportunity. The financial opportunities here were plain to see.

Trinity Hill was chosen as a potential vineyard in 1987, but the first plantings weren't made until 1994, making it a young winery even compared with those I'd seen in Martinborough. Their tasting room was housed in a building designed for them by Auckland architect Richard Priest, and in 2002 the New Zealand Institute Of Architects honoured it as a 'stand out' building. It stood out a little too much for my liking, looking like a large concrete brick that had been hollowed out and tethered to the ground. I had nothing against modern architecture, but it didn't have to look ugly to impress.

Fortunately the wines made up for the concrete bunker they were housed in. Their Chardonnay rivalled any I'd tried, and their Rosé reminded me of the one I'd bought at Winslow, very dark and dry compared with the European pinks. As we moved on to taste the reds I noticed that the whites had Stelvin screw caps, but that the red wines were closed with traditional corks. I asked our host why this was.

'We'd be happy to move to Stelvins on all our wines,' he replied with a look of frustration, 'but unfortunately we just can't sell them to the overseas market. It looks like most people drink their whites pretty soon after buying them, but they tend to cellar their reds a bit longer, and there's some suspicion that the reds don't cellar so well with Stelvins. It's not true, but if we can't sell it then it causes a problem. We really struggled selling the screw caps in America too. They've been taught for years that if it has a screw cap then the wine isn't any good, and we can't get beyond that, no matter how much we try. I suspect we'll be putting corks in our reds for a good few years yet.'

An American couple were also enjoying a tasting at the counter, and they confirmed for me that bottles with screw caps just wouldn't sell in the States. In the past the only screw caps they'd encountered had been on poor quality wines, often from South America, and the cork had come to be seen as an indicator of quality. No matter how good the wine was, they couldn't be convinced of its quality as long as it sported a metal cap. I harboured vague hopes that they might act as ambassadors for the Stelvin cap once they returned home, but as they didn't appear to be buying anything it looked unlikely. It seemed that the humble cork had some life left in it yet.

When we reached the last of the reds the label declared it to be a Shiraz, although I was fairly sure that the term was only used for Australian wines, and that the grape was usually called Syrah.

'Yeah, that's a marketing thing again,' our host confessed. 'This wine falls into the lower price bracket, and people at the cheaper end of the market are more used to buying Shiraz than Syrah. If we called it a Syrah the top end of the market would see it as being too cheap, and the bottom end wouldn't know what the hell it was. We hate to throw our lot in with the Aussies, but it sells better as a Shiraz.'

It might fall into the cheaper end of the market as far as he was concerned, but it was still rather pricey for my budget, so I settled for a bottle of the Chardonnay. It was my first purchase today, and I was conscious of the bottles from Martinborough sitting unopened in my hostel room. I vowed not to buy too much on my tour of the Gimblett Gravels.

The next stop was Ngatarawa Wines, owned by the Corban family. The Corbans traced their roots back to the Lebanon, and specifically to Assid Abraham Corban, who migrated to New Zealand in 1891. His family was already renowned for winemaking in their home country, and in 1902 he planted his first vineyard in Henderson, on the outskirts of Auckland. At first I was surprised to encounter a Lebanese winemaking family here in the New World, but upon further consideration it made perfect sense. I'd already encountered Scots and Dalmatians living in the North Island – it felt quite natural to be adding the Lebanese to the list.

Despite the family vintage my hopes of this being an older vineyard were dashed when I discovered that it was planted in 1981. The Prohibition movement had stalled the wine industry here in the same way that it had in Martinborough, and the resurgence of New Zealand wines was a fairly modern phenomenon. The name Ngatarawa translated roughly as 'between the ridges', alluding to the vineyard's position on the valley floor, but the labels on the bottles displayed a stylised horse logo, a legacy from the days when the land was used for stables. Like Trinity Hill, the vines were grown on the gravely soils of an old stream bed, although their tasting room was located in a much more tasteful whitewashed barn, part of the old stables complex. I was glad to note that there wasn't an inch of concrete in sight.

I tried two Sauvignon Blancs, one made from the local grapes, the other produced with grapes they bought from the Marlborough region on the South Island. Marlborough was widely considered to be one of the best regions for Sauvignon Blanc in the world, and by purchasing fruit from the area Ngatarawa were able to cash in on some of that international renown. Personally I preferred the local Hawkes Bay Sauvignon Blanc, but the Marlborough version sold considerably better to the export market. The power of marketing was at work once again.

While I'd tasted wines in the barn Imogen, my guide, had been sitting outside with an ice cream from the café. Before we headed off again I mentioned that I'd heard the Sileni vineyard was near here. It was one of the few New Zealand labels that I was used to seeing back home, although the high price tag in Britain meant that I hadn't tried it.

'Ah yeah, Sileni's nearby,' she managed between spoonfuls of ice cream, 'although they've become so popular that they charge for tastings nowadays. They've got some really special wines there, though, and they usually give you some cheese and crackers with the tasting too. Might slow down the drunkenness at least!'

As we entered the Sileni vineyard I noticed with a barely audible groan that this was a return to the concrete bunker school of tasting room design. Despite the fact that it looked like a hospital, however, some of their reds were spectacular, although they were placed firmly outside my price range. My judgement was amateurish at the best of times, but with several pints of alcohol soaking my brain I doubted that I could tell a Chardonnay from a Riesling, or a Merlot from a glass of grape juice

In the end it was the cheeses that blew me away. The counter held samples of two cheeses, both from local dairies, and they exhibited an amazing depth of flavour. One of them in particular had a beautiful nutty aftertaste. While Imogen tasted the wines I quite happily worked my way through the plate of cheese, stopping from time to time to wash it down with a mouthful of Chardonnay or Pinot Noir. When the plate was nearly empty I made sure to leave a few pieces behind, just in case anybody else wanted them. But they were still there as we turned to leave, so I made short work of those too. All this drinking had given me the munchies.

By the time we returned to central Napier I was almost asleep, and I returned wearily to my room just in time for my head to hit the pillow. I managed to drag myself out for a paper sack of calorie-laden fast food at some point during the evening, but otherwise sleep was the first thing on my agenda. Napier had always been just a stopping point to refuel and relax – tomorrow I'd finally head into the island's interior, and the heart of the nation's Maori culture.

Ka Mate

8
Taupo - Rotorua

As I drove out of Napier, heading inland towards Taupo and the giant lake I'd skirted on my trek down to Wellington, I took stock of what I'd achieved over the past few days. In the final analysis I came up disappointingly empty-handed. The wine regions I'd passed through had acted as a pleasant diversion, but nothing more than that, and since leaving the city I'd seen little of Maori culture. I hadn't even encountered any spectacular scenery, surely the one thing that New Zealand had in abundance. I couldn't help feeling that I'd been led astray by the ready availability of reasonably priced premium wines: perhaps the Prohibition movement had had a valid point after all.

Fortunately the region I was entering had always maintained a strong Maori presence, harking back to the first settlement by the crew of the Arawa canoe, part of the Great Migration that first brought the Polynesians to Aotearoa's shores. After Taupo I intended to travel up to Rotorua, still a thriving Maori community and one of the North Island's main tourist destinations, and then north through Tauranga to the picturesque scenery of the Coromandel Peninsula. There should be sufficient cultural experiences and breathtaking vistas to make up for my recent hedonism.

It took a little under two hours to drive to Taupo, through an unspectacular but calming landscape of rolling hills and pine forests. I began to see more logging trucks on the roads, and I recalled that I'd encountered them in this area when I'd passed through before, during my eight-hour drive down to Wellington for the Rugby Sevens. With all the pine trees around it made sense that the logging industry should have a stronghold here.

I remembered the basic layout of Taupo from my earlier visit, with the centre of town stretching around the northern shore of the lake, and I made the Information Centre my first port of call, to book a room for the night. The hotels along the lakefront were out of my price range, but in the end I found a pleasant motel only fifteen minutes' walk from the centre. Not only did my room have full kitchen facilities and an *en suite* bathroom, it also included a separate lounge. When I discovered upon check-in that they provided sachets of real ground coffee and a large French press it started to feel like home.

I picked up a map of the town at reception, and was overjoyed to discover a list of free things to do in Taupo and the surrounding area. Any tourist destination that actively encouraged visitors not to spend their money was okay by me. As it was a warm, clear afternoon I decided to walk to the first place on the list, the Huka Falls.

It was a pleasant stroll to the falls from the motel, passing through well-kept parkland at first, then trailing along the riverbank the rest of the way. It was sheltered from the wind down by the river, and surprisingly warm. The sweat trickled past my ears, cooling the side of my neck. Insects hummed in the trees, sounding like a live electrical cable in the undergrowth, and to my left the river gurgled and sparkled in the sunlight. On such a beautiful day I found it hard to believe that more people weren't out walking, but for long stretches I had the path to myself.

This solitude vanished as soon as I drew near to the falls, the dirt path rapidly turning into expanses of gravel and concrete. I counted five tour coaches in the parking lot.

There was even a small souvenir and refreshments stand, and I used the opportunity to buy some more water for my return trip. I felt certain that I'd lost several pints in sweat, and common sense told me that I ought to replace it.

The most remarkable thing about the Huka Falls was that they didn't actually fall very far at all. Instead the flow of the river squeezed between two sheer cliffs, turning into some extremely violent rapids. The still water to either end of the 'falls' was unusually blue, but that turned to a chaotic white as it was funnelled inwards by the cliffs. I spent a few minutes walking up and down the fence searching for the perfect photo, balancing the relatively placid flow of the river with the frenetic turbulence of the falls. Eventually I chose a position close to the mouth of the falls, where the white water started to settle down to a calm blue again.

I was about to press the shutter release button when a large red jetboat suddenly darted into the frame. It powered up to the start of the white water then executed a precise u-turn, zipping back down the river. It performed this manoeuvre four or five times, the plastic-clad tourists inside screaming at each hair-raising turn, then it vanished back up the river. I tried to line the same photo up again, but the calm blue waters had been churned to a muddy brown. After a few minutes of waiting I decided that the moment had vanished. I walked back through the parking lot to the start of the path, eager to get away from the crowds.

On the way back to the motel I considered what had just happened. David Bellamy might be concerned about the environmental impact of wind farms, but surely the impact of this single jetboat had been equally damaging, and considerably more frivolous. In my head I was beginning to sound like a middle-aged killjoy – but why should the adrenaline rush enjoyed by the fifteen people in the boat be allowed to taint the enjoyment of the falls for everyone else? I fully intended to go jetboating before my trip was over, but there needed to be tighter controls if they weren't to upset the wonderful scenery this country had to offer.

When I got back to my room I reluctantly put my soapbox away and started to plan the next day's excursions. It was already too late to do much else, so I opted for an early night followed by an early start, and I placed a booking for a slow, peaceful boat trip out on the lake. I intended to be in Rotorua by the following afternoon, so I also booked myself onto the Tamaki Village cultural evening. Their leaflet looked a little tacky, aimed squarely at the visiting tourist market, but I was keen to see some more Maori culture while I was here, even if it was the commercialised version.

* * *

I slept well in my new room, and although I'm never at my best first thing in the morning I had the French press and the ground coffee to revive me. During the night the temperature had dropped, but the following morning I was still quite comfortable in a t-shirt and jeans. As I drove down to the lake I noticed a fine layer of mist floating above the water. It was already starting to clear, however, as the morning sun warmed the air – hopefully it wouldn't cause any delay to my sightseeing.

When I arrived the boat was already waiting at the Taupo marina. Our vessel was a replica steamer called the Ernest Kemp, a remarkably prosaic name for such a lovely little wooden boat. I shared the main cabin with two French couples, who seemed to be under the mistaken impression that we were about to embark on a cruise of the Antarctic. All of them were wearing at least four layers of clothing, and they cradled cups of hot chocolate as if their lives depended on it. I sat opposite them in my t-shirt feeling decidedly manly, wilfully ignoring the gooseflesh on my arms. Hopefully the air would warm up and the mist would clear soon. The view of the mountains from the lake should be breathtaking.

As the boat slowly moved away from the jetty, seeming to drift across the surface of the water in stark contrast with yesterday's jetboat, our skipper came on the P.A. system to introduce himself. His name was Miles Poananga, a mixture of European and Maori that seemed to be fairly common. I'd thought I was getting better at identifying the Maori and the Pacific Islanders, but looking at him I wouldn't have guessed his Maori heritage. It was only when he laughed that his ancestry became clear: he had the same high-pitched chuckle as Robin from the Northland tour. It seemed strange that something as personal as laughter could be genetically inherited, but it certainly sounded that way. For a moment I almost believed that Robin was driving the boat.

Maori history in the area stretched right back to the settlers from the first migration, and the lake itself was named around 1300 A.D. by one of the Maori chiefs. Taupo meant 'great cloak', and it was a reference to the layer of mist that he'd seen above the water, a feature that weather conditions had kindly reproduced for us today. The lake with its cloak of mist and the mountains rising in the distance must have been a spectacular sight to these early settlers, although they might have been shivering almost as much as my French companions if they were freshly arrived from the Pacific.

Even before its discovery by the Maori, however, the lake had boasted an intriguing and eventful history. There used to be a large volcano on the site, part of a wider volcanic field that still peppered the area with mountains and volcanic cones. In 186 A.D. this volcano exploded, and the eruption is still the largest in known history, its effects being recorded by historians as far away as China and Rome. In addition to creating the lake, the ash from the fallout darkened the skies in the northern hemisphere for two years and caused a mini ice age, the effects of which were still geologically visible today. Lake Taupo was in fact a large volcanic crater filled with water, and its past still manifested itself from time to time when certain areas of the lake began to boil and steam. None of this made me feel any more secure on our tiny boat, but I suspected that the French might appreciate the extra warmth of some boiling water.

As we chugged past Acacia Bay South, Miles came on the P.A. system again to give us a brief history of the lake, although the French couples were more interested in wrapping scarves around their heads. The confidence with which he spoke suggested that he was used to telling this story, and he added several pauses for dramatic effect. The Maori have always relied on the passing down of oral histories from generation to generation, and I liked to think that Miles was living proof of this tradition's survival in the modern age.

During the period of European settlement there had been both Protestant and Catholic missionaries operating in the area, Miles told us, and one of the local chiefs had had difficulty deciding which faith to convert to. He was an educated man, having read a number of European histories, and he was naturally confused by the way the various Christian sects fought amongst themselves while worshipping the same God. One day, when the Protestant and the Catholic missionaries were both present for a feast, he decided to test their faith. He told them both to drop their pants and squat over the hot coals of the fire. He who remained there longest would have proved his faith, and would win the chief's conversion. Miles told us that the Protestant refused to take part, but that the Catholic missionary began to untie his belt and lower his pants. Before he could go any further the chief stepped forward to stop him. Since he was the only one prepared to take the challenge he declared the winner, and the chief converted to Catholicism along with most of his tribe. To this day most of the local Maori were Catholic, and the story of their conversion was passed from generation to generation. I wasn't sure how historically accurate it was, but it was certainly an excellent tale. Perhaps this was the only time in history that a Catholic priest had actually *gained* respect by dropping his pants.

The main aim of our trip was to visit a group of Maori rock carvings further round the shore, and it took us almost half an hour to reach them. At one point we were overtaken by a small yacht, and I wondered if I'd made a mistake opting for such slow transportation as a backlash against yesterday's jetboat incident. When we drew closer, however, the water became quite choppy, and the sight of the yacht rolling in the swell vindicated my decision.

Despite the rough conditions we managed to get within close range of the rock wall, our boat pitching violently from side to side. Once there we were afforded a front row view of the carvings. To the right was a large face, at least twenty feet high and set back into a slight recess in the rock. It was decorated with swirling patterns echoing the forms of the traditional facial tattoos, and the mouth was rendered as a stylised figure-of-eight. It wasn't just imposing in its demeanour and impressive due to its size – it was also a remarkable achievement, given that the cliff presented a sheer drop down to the water. To have achieved such precision and detail in such an inaccessible place showed incredible skill and resourcefulness.

The rocks to the left of the face were also adorned with a variety of carvings. Miles told me that they were originally made as decoration for an altar that used to stand there. Today's carvings were a mixture of the traditional and the modern, the original work having been renovated and supplemented by a local artist. Some of the shallower etchings on the back wall looked more traditional in form, echoing the woodcarvings I'd seen at Waitangi, while I assumed that a large lizard carved from a rock in the foreground was a more recent addition.

Once everyone had taken their photographs we turned back towards the Marina. Miles said that he'd normally have taken us out across the lake to see the far shore, but the waters were too choppy today for him to risk it. We passed the yacht again on the return trip and everyone on board looked pale, their complexions occasionally brightened with a hint of green. It certainly wasn't a day for boating.

When we were back on dry land I thanked Miles for his commentary, and I just had time to see one of the French men finally removing his woolly hat before I left town. As I drove I glimpsed the mist gradually lifting from the lake in my rearview mirror, unveiling the wonderful views of the mountains again. It was hard to believe that such beauty was created by the largest volcanic explosion in history: today Lake Taupo looked majestic and serene as I left on the road to Rotorua.

* * *

There has always been an abundance of geothermal activity in and around Rotorua, but until the 1950s Taupo only had the Karapiti fumarole, a small opening in the ground just north of the town that emitted wisps of steam and volcanic gases. This changed in 1958 when the Geothermal Power Station opened. Because the Power Station utilised boiling water from nearby underground lakes the overall water pressure reduced considerably, extinguishing several springs and geysers close to Rotorua. The reduced volume of water in the lakes caused the remaining water to boil more vigorously, and as the steam struggled to escape, the thermal activity near the Power Station increased. These geothermal features had become an attraction in their own right in recent years, earning the curious but evocative title 'The Craters Of

The Moon'. With a name like that they were simply too good to miss, and I stopped for a brief moonwalk on my way out of Taupo.

Even from a distance I could see clouds of steam drifting among the hills, and as I left the parking lot and started out on the circular trail there was a definite smell of sulphur on the breeze. The ground was often unstable and extremely hot, and signs warned visitors not to step off the boardwalks and paths provided. Given the sudden bursts of steam and gas I wouldn't have risked it anyway.

It wasn't long before I passed a large crater on my left, and a sign informed me that it had last erupted in 1983. It had once been a fumarole – a hole in the ground that acts as a vent for steam and volcanic gases – but at some point it had become blocked. Pressure had built up behind the blockage, eventually causing the explosion that formed the crater. Within a minute I passed another two craters that had erupted as recently as 2002, covering the boardwalk I was now standing on with several inches of ash, mud and pumice stone. This information didn't fill me with confidence, and I hurried along the path just in case they decided to repeat the performance. The fumaroles were all regularly monitored for safety purposes, but I didn't want to take any chances. While some people would probably pay to be covered from head to toe in sulphurous mud, I didn't include myself among them.

As I passed further into the area of geothermal activity there were fumaroles and small craters along either side of the path, and the smell of sulphur made me gag. There was also an amazing abundance of greenery, many of the rocks covered with ferns and mosses that thrived in the damp, warm conditions the escaping steam provided. I was fairly sure that the actual craters of the moon weren't this green, and I couldn't recall ever seeing them belch clouds of foul-smelling steam into the moon's atmosphere, but I figured that we could allow the area's promoters some creative license. There was certainly something otherworldly about the landscape, and many of the crater rims were stained pink, green and blue by the escaping gases. It might not be the moon, but it didn't quite feel like Planet Earth either.

Eventually the persistent smell of sulphur – best described as rotten eggs combined with a chemical burning at the back of the nose – forced me to move on, and I followed the rest of the walkway back to the parking lot. It took just over an hour to drive to Rotorua, and as I drew closer there were increasing signs of geothermal activity. Occasionally I glimpsed a pillar of steam among the trees by the roadside, or caught a hint of something sulphurous making its way through the air conditioning system. There was even a large neon sign for the *Sulphur City Motel* as I drove through the outskirts of town, although I couldn't believe that they attracted many customers with a name like that.

Passing over a bridge I noticed two large wooden carvings flanking it on either side, an indication of the strength of the Maori community here. Rotorua was considered by many to be the centre of Maori culture on the North Island, or at least the centre of the culture's tourist industry. It was encouraging to see these traditional art forms being incorporated into the modern town.

There were several different accounts of how the Maori came to Aotearoa, and even in this age of carbon dating the arguments were still unresolved. Some of the facts were more solid than others, however. It was generally agreed that the Maori first settled on the shores of Aotearoa around 1350 A.D., and that their heritage was Polynesian in origin. Maori culture gradually grew as the Polynesians spent more time away from their homeland, developing a distinctive artistic style that owed a lot to the natural swirls of the bracken ferns that surrounded them. By the time the first Europeans arrived they were a settled society, relying more heavily on agriculture than their cousins on the Pacific Islands.

Maori mythology, however, offered a more poetic rendering of the first arrival. It told us that the Maori arrived from Hawaiki, the spiritual homeland of the Polynesians. The concept of Hawaiki was common to most Polynesian cultures, sometimes appearing as Havai'I, Hawai'ti, or Ra'iatea, and there were suggestions that Hawai'i was named in memory of this homeland. The Maori first settled in Aotearoa during the Great Migration from this mythical country. Five canoes were chosen for the journey: Arawa, the Shark; Tainui, the Great Tide; Mata-atua, the Face of a God; Kura-haupo, the Storm Cloud; and Tokomaru, the Shade of the South.

According to the legend, all five canoes arrived at more or less the same time, pulling up on a beach where a sperm whale was stranded. The captain of each canoe claimed the whale as his own, and arguments broke out over who had arrived first on the shore. Each canoe had set up a shrine on the sands, and after a detailed inspection of these shrines it was discovered that the one belonging to the Tainui canoe was more withered and dried by the sun, a sign that it had been erected before the others. The Tainui canoe claimed the whale, as well as the honour of being the first to land on Aotearoa's shores. Today the bay was known as Whangaparoa, the Bay of the Sperm Whale.

Once the dispute was settled, the people of the Arawa canoe planted the first kumara (sweet potato) plant on the shoreline near Whangaparoa, then they moved inland to find themselves somewhere to settle. Eventually, after journeying for several months, they stopped near the hot pools in the centre of the island, and in outlying communities along the shores of Lake Taupo. The Mata-atua canoe also settled nearby, along the northern shore of the island.

More conventional history also places the first settlement of the Rotorua area in the fourteenth century, although the initial settlement, Ohinemutu, was south of the current town. Te Arawa, the crew of the Arawa canoe, were attracted to the area by the benefits of the geothermal activity. Not only did it provide a source of heat during the cold winter months, but they also adapted their cooking methods to make use of the boiling pools. It seemed inevitable that much of their history would be tied to these natural features.

When Europeans began to settle in the area local relations became turbulent, however, and the tribe sided with the Government during the internal New Zealand Wars. It was only after the fighting subsided that Europeans once again began to settle in Rotorua. In 1838 a group of European visitors came to view the Pink and White Terraces, one of the features created by the escaping volcanic gases, and by the 1870s there was a flourishing tourist trade, with many of the Te Arawa tribe accommodating the visitors before the first hotels were built. This developing trade was halted abruptly by the eruption of Mount Tarawera in 1886. The explosion buried the Terraces forever beneath layers of mud and rock, and killed around a hundred and fifty people – but it didn't take long for the tourists to start returning.

Today the local Maori were still a driving force in the tourism industry, and Rotorua was proud to claim that it was the most visited tourist destination in the country. I had some concerns about this – at times the advertising made it look like a Maori theme park – but it seemed fitting that the people of Te Arawa should benefit from the current resurgence of interest in New Zealand.

Rotorua was itself a Maori name meaning 'two lakes', and I had to drive past the shores of these lakes to reach the YHA hostel. The hostel was noisy but cheap, and one of the few budget options in a town that attracted tourists from across the globe. I just about managed to squeeze my bags into my room, having to tuck one beneath the miniscule desk they'd provided, but I was forced to leave the bottles of wine in the car. It made me glad that I'd already booked the cultural evening, as I could easily have become claustrophobic in such a small room, but thankfully I managed to contort my body enough to make it back to the door, and eventually I was able to escape into the open air. It was a short drive back into the centre, so having picked up a map and some leaflets from reception I returned to the car and retraced my route.

A quick glance at the map told me that the carvings I'd seen on the way into town were part of the New Zealand Maori Arts And Crafts Institute, and given its grand name I couldn't resist a visit. I was simply hoping to have a quick look around their store, but when I arrived I discovered that you had to pay, even just to enter the shop. Reluctantly I purchased an all-inclusive ticket for the reserve.

Once past the ticket booth I was directed across to the *wharenui*, or meeting house, where the cultural performance was about to begin. The *wharenui* itself was particularly beautiful and intricately carved, and there was already a large crowd gathered for the start of the performance. I hung back for a moment to separate myself from mob, and also to look at the *pataka*, or storehouse, that stood on the other side of the *wharenui*. Like the meeting house itself this was constructed entirely of wood, and it stood on four stilts that raised the food off the ground to protect it from predators. This particular *pataka* had been constructed for the international exhibition in Christchurch in 1906, and there were wonderfully intricate carvings on every available surface. Some of the roof panels looked rather weathered and eroded, but all in all it was in remarkable condition for a wooden building that was almost a hundred years old. I was fascinated by two large carved figures of a man and a woman on the rear wall, and spent several minutes studying them while the crowds slowly cleared. The man appeared to be playing a flute, and it was only when I stepped back to get a clearer view that I realised the flute was actually his penis. I wasn't sure why this remarkably endowed gentleman was blowing his own trumpet, although I liked the idea that it might be a satirical depiction of a particularly narcissistic ancestor. Either that or they used to have some really wild parties.

By the time I'd finished marvelling at this unique feat the crowds had almost dissipated, and I followed the signposts round to the Kiwi House. Long before the New Zealanders acquired their nickname, or the fruit marketing board decided to rename the Chinese gooseberry during a moment of divine inspiration, the kiwi was a small flightless bird, the closest living relative of the giant moa that the first Maori settlers hunted to extinction. It felt like cheating to see my first kiwi in such a controlled environment, but as their numbers were dwindling and they only emerged at night it might be the only chance I'd get.

The statistics surrounding the disappearance of this iconic bird were quite staggering. Two hundred years ago there were around twelve million kiwi in New Zealand, a number that had now dropped to under seventy thousand. The main threat to their survival was the stoat, the predatory mammal having been introduced to the country by European settlers. A female stoat could kill a kiwi up to four times her own weight, and their tendency to ravage nests could easily destroy not only the living population, but also their potential offspring. Dogs were another problem, with one dog in Northland having killed over five hundred of the birds, totalling almost half the local kiwi population. Add to this the threat from wild cats, ferrets, wild pigs and possums, and it's easy to see why the species was dying out. The adult kiwi could live up to forty years, but in the face of this onslaught around ninety-five percent were killed within the first six months of their life.

Fortunately there were now conservation schemes underway to protect the species, although it might already be too late. It was sobering to think that we might be experiencing their last years on the planet. They were thought to have evolved up to seventy million years ago, and although officially members of the bird family they shared several characteristics with mammals, including the fact that they lived in burrows. The name was originally thought to be a crude representation of their call, but today linguists tended to trace it back to a Pacific curlew known as the *kivi*, a similar-looking bird with brown plumage and a long bill. When the Maori first arrived they are thought to have confused the two species, and over the intervening years the name had stuck.

It took me a few minutes to spot the birds in the glass cage, reinforcing my concerns that I might not get to see them at all in the wild. Their brown feathers quite closely matched the vegetation, and it was only when one started to dig into the dirt with its feet that I was able to distinguish it from the background. It was considerably larger than I'd expected, built like a hedgehog on stilts, but unfortunately it was busily engaged in digging a burrow and I only managed a rather unspectacular view of its backside. The scraping motions it made with its feet threw the displaced dirt a good two or three feet in the air, though, which at least added some dynamism to the performance. After a few minutes it became clear that this was the only view I would get, so bidding farewell to the kiwi's backside I headed back outside into the daylight.

The store was attached to a carving school, *Te Wananga Whakairo*, the real reason behind the rather contrived New Zealand theme park I'd just spent an hour wandering around. Traditionally carving was only undertaken by a chosen few known as *tauira*, roughly translated as 'disciples'. These men dedicated their lives to perfecting the art of carving, and when the time came they would pass their skills and knowledge on to a new disciple. Since 1966 *Te Wananga Whakairo* had preserved this ancient art form, and provided a modern framework for passing on traditional techniques and practices. Once again I was impressed at the ways in which the Maori community was adapting traditions to fit in with the modern world, ensuring that the old ways didn't die out by passing them on to younger generations. Some might view it as a dilution of their traditional culture, but throughout history evolution had been necessary for the survival of tradition. Initiatives such as this had ensured that the old ways were still a part of modern life for the Maori communities.

Some of the pieces produced by the students at the Institute were intended for buildings or outdoor display, such as the two carved heads I'd seen on my way into town, but many of the smaller pieces found their way into the store. Over a three year course the students learned how to use six different types of chisel, and were educated in the techniques for carving timber from the native totara tree, as well as other woods. About a third of their course was spent studying the origins of the most common patterns, as well as their various tribal characteristics, and the carvings were still used to convey local stories and legends as an aid to oral history.

In the end I bought a carved figure from the shop to take home with me, although as an outsider I was blind to its cultural significance. I asked the lady behind the counter and she informed me that it was a *tiki*, traditionally a representation of the first man created by the gods, and often shown in a foetus-like position. He was about nine inches long and in true Maori fashion was sticking his tongue out. The shop assistant also told me that he was supposed to bring good luck, but I was pretty sure that this was simply a sales pitch for ignorant tourists like myself.

In recent years the *tiki* had stirred up a fair degree of controversy in New Zealand. As part of Waitangi Tribunal Claim 262 the traditional images, emblems, and art forms of the Maori people were to be protected in accordance with their cultural views, but the *tiki* had a habit of appearing on postcards, stickers, and t-shirts across the country. No one had suggested that this should stop, but the ruling was a legal recognition of the fact that this image was the cultural property of the Maori people. For my own part I was glad that I'd bought my *tiki* from a Maori-run institution, if only because it felt more genuine than the many reproductions flooding the market. Hopefully it helped protect their cultural rights too.

As I left the reserve I saw five large coaches full of tourists unloading in the parking lot. The reserve had been fairly subdued during my hour there, so perhaps my *tiki* was working for me after all. Once I was back in my room I unpacked him from the tissue paper and examined him one last time before consigning him to the bottom of my backpack. He might bring good luck, but I still didn't want to wake up next to him in the morning.

* * *

'My name's Dennis, like Dennis the Menace can't play tennis.'

Our coach driver for the Tamaki Village cultural evening laughed at his own joke, a high-pitched chuckle that I'd grown used to hearing from Maori tour guides since my arrival in New Zealand. He looked more obviously Maori than either Robin or Miles, his thickset body verging on the overweight, his grizzled face framed by long, wavy grey hair.

'I'll be your driver all night tonight, so when you're coming back from the village look for bus ninety-two, or just ask for Dennis. On our way out to Tamaki I'll give you a quick rundown on the protocol for visiting a Maori *marae*. It's customary for the people of the *marae* to address their greetings to the visiting chief, so we're gonna need someone to be a chief from you lot. Anybody here want to volunteer?'

I was fairly confident of the correct procedures for the traditional greeting known as the *powhiri,* and I was tempted to raise my own hand, but before I had a chance a young man to my left was pushed out into the aisle by his partner.

'Well volunteered, mate. Why don't you tell us all what your name is, where you're from, and what brings you to beautiful Rotorua.'

Our 'volunteer' was obviously nervous, but he summoned his courage and turned around to address the coach. 'I'm Colin, from Loughborough in the UK, and we're here in New Zealand on our honeymoon.'

There was a spontaneous round of applause from the rest of us, which Colin accepted in a typically timid English manner, then Dennis ran through the *powhiri* with him. This was the official Maori welcome, and it opened with a *wero*, or challenge, from one of the tribe's warriors. He would emerge from the meeting house and advance towards us at a trot, slashing the air around him with a large wooden stave as he went. This stave, known as the *taiaha*, had become an important symbol of Maori tradition in recent years, and could be seen across New Zealand, from replicas in gift shops to abstract designs on buildings. Its use in *The Whale Rider*, the award-winning film based on Witi Ihimaera's novel, had even brought the *taiaha* to an international audience. At one end it flattened out to create a striking edge, and at the other it was topped with a decorative carving. This was usually the aggressive face of a warrior sticking his tongue out at his foes. The idea of a warrior sticking his tongue out at you might seem comical, but when combined with facial tattoos and the eyes rolling back in their sockets to show the whites it could look incredibly frightening.

Once we were all sufficiently intimidated the warrior would bend down and place a short branch on the ground. This was the *teka*, a peace offering to the visitors, and our chief would have to collect it without taking his eyes off the opposing warrior for the *powhiri* to be complete. Tonight the only change to this traditional ceremony was that there would be a number of chiefs at the ceremony – one from each coach – and only one of them would be selected to participate in the official greeting. I hoped for Colin's sake that it wasn't him, as the poor boy looked as if he might turn on his heels and run away screaming at the sight of a *taiaha*-wielding Maori warrior.

The village itself was a recreation of a traditional Maori settlement, complete with a high wooden external wall that we gathered outside in preparation for our *powhiri*. The chiefs selected from the evening's coach parties were asked to step forward into the open courtyard in front of the gates, and I was pleased to see that Colin hadn't been chosen as the senior chief for the ceremony. I was sure he'd never live it down if his honeymoon turned into an international incident.

When the Maori warrior emerged from the gate he was naked apart from a belt and a short grass skirt, and his *taiaha* looked plain and worrying functional. Throughout the ritual he maintained eye contact with our chief, who managed not to turn away or divert his gaze despite the scantily-clad man trying his best to intimidate him. When the peace offering was finally laid on the ground our representative walked slowly forward to collect it. I released an involuntary sigh, and I suddenly realised that I'd been holding my breath throughout the performance. Given that this was only for show – a highly dramatic representation of the Maori traditions, but a representation nonetheless – it occurred to me that the early European settlers would have thought twice before setting foot on a *marae*. We had the comfort now of knowing that the people of the village were unlikely to kill us, but in the early days of the settlement this wouldn't have been taken for granted. Calling round to visit your neighbours could be a life-threatening business.

Once our chief had collected the peace offering from the ground the warrior retreated, and a welcoming call known as the *karanga* went up from behind the wall. Usually we'd move to the *wharenui* next, but the Tamaki villagers offered demonstrations of cultural activities first. This seemed to involve the men grunting a lot and pretending to fight, reinforcing the common perception of the Maori as a great warrior race, although some of the women also gave dancing and singing demonstrations. The interval offered some good photo opportunities, but few cultural insights, and there were so many cameras around that I was fearful of walking anywhere in case I was shouted at for ruining someone's shot. Finally there was a call for us to move through to the meeting house, and I did my best to fight my way to the front in an effort to avoid the many camcorders.

The songs and dances were slickly presented, and there was even a commentary accompanying some of the routines, including an introduction to the *haka* that reminded us all that it was intended as a challenge in war, not as entertainment for spectators at sporting events. Strictly speaking this wasn't entirely true, as I'd learned that there were also *hakas* for funerals, welcomes, protests, and a variety of other occasions. The idea of the *haka* as a war dance played nicely to our preconceptions of the Maori as a warrior race, however. According to our hosts the last true performance of the *haka* was by the Maori Anzacs stationed in Vietnam, and I couldn't help wondering what the Vietnamese people had made of these fearsome warriors. They might not have understood their language, but the aggression of the *haka* spoke for itself.

When the performance was over we filed outside again, this time being led to a modern building for our meal. I'd been looking forward to this part of the evening for some time, as we were to be fed from a traditional Maori *hangi*, an underground oven of the type used by many Polynesian cultures. There was an open *hangi* in front of the dining

Ka Mate

building to demonstrate the process, showing how large volcanic rocks were heated on an open wood fire then placed in the bottom of the pit, several feet below ground level. The food was then arranged inside specially woven baskets, with the meat and fish sitting closest to the stones, then the vegetables, then the pudding on top. This ensured that the meat cooked thoroughly, while the vegetables and pudding steamed slowly in the heat. Finally hessian cloths made up the top layer, having been soaked in water overnight, and the oven was covered with soil. Five hours later it was all dug up again and was ready to eat.

The manner of its preparation made the meal sound exotic, but once we were inside I was disappointed to be confronted with roast lamb, potatoes, and gravy at the buffet table. The spread also included fish, chicken, mussels, carrot, and sweet potato, all of which were beautifully tender, but otherwise it wasn't vastly different to many roast dinners I'd enjoyed at home. Even the fish was served in a very European-looking white sauce, and I discovered that all the food had been prepared in modern metal trays rather than baskets, for reasons of hygiene and convenience. Having been on the road for a while I enjoyed the quality of the food and even went back for seconds, but it was no different to any hotel buffet or cheap restaurant. There was certainly no indication that it had spent five hours buried underground.

We were given half an hour before the bus left to look around the craft shops, but by then I'd grown disillusioned with the evening, and I was in no mood to part with even more money. The shops were mainly filled with the same cheap souvenirs I'd seen throughout the North Island, much of it vastly inferior to the carvings at the New Zealand Maori Arts And Crafts Institute. I'd entertained hopes that the Tamaki Village would offer some genuine cultural insights, but instead it felt like yet another Maori theme park – I should have taken the hint when I first picked up their glossy brochures.

Fortunately Dennis was on hand to cheer me up on the coach journey back to town.

'You all remember my name? It's easy to remember: Dennis, like Dennis the Menace can't play tennis.' I was starting to wonder if this was actually his surname. 'Now, while we drive back home I want to tell you a story about a Maori girl from here in Rotorua who really made it good. She lived here during the war, and she ended up marrying an American soldier who was stationed in New Zealand. They were really in love, and when the war finished she moved back with him to the United States. She became interested in all the great movies they make over there, and being a good Maori girl she figured she could sing and dance as well as anyone else, so she tried her hand at the movies. Eventually she became a huge success all across the world, and she was one of the greatest actresses of her generation. And that Maori girl's name was Doris Day.'

His infectious chuckle pierced the encroaching darkness and I found that I was smiling despite myself. It was hard to stay peevish in the face of such unrelenting goodwill, and before long I was singing along with 'She'll Be Coming Round The Mountain' while Dennis wrenched the coach through five full circuits of a roundabout on the edge of town. By the time I was delivered back to my hostel, the last drop-off on his route, I'd decided that I didn't mind the tackiness of the Tamaki Village as long as the profits were going to people like Dennis. The local communities benefited enormously from cultural performances like the one I'd seen tonight, and if they had to popularise their age-old traditions in order to fill their seats then so be it. At least they were vulgarising in a good cause.

As Dennis drove off into the night I thought I could hear him still singing to himself, although it might just have been the drunken teenagers in the hostel bar. I eventually fell asleep to the sound of thumping bass from downstairs, with the words 'Dennis the Menace can't play tennis' ringing in my ears.

9
Te Paeroa-o-Toi *(Coromandel Peninsula)*

It will come as no great shock to hear that I first met Sarah and Peter on a wine tour – this time in the Yarra Valley, just east of Melbourne. We'd swapped contact details in case our paths should cross again, although being British I'd never truly had any intention of looking them up. The wonderful time I'd had with Ian and Heather in Wellington had broken down some of my cultural inhibitions, however, and before leaving Rotorua the next morning I dug out the business card Sarah had given me. I vaguely recalled that they owned an avocado farm in Tauranga, which just happened to lie directly on the route I was taking to the Coromandel Peninsula. Almost everything else I'd learned about them had vanished in an alcoholic haze, but I was looking forward to seeing some familiar faces again, even if the familiarity was only fleeting. I just hoped they remembered me.

The weather was appalling as I left Rotorua and I kept the windscreen wipers on for most of the journey, although at times the torrential downpour threatened to obscure the road completely. It took almost two hours to reach Tauranga, despite the fact that I'd only travelled about fifty miles. The town centre looked grey and dismal, the persistent rain doing it no favours. Part of me couldn't help wondering why I'd come here.

Sarah worked in a jewellery store on the high street, but because of the local parking restrictions I had to leave the car near the waterfront and wander back into town. I wasn't sure whether I'd recognise her, or, indeed, if she'd recognise me. I thought I could recall Peter's face, but on closer consideration I discovered that I'd confused him with someone I used to work with. In fact I could remember almost nothing about him.

As it turned out, however, I recognised Sarah as soon as I walked through the door, and she seemed to recognise me too. She was serving a customer but she waved in my direction, so I killed some time browsing through their glass cabinets until she was finished. Once she was free she ushered me over.

'You know, I was just saying to Peter the other night that it's about now that you said you'd be here. We were wondering when you'd show up. So how are you? Where have you been since we saw you?'

I told her about my two weeks in Fiji and my travels around the North Island, placing special emphasis on the Wellington Sevens as I remembered that Peter was a rugby fan. He was a Kiwi, after all.

'You sound like you've been having a fantastic time. We've just been back here I'm afraid, so there's not so much to tell really. What are your plans now you're here? Where are you staying tonight?'

'I'm not sure,' I confessed, 'I thought I'd try to check in at a hostel or a motel, if you know a good one.'

'Nonsense: you must come and stay with us. We've got plenty of room now the kids have left home. I finish here at five-thirty, then we can drive out to the house. It's near Katikati, I don't know if you've heard of it, it's just north of here. Have you got your own car? You can follow me out there, I'll just need to stop for some food on the way. Now, what are you doing this afternoon? Have you been to the Mount yet?'

I shook my head – I'd not even heard of the Mount before, although I had a suspicion that it might involve some walking.

'Well that's worth seeing then, especially if you've got a car. If you pick up a map at the Information Centre that'll show you where to go, and you can park right at the foot of it. It's a lovely walk around there, you'll definitely enjoy it. Then if you come back here for five-thirty we'll drive back together. How does that sound? Peter's out of town today anyway, helping our daughter do her new house up, so it'll be more exciting than moping around the place on my own. Alright then? And I'll see you about five-thirty?'

It was nice to have my day planned out for me for a change, and I wished that Sarah had been on hand to plan my entire trip. I wasn't convinced that it was a good day for walking, but as soon as I stepped outside the showers dried up, and chinks of sunlight appeared between the clouds. I took this as a sign that the Mount was calling me, and I hurried back to the car.

The Mount in question was Mount Maunganui, and it was only a short drive from central Tauranga. As I crossed the bridge from Tauranga to Maunganui I could see the Mount looming in the distance, a perfectly triangular volcanic cone that dominated the skyline. Beyond it lay the Bay of Plenty and the open sea.

By the time I'd found a parking space and had walked the short distance to the base of the Mount the sky had cleared, and the ground was drying quickly in the heat. The base walk allowed a pleasant stroll through well-kept woodland, affording occasional glimpses of the coastline through the trees. After about ten minutes I came to a fork in the path, with the right-hand turning marked as a twenty-five minute path to the summit, and I found myself unable to resist the challenge. The gradient didn't look too steep as I started out in this new direction, and I assumed that the path would zigzag up the side of the Mount on its way to the summit.

It soon became clear that whoever had designed the path had more vigorous exercise in mind. Rather than zigzagging from left to right and avoiding the steeper gradients it began to head straight up the hillside, as if the planners had simply taken a ruler and drawn a line between the two points. Fortunately they'd had the decency to cut steps into the path, but some of these were a couple of feet high, and I strained to haul myself up them. Now that the clouds had gone the heat was rising too, and after ten minutes I could feel my t-shirt clinging damply to my back. So much for my pleasant stroll.

I finally reached the summit after half an hour's vigorous climbing, having been overtaken on the way by a bronzed gentleman in his sixties who put my fitness levels to shame. Not only were there amazing views in every direction but there was also a fresh, cool breeze blowing in off the sea, and I spent the first five minutes restoring my body temperature to something approaching normality. From up here I could see that Tauranga lay slightly inland, while Maunganui stretched along a spit of land by the entrance to Tauranga Harbour. I could even trace the route that I'd taken from Sarah's store. A quick glance at my watch told me that it was about time I started heading back if I was to meet her as planned, and I decided to return via the other side of the Mount on a slightly wider gravel path.

Fortunately it was much easier going downhill, although my legs were starting to burn from the earlier exertion, and my thighs struggled to cope with so many steps. I made it back to Tauranga just in time to catch Sarah as she was locking up, and we arranged to meet in a small lay-by on the way out of town, so that I could follow her home. For a few nervous minutes I was concerned that I might have misunderstood her directions, but then I saw her pull alongside me in a rather expensive-looking car, and we headed out to Katikati.

Their house was large and impressive, and it was no wonder that Sarah hadn't been keen on filling the space by herself that evening. After I'd dropped my bags off in the guest bedroom she kindly took me on a tour of their avocado orchard. The orchard was one of two that they owned, the other located further east on land that they rented off the local Maori tribe. In the distance I could still see the Mount rising up against the backdrop of the sea, even though it was now over ten miles away. Sarah told me that their last harvest had been a poor one, and she apologised, as there were no avocadoes left for me to try. The trees were heavily laden with small green fruit, however, and it looked as if the next picking would be good.

As we walked around she repeatedly bent down to check small panels at the bases of some of the trees, and after this had happened several times I finally plucked up the courage to ask about them.

'All our irrigation here's computerised now,' she explained, stopping to check another one, 'so I just have to check that the settings are right while Peter's away, and the rest looks after itself. These tell me the moisture levels in the soil, so that the irrigation can give them the right amount of water.'

The tree nearest to us had several fruit with large raised ridges on the skin, and I asked her what had caused this.

'We get that on the avocadoes when there have been high winds, especially when the fruit's still small. Unfortunately it means that we can't sell those along with the rest, although they can be used for avocado oil instead.'

I cupped one of the golf ball-sized avocadoes in my hand and was surprised at how heavy they already were. They were no bigger than plums or small nectarines, but their weight felt more like that of a small potato.

'We export mainly to the US and Australia now,' Sarah explained as we wandered among the trees. 'We'll aim to get about twenty-five thousand crates from this orchard at the next harvest, and probably another ten thousand from the other one. It's going to be a big job. Peter won't be able to do it by himself, so we'll have to hire some casual labour to help us with it, possibly from the hostels. It's a shame you didn't arrive here later, or we could have used a hand.'

Once the moisture levels had been checked we headed back inside, and Sarah prepared dinner while we shared a bottle of wine as an aperitif. Peter called to say that he was heading back tonight and would join us for dinner, which meant that I'd get to share rugby stories with him. Fortunately there was a photograph of the two of them in the living room, and I was finally able to locate him in my hazy memories of the Yarra Valley.

He arrived just as the meal was nearing completion and I helped them set the table. I asked if they ate many of the avocadoes themselves, and Peter told me that they often just ate them out of the skin with a spoon, or spread the ripe ones on bread instead of butter. At home I'd always considered avocadoes to be something of a luxury, and it seemed rather decadent to make such liberal use of them. I imagined that if you had thirty-five thousand crates of them, though, the novelty would soon wear off.

We chatted more over dinner, and Peter mentioned the other orchard they owned to the east of Katikati. I asked him how well that worked, with the land being rented from the local tribe.

'Well, officially I own a quarter; my accountant – who went into partnership with us – owns a quarter; and the other half remains with the tribe. That way they keep a controlling share, you see, so it's still their land. We never see them there, though, so they basically get their money for nothing. In the six years we've been growing I've only seen them actually come onto the land once. They always seem to know when we've been there, though, and if we go to the local pub they always say that they've heard we're in town.

'When I first looked into buying the land the local chief showed us around,' he continued, chuckling. 'He's a big fella, so overweight that he couldn't walk all the way through the orchard, so he dropped us off on one side and we walked through. The other end backed onto the local school, and he drove round there to pick us up. Even then he didn't actually set foot in the orchard. As long as their money keeps coming in we're more or less left to look after ourselves.'

Sarah joined in, telling me how she loved the Maori sense of humour. 'We've had a few work in the shop over the years, and they were such funny guys, it was always a joy working with our Maori staff. They're always smiling and joking, it was great for the rest of us.'

'A lot of the Maori families outside of the towns seem to be stuck in a bit of a rut, though,' Peter added. 'Most of them are on income support, living in rundown old caravans, and because they've got such a relaxed attitude all the time they look like they're never going to lift themselves out of it. There's a real problem with drugs too, especially in Northland and down the east coast. A lot of them use their vacant plots to grow dope, and the Police have to get involved when it reaches the local schools. It means these communities are getting a bad reputation and it makes it even harder for them to move on. We employ some of the guys from the local tribe to help in the orchard occasionally, and I think that's all the work they do all year. We have to pay them in cash too, so they can keep claiming their money from the government. It's a way of life that most of them are stuck in for good.'

To lift the atmosphere I mentioned the Sevens rugby tournament in Wellington, and Peter immediately brightened.

'Christian Cullen came to the All Blacks side from the Sevens competition you know,' he said, leaning forward in his seat, 'and I'd rate him as one of our best players ever. He's only a little guy, but apparently he used to be able to bench press more than the big forwards. That's your ultimate Sevens player for me – fast and strong. Our Sevens side is one of the reasons the All Blacks have stayed such a strong team.'

The All Blacks *haka* was one of the things that had brought me to New Zealand in the first place, and it seemed to have become such an icon for the country – even people who never watched rugby knew about the *haka*.

'Taine Randell was the best at doing the *haka*. He was so scary, you know? I wouldn't want to face him after seeing that!'

'When I was young they always used to spook me,' Sarah added as she cleared my plate away. 'I used to get so frightened at the Maori cultural displays, they can be pretty scary when you're a kid. Nowadays I think they tone them down a bit for the tourists, especially if there are children in the audience. They don't want to send people home from their holidays in tears, after all.'

Before heading to bed I couldn't resist asking about the Super Rugby competition, played between teams from New Zealand, Australia, and South Africa. I was eager to see a match while I was in New Zealand, but I hadn't had the chance up in Auckland.

'Our local team here's the Chiefs, although we do support other teams sometimes. We never support Auckland though,' he laughed, 'round here we call them Jafas.'

Jafas?

'Just Another Fucking Aucklander. All their fans are either super-rich or spoilt brats, so you won't find many Auckland fans around. At least not ones that'll admit it.'

I could tell that I'd have to pick my team very carefully. I certainly didn't want to be mistaken for a Jafa.

* * *

As I loaded my bags back into the car the following morning the cicadas were humming in the surrounding trees, their empty body casings hanging from the trunks on either side of the driveway. The Coromandel Peninsula had a reputation for enjoying some of the most beautiful scenery in the North Island, and I couldn't leave without paying it a visit. After saying our goodbyes I drove through Katikati, joining the road that would take me up the Peninsula's east coast.

In the past the Coromandel Peninsula had been renowned for its gold mining and kauri logging, with Waihi on the east coast producing half of New Zealand's gold at the height of the gold rush. The kauri industry had made a lasting impact on the area too: when the HMS Coromandel stopped there in 1820 to collect kauri spurs its name was adopted for the region. Now those industries had vanished, and tourism had taken their place.

A few black clouds squatted on the horizon, but otherwise the weather remained clear as I headed north along the coastal route. Before long I was back on the small winding roads I'd driven around Paihia and Kaitaia, including the rickety one-lane bridges held together by a crumbling layer of asphalt. My route looked insignificant on the map, but the small roads and regular stops for bridges added an hour to my journey time. By the time I reached Hahei it was already midday.

In order to reach the infamous Cathedral Cove I knew that I'd have to turn off soon, but after fifteen minutes I still hadn't seen a signpost, and I was forced to retrace my steps. Fortunately there weren't many roads to choose from, and on a hunch I took an unmarked sharp left turn that seemed to be heading in roughly the right direction. A hundred yards up the road I finally came across a sign confirming that I was on the right track, possibly the worst piece of signposting I'd ever encountered. It led me to hope that Cathedral Cove might be off the beaten track. Given the number of postcards that I'd seen of it in gift stores, though, that didn't seem likely.

When I eventually reached the parking lot all my hopes were dashed. Not only was it jammed to capacity with white rental cars and unnecessary off-road vehicles, but the Kiwi Experience bus had just turned up and was disgorging its contents. Along with two other companies Kiwi Experience offered cheap transportation across New Zealand and 'entertainment' aimed squarely at the teen backpacker market, like a less polished 18-30 holiday with travellers sandals and rucksacks. Nicknamed the 'fuck truck', their reputation attracted as many tourists as it repelled, although most of them saw more of New Zealand's bars than its sights.

As fifty or so hungover, dishevelled teenagers disembarked from the coach I realised that there were at least another twenty still inside, lolling across empty seats or crushed up against the windows as they tried to sleep off last night's excesses. On the surface it looked like a cheap way to see the country, but in reality most of them were more likely to see the inside of a toilet bowl. I was fairly sure that it wasn't what my teachers had in mind when they'd talked to us about travelling the world.

I waited for a few minutes and let the huddle of teenagers slouch a short distance along the path. It took forty-five minutes to walk from the parking lot to the cove, and the scenery was so beautifully tranquil that I didn't want to run the risk of them ruining the atmosphere. When the air was finally clear of the scent of second-hand alcohol I began to walk, taking my time to ensure that I didn't bump into their rearguard. It was easy to slow my pace as the path undulated dramatically, running downhill at first only to rise up a steep incline shortly afterwards, and I couldn't help wondering whether the planners should have done a better job of levelling it out. I probably needed the exercise after my long drive, but as the sweat began to trickle down behind my ears I found myself hoping desperately for a flat stretch. My prayers went unanswered, and by the time I reached the first smattering of sand my hair was plastered to my forehead.

Cathedral Cove proved to be worth the exertion. It was not one cove but two, formed from two adjacent beaches joined together by a large hole in the separating headland. Fortunately it was low tide when I arrived, and I was able to walk through the gap to the far beach. I'd taken my shoes off once the grains started to encroach into my socks, and as I walked under the natural sandstone arch I could feel the sand growing cool between my toes; clumps of seaweed lay strewn around in the shade, left behind by the receding tide, and I took care to step around or over them whenever possible. The natural arch overhead had an almost Gothic quality about it, and it was easy to see how the name Cathedral Cove came into use.

The second beach was even more beautiful than the first, with fine pale sand and gently rolling surf. It also boasted a second sandstone feature known as Te Hoho, or Sail Rock, a lone pinnacle standing several meters out in the water. The erosive action of the sea at the pinnacle's base had given it the triangular shape that earned it its name, although the sides were pitted with a number of small circular indentations, as if someone had taken chunks out of it with an ice cream scoop. This was known as honeycomb weathering, and was caused by the salt water soaking into soft rock, then breaking chunks off as the water dried and salt crystals formed. The wind also contributed, rolling loose particles around these indentations until they formed shallow, circular depressions. Here it had produced a feature that was almost as impressive as the arch I'd just walked through.

I found myself a clear spot to rest for a moment, and as I sat down on a flat rock the sun broke through the clouds, bathing the beach in a warm glow. The Kiwi Experience group, situated further down the beach, appeared to be getting ready to go kayaking, although most of them were already drowning themselves with much-needed bottles of water. I was sure that their hungover expressions hinted at some health and safety issues, but at least they were getting some daylight and a modicum of physical exercise. It would give them another story to tell in the pub tonight, anyway.

I'd never really seen the attraction of lying on beaches, so after ten minutes I gathered my things together and moved back the way I'd come. The views were undoubtedly spectacular, but there were too many people around to feel completely relaxed. I was surprised that so many people had made the forty-five minute walk to get here, especially since so many of them were now lying on their backs with their eyes closed. My experiences so far suggested that there weren't many beaches suitable for sunbathing in New Zealand, however, and there certainly wouldn't be many south of Wellington. I could only assume that the Kiwis felt a little sun-starved.

Eventually I returned to the parking lot, after another trek along the undulating pathway. Fortunately I had some water in the car to cool off with, and once I'd rehydrated I drove back to the main road. There was still no signpost telling me which way to go, but having driven in both directions already it didn't cause a problem, and I headed north, continuing around the east coast and up towards Coromandel Town.

I ended up driving through the town and staying overnight in a cabin about seven miles further north, near Papa Aroha. The clouds I'd seen earlier in the day had completely cleared, leaving a beautiful, bright evening, and I could sit outside on my private balcony with a glass of wine and watch the sun set over the sea. There was no sign of the Kiwi Experience bus, and no obvious reason for it to come this far up the peninsula. For once I felt that I'd escaped from the well-trodden tourist track. Later that evening, as I fell into a peaceful slumber, I could hear a lone sheep bleating in the dark.

Ka Mate

10
Waitomo

It was no great surprise that I managed to find a sports station on the radio the following morning, as I drove back down the peninsula. The New Zealanders were renowned for their fanaticism when it came to most competitive endeavours, but especially when a ball was involved. If the ball in question was an irregular shape, then all the better. It was this fiercely competitive streak that had made the All Blacks one of the most recognizable franchises in world sport, despite the fact that they'd struggled to win the Rugby World Cup since their victory in its inaugural competition, and if national stereotypes were to be believed then there was nothing a Kiwi bloke liked more than throwing his body into a bone-crunching tackle on the rugby pitch – except, perhaps, the beers in the clubhouse afterwards.

As I drove back through Coromandel Town it was clear that there would be only one topic of conversation on today's show: Vinnie Anderson, a player with local Rugby League side the Warriors, had been dropped by the club, and allegations made in the press had fired up the nation. Anderson still had a year to run on his contract, but because he'd opted to join the touring national side without asking his club's permission they'd queried his commitment. As soon as he was dropped by the Warriors the London Broncos had signed him up, compounding the problem as it meant that he was now set to leave the country. It probably didn't help that the Warriors were an Auckland team, either.

There was little sympathy for the club's point of view. The true reasons for Anderson's departure were still a subject for debate, but the New Zealand public felt they were owed an explanation. If it was true that he'd been dropped because of his commitments to the national side then it sounded as if the Warriors' management might get lynched. At the very least their jobs were on the line.

The attitudes on display intrigued me as I drove slowly south. Callers repeatedly argued that as fans of the club they were effectively shareholders, and therefore they were owed a full explanation by the management. It never entered the equation that the Warriors had *actual* shareholders, who were likely to receive an explanation ahead of the public – to be a fan was to invest something of yourself, in return for which you were owed a say in the running of the team. Even more intriguing was their relationship with the national side. Time after time people were calling in to express the same sentiment: it was an honour to represent New Zealand at any level, and no player should be penalised for putting their country first. The fact that Anderson hadn't followed his club's protocol for taking time out was largely ignored, and instead he was portrayed as an ill-treated hero. If you played for the national side, it seemed, you could do no wrong.

It took me about an hour to drive down to Thames, after which I officially left the Coromandel Peninsula and began heading west towards Hamilton. As the argument continued to rage across the airwaves there were few variations from these two basic positions; Anderson's father even called in to add his own expressions of disgust to the chorus of disgruntled voices, and you'd have been forgiven for assuming that the country was on the brink of civil war. New Zealand certainly took its rugby seriously.

I aimed to reach Waitomo before nightfall, having failed to reach the west coast before because of the Wellington Sevens. This time there was nothing to distract me from my task. Once again it took a disproportionately long time to navigate my way out of Hamilton, and I'd almost reached the conclusion that the town planners had designed a maze to keep visitors trapped there when I finally emerged on State Highway Three, heading towards Otorohanga. My spectacular escape would probably be talked about for years to come.

It was already late in the afternoon by the time I reached my destination, so I wasted no time in checking into a motel. I still had about ten miles to go to Waitomo, but you had to pay a premium to sleep that close to the caves, and for less than the price of a hostel room in Waitomo I managed to rent myself a large lounge-slash-bedroom, with a separate shower and cooking facilities too. If it wasn't for a densely patterned bedspread resembling the Magic Eye pictures that were so popular during the Nineties, it could almost have felt like home.

Otorohanga had an intriguing history of its own, although without the glowworm caves at Waitomo it would have struggled to attract tourists. The name Otorohanga translates only clumsily into English: 'O' means the food carried for a journey, while 'torohanga' translates as 'extended over a long distance'. This title came from the exploits of a local Maori chief who had reputedly travelled to Taupo on foot, carrying his rations on his back, and it made my car full of wine look positively decadent. It was estimated that up to five thousand Maori used to live in the town and its surrounds, compared with a total of less than three thousand people in the modern settlement. When timber millers settled here in 1890 they marked the first real intrusion into the area by Europeans, and it took less than a hundred years for the Maori traditions to disappear and the town to fall into decline.

The fate of Otorohanga was typical of this region of the North Island. Known as King Country, it was one of the last areas to resist European intrusion, and was still a stronghold for many Maori communities. The name came from the self-proclaimed Maori King Potatau I, previously the leader of one of the Waikato tribes. Following the aggressive occupation of the Waikato by British forces in the 1860s, the Tainui, under Potatau's leadership, withdrew into what was now known as King Country. For several decades they resisted European influence, and King Country acted as a haven for homeless refugees fleeing the wrath of the government's army.

It was easy to emphasise the aggressive role of the British Government in the colonization of New Zealand, and of King Country in particular, but the negotiations weren't entirely one-sided. In the early 1870s there were genuine attempts to reach an agreement concerning the land that the tribes laid claim to, but the two points of view were impossible to reconcile. The Maori refugees wanted the return of their traditional lands, but by this stage things had already moved on across the rest of the country. Their homeland was slowly slipping through their fingers.

Today Otorohanga was pleasant enough, although it had few attractions of its own, preferring to survive on the fringes of Waitomo. I saw no Maori faces as I walked through the town, and its turbulent history seemed to have been forgotten. Instead the main road was lined with motels, accommodating yet another European invasion. That the current invasion arrived in white rental cars made it only slightly less intrusive.

Depressed by my own complicity I retreated to my motel room as the sun went down, preparing myself a quick meal in the cramped kitchen. Tomorrow I would descend into the damp, dark recesses of Waitomo's caves. I'd need all the energy I could muster.

Ka Mate

* * *

Driving through the centre of Waitomo the following morning I was disappointed to find that it consisted of little more than a cluster of small, shabby buildings along one side of the road. On the other side an entire fleet of coaches was parked, including my old friends from the Kiwi Experience tour, and their human cargo had already been unloaded into the handful of buildings that comprised the Visitors' Centre. I'd waited two weeks to reach Waitomo, and now that I was finally here my sense of anticipation was deflating rapidly. It felt more like a theme park than a natural attraction, bringing back unwelcome memories of Rotorua.

Fortunately Waitomo's true treasures lay buried beneath the surface. Waitomo translated roughly as 'the place where water enters', and this provided a surprisingly succinct account of how the area was formed. It sat in the middle of a karst region, a landscape that was estimated to cover almost ten percent of the world's land area. In Waitomo's case the karst area was created approximately thirty million years ago, when the region sat beneath a shallow sea; because of this prolonged submersion, layers of coal, sandstone, limestone and siltstone were laid down on top of the less porous base rock, gradually accumulating over a period of twenty million years. Then, around ten million years ago, movements in the earth's crust pushed this new land back up above sea level, tilting and twisting it as it did so.

It's what happened next that made this area such a perfect example of a karst landscape, and helped to attract coaches full of hungover teens. As rain fell on the newly raised land over the passing centuries it absorbed carbon dioxide from the atmosphere and the soil, making it slightly acidic. Not only did this acidity gradually erode away at the soft stone of the surface, carving it into unusual natural 'sculptures', but it also achieved a similar effect below the surface. Water seeped slowly through cracks and holes, and over the millennia these widened to create a vast cave network. It was these caves that we'd all come to see.

I eventually found somewhere to park and elbowed my way into the Visitors' Centre, trying to wind an erratic course through the clusters of gossiping teenagers. The most popular caving option seemed to be black-water rafting, which went partway towards explaining the damp smell sitting heavily in the air. It appeared to involve throwing yourself into an unlit cave on a small inflatable ring and hoping that the underwater current carried you through to the other side, something that really didn't appeal to my sense of self-preservation. Hurtling through an enclosed space in absolute darkness on what looked like a child's beach toy just wasn't my idea of fun, although by the look of it the Kiwi Experience bus would qualify for a group discount. Their interest was enough to cement my conviction.

Instead I settled on a trip through St. Benedict's Cavern. The brochure said that it involved a hundred foot abseil into the cave, then a guided walk through the interior to an exit on the other side. I'd never abseiled before, but since there wasn't any water involved, and they generously provided you with torches to light your way, it still sounded safer than the black-water rafting. St. Benedict's was also rumoured to be the most beautiful of the caves at Waitomo. My mind was set.

Unfortunately the morning tour of the cave had already left, and I had a few hours to kill before I began my descent into the depths of the earth. It gave me enough time to check out the other main attraction in Waitomo, and one of the reasons that it drew far more visitors than your average karst region: the glowworms.

In 1887, when the area was still largely closed to European settlers, a government surveyor called Fred Mace and the local Maori chief, Tane Tinorau, stumbled across a cave entrance. A river flowed from the cave mouth, so they assembled a makeshift raft from flax stems and pushed themselves into the underground chamber. What they saw there changed the character of the area forever. At first there was just a tiny pinprick of light on the ceiling, as if a hole in the roof was allowing them to catch a glimpse of the night sky. Then there was another, and another, twinkling above their heads like the stars in a nursery rhyme, yet somehow contained within the craggy dome of the cave. Before long the entire cavern ceiling was twinkling with hundreds of lights. They must have thought they were witnessing a miracle.

In many ways they were. What they saw on that day were *Arachnocampa luminosa*, or glowworms. The species spends between six and nine months in its larval stage, during which time each larva lets down about twenty sticky threads from the ceiling to catch its meals. Once they've caught and eaten a fly their body processes it, and excretes the waste matter from the other end. A chemical reaction in this excrement causes it to glow in the dark, which in turn attracts more flies to the sticky threads, thinking that they're flying into the night sky. Within the confines of these caves the majority of the flies that the larvae ate were from previous generations of *Arachnocampa luminosa*, having hatched in the darkness at the end of their nine months in larval form. As cannibalistic orgies go it was astoundingly beautiful.

When Mace and Tinorau emerged back into the daylight they realised that they had a natural wonder on their hands. In 1889 Tane Tinorau conducted the first guided tour of the cave, and until 1904 the local Maori resisted attempts to take this virtual goldmine away from them. In 1904, however, the Crown made a compulsory purchase of the land under the Scenery Preservation Act, and it passed out of their hands. At that time the authorities had reasonable cause for concern: many of the early visitors were in the habit of breaking off stalactites to take home as souvenirs, and the caves had already been plundered to the point of destruction. In 1990 three of the four caves were returned to the local tribe as part of the Treaty Of Waitangi settlement, and, echoing Mace and Tinorau's early collaboration, control was currently shared between the Department of Conservation and the Maori trust. Strict restraints were placed on the number of visitors, and all the caves were carefully monitored. The glowworms were too important a part of Waitomo's tourist industry to be ignored.

Before we were allowed to see the glowworms we were taken on a tour of the few caves that sat above water level. Our group was large and noisy, and I found myself straggling at the back, not really paying attention to our guide. The restrictions on numbers weren't strict enough for my liking, and I only managed occasional glimpses of the cave's slender stalactites between my fellow tourists. We might not have a significant impact on the humidity or carbon dioxide levels in the cave, but we managed to ruin its atmosphere in other ways. I clung onto the promise of unspoiled St. Benedict's while we were herded through to the boats.

Our final stop before the jetty was their so-called 'cathedral cave', the largest of the caves that we'd passed through in the complex. Its soaring ceiling was certainly impressive, but I cringed when I heard that they'd packed in crowds of two hundred people for concerts by Dame Kiri Te Kanawa and, bizarrely, Rod Stewart. What had once been a stunning feature of the natural landscape had slowly been turned into just another concert hall, complete with paving stones and metal handrails. A glitterball must surely be on the way.

This new information provoked a German group to burst spontaneously into several indecipherable folk songs, and we had to wait five minutes for them to simmer down again. I'm not sure whether Dame Kiri would have been proud or appalled, but there was no such confusion over my own reaction. If anyone had dared to unsheathe a camcorder I might have stormed out in protest.

Eventually the Germans ran out of songs, much to everyone's relief, and we were ushered through to the boats. The landing stage was only half-visible in the darkness, but after some desperate clambering and jostling we all managed to fit into a shallow, metal-hulled boat and our guide pushed us off. He slowly fed an overhead rope between his hands, sending our craft gliding smoothly through the water, and for the first time since we'd entered the caves silence descended. Water lapped quietly at the boat as it rocked gently from side to side, and as I relaxed I almost found myself falling asleep.

I had nearly lapsed into disturbing dreams of gravely-voiced Scottish crooners and Germanic beer halls when I saw a tiny light above my head, as if someone had punctured the ceiling with a pin and the daylight was struggling to shine through. Then there was another, and another. As we rounded the corner the ceiling was suddenly aglow with hundreds of these pinpricks of light, some gathered in small clusters, others sitting in patches of comparative darkness. Each light seemed to flicker slightly as you stared at it, and the overall effect was remarkably like a clear night sky. It was easy to see how the cave-dwelling flies were deceived. I found myself trying to make out constellations of my own devising, a game usually rendered necessary by my own poor knowledge of astronomy. In here I constructed dot-to-dot patterns from the luminescent excrement of maggots, yet my joy at finding a shape like an umbrella or a teapot remained undiminished. This unconventional star map kept me entranced, my neck craned upwards, as we drifted slowly beneath them. It was almost worth enduring the German folk songs for this.

Eventually we passed out of the main glowworm cave, their presence reduced to an occasional flickering blip on the ceiling, and before long we emerged into daylight. Once we'd all disembarked I paused for a moment on the jetty, partly to allow the German group to pass, and partly to look at the cave mouth. It was here that Fred Mace and Tane Tinorau had first entered the glowworm caves over a hundred years ago, floating into this dank, moss-covered entrance on a crude hand-made raft. Only the slow, steady flow of water from underground hinted at the complex of caves they were to uncover, and nothing could have prepared them for the sight of the glowworms. They must have felt like they'd discovered another planet.

By the time I returned to the main road our group had cleared, although I thought I could hear the chorus of a folk song drifting on the breeze. I returned to the Visitors' Centre with a twinge of trepidation. Soon I would be descending a hundred feet into another of Waitomo's caves, and there would be no paving stones or handrails down there. I was pretty certain that Rod Stewart had never abseiled into St. Benedict's in his trademark skin-tight pants, either. Nothing in the Glowworm Caves had prepared me for this adventure.

* * *

'You know, the abseil's not too difficult. We'll run through it before we go down, give you a practice run and everything. Billy Connelly even came down to the cave for his recent New Zealand program, so there's nothing to be scared about. He just walked in through the door at the far end, mind you, he didn't take the hundred foot drop. But for a young guy like you the abseil should be easy.'

Robbie hardly paused for breath as our minibus hurtled around the small, winding roads of Waitomo, his driving almost as frantic as his conversation. I suspected that he could sense my nervousness and was trying to take my mind off what lay ahead, although my carsickness was doing a much better job. He exuded confidence, but I got the feeling that he'd have looked just as comfortable if he was about to jump into a swimming pool full of sharks. Robbie was one of the adrenaline-junkies that both Australia and New Zealand seemed to produce in abundance. Given the thin ozone layers in this part of the world I figured that it might be an unusual form of sunstroke.

When he heard that I'd visited the glowworm cave earlier that day he grinned.

'And what did you make of that? Packed with tourists, was it? All to see those cannibalistic maggots with shiny shit. Well, we might not have any maggots for you, but we'll have the cave to ourselves this afternoon. It's gonna be awesome.'

I was the only person on the tour of St. Benedict's Cavern, the rest having been seduced by the near-death experience of black-water rafting or, as Robbie put it, by the cannibalistic maggots. What made the contrast with the morning's tour even more pronounced, and slightly embarrassing, was the fact that Robbie had been joined in the front of the minibus by a second guide. Paerau came from one of the local Maori tribes, and I was reminded yet again of Mace and Tinorau, and the ongoing spirit of co-operation in Waitomo. Robbie and Paerau outnumbered me two-to-one, and had more caving experience between them than I'd accumulate in a lifetime: it was nice to have so much attention, but it was also more than a little intimidating.

Once we'd passed out of town Robbie wrenched the car off the main road and onto a small track that snaked through the fields. I couldn't help noticing that this manoeuvre didn't cause him to slow down, and I wondered whether he also dabbled in rally driving during his spare time. His sudden twists of the wheel to avoid large potholes sent sheep scuttling away on both sides, and occasionally sent judders up my spine as we hit a small rock or patch of stony ground, so I was secretly rather relieved when we pulled up outside a modern corrugated iron shed. Paerau jumped out and opened the door for me, and I stepped shakily outside onto solid ground. At least it had taken my mind off the caving.

It took a few minutes to get me kitted out in white gumboots, blue overalls and a very fetching orange helmet, then Robbie helped me into the abseiling harness. It was smaller than I'd expected, the complex web of black straps shaped like the outline of an oversized diaper. It was perturbing to think that I'd soon be suspended above a hundred foot drop by these thin straps, and I didn't mind when Robbie decided to double-check that I was secure. Apart from anything else, an ill-fitting strap could pinch you in some very uncomfortable places.

As we walked down to the cave entrance he talked me through the basics of abseiling. The rope fed through a complex buckle system that looked like one of those frustrating mechanical puzzles that gift shops sell at Christmas, and although he told me the name of it my attention was wandering elsewhere. I could see the ropes slung over his shoulder, and they looked awfully slender. Was I really going to be suspended above a hundred foot drop by nothing more than some straps and a length of cord? And should I have eaten that ice cream while I waited for the tour to start?

I received some answers when we paused on a steep section of the hill to practice. Robbie attached the rope to a hook set into the hillside, helped me thread it through the unfamiliar buckle system, and with some gentle cajoling convinced me to step out over the edge. My first few steps were awkward, not being used to walking backwards down steep hills, but once my brain had grown used to it the descent became relatively easy. I tucked one hand beneath me as instructed and fed the rope slowly through, trying to remember to walk down the slope as I did so. Before long I was at the bottom, and after a couple more descents, carefully dodging the sheep turds each time, I was confident that I knew what I was doing. Abseiling, it seemed, was easier than I'd thought.

Abseiling down a hill might have been easy, but I soon regretted my premature optimism as Robbie and Paerau led me to the cave entrance. To call it an entrance is probably misleading, summoning images of grand openings rimmed with overhanging mosses and root networks. This was a crack between two boulders, no wider than a few feet. And it headed straight down.

Robbie turned at me and grinned.

'Okay. You ready?'

Ready wasn't the word, but I didn't want these Kiwis doubting the British appetite for adventure. I stepped slowly forward to the edge of the crack, peering down into the darkness. There was no sign of the bottom.

'Don't worry,' Robbie said, clipping his own harness onto the line. 'I'm going down first, to make sure everything's okay. There's a ledge about halfway down, so I'll see you there in a few minutes. Paerau will look after you up here, and take some nice pictures to remind you of your first caving experience. I'll see you in five.'

With that he leant out over the edge and lifted his feet off the ground, disappearing rapidly into the darkness below with the rope whirring through his hands. He was visible for a few seconds, then a protruding rock hid him from view. It was as if the earth had swallowed him up.

Paerau smiled and nodded to me, waving his camera. 'You want to step a bit closer to the edge there? I'll take your picture for you, then we'll do another when you're in the hole. It'll give Robbie a minute to get things ready for you, then it's your turn. You excited?'

Contrary to my expectations I did feel surprisingly elated, and I finally realised why they called these adrenaline sports. I'd always assumed that the rush came during the activity, but it seemed that the anticipation was more than enough to start the hormones flowing. I was nervous, even a little jittery, but I couldn't keep the smile off my face, and I had to make a conscious effort to turn the corners of my mouth down. This was what I'd come here to do.

When the time came to descend, Robbie having sent us a signal that he was ready, I carefully clipped myself onto the line. I was surprised to see that Paerau didn't have a harness on, and as I sat suspended over the drop I asked if he was coming with us.

'Nah, I'm not that stupid, no matter how I look. I'm gonna get some supplies and meet you halfway. I'll move the bus round to the exit too, so we don't have to walk too far. You have fun though, won't you.' He laughed that Maori laugh again, the high-pitched giggle that I'd heard in Taupo and Rotorua, and it occurred to me that it was almost exactly as I imagined a hyena would sound. The thought didn't fill me with confidence.

The first few steps weren't too bad, and I concentrated on moving my feet in time with my hands, slowly feeding the rope through as I walked down the sides. It grew noticeably colder as soon as I left the surface, the rocks seeming to drain all warmth from the atmosphere; it was also damp and musty, and my feet occasionally skidded over patches of lichen or wet moss. The entrance was still visible above me, but I stopped for a second to flick my helmet light on and its strength surprised me, lighting the nearby rock wall with a sterile white glow. There was nothing much to see, so I started to descend again.

At first I thought it was my imagination, but after I'd dropped a few more feet it became clear that the crack was narrowing. I took a few steps down and the space constricted even further, squeezing me between two solid rock walls. It wasn't panic, but there was a definite feeling of discomfort swelling in my brain. Daylight was only just visible above me, and the walls were growing tighter and tighter as I descended, until it felt as if I could go no further. It stood to reason that Robbie must have got through somehow, so I twisted and contorted myself in the restricted space. It still wasn't comfortable, but at least there was some room for manoeuvre. The harness pinched the insides of my thighs as I slowly inched my way down, my toes only scraping the rock as I struggled to get through the gap. There was, after all, no way back up. Down was the only option.

Then, like a cork being released from a bottle, I was through. The crack suddenly widened again, and in the light from my helmet I could see Robbie standing on a narrow ledge a few feet below me. I whizzed down the line with barely-contained abandon, trying to pretend to myself that abseiling was a breeze. I was still glad when my feet touched the solid surface of the ledge, however, and Robbie moved my clip from one line to another: the overhang that I'd just squeezed past blocked out all daylight from above, leaving us suspended halfway down the crack in a pool of torchlight. My hands were shaking a little, but not too much. Fifty feet gone, fifty to go.

It might just have been the adrenaline, but the second half of the descent felt much easier than the first. There were no narrow passages to squeeze through, no uncomfortable overhangs, and I allowed myself to enjoy the experience a little more. By the time my feet hit the bottom, a slippery surface of what felt like wet clay, I was confident that I knew what I was doing. Robbie had been right, abseiling was easy. I might give the ice cream a miss if I tried it again, though.

I waited at the bottom while Robbie slid down to join me, whizzing so quickly down the line that my newfound confidence deflated a little. It seemed that I still had a lot to learn.

While I waited for him to gather the lines together I looked around the chamber that we'd ended up in, everything pale and overexposed under our artificial light. It was as I did so that I noticed a large, ugly creature sitting a few inches away on the cave wall, within easy touching distance if I'd been foolish enough to reach out. It looked like a giant, mutant grasshopper, about two inches long and as thick as my little finger, with long antennae that were slowly probing the darkness. I wasn't jumpy enough to scream, but it certainly made me start. No one had told me to expect company.

It turned out that our unattractive host was a cave weta, a distant relative of the grasshopper and a species unique to New Zealand. Wetas came in many shapes and sizes, although Robbie informed me that this was an unusually large one for these caves. They were thought to have remained more or less unchanged for the last hundred million years, New Zealand having had very few natural predators to feed on them, and it was easy to imagine our new friend sharing the Earth with the dinosaurs. Angular, heavily armoured, and boasting an impressive pair of mandibles: I should have guessed that he was a prehistoric leftover.

Once the ropes were tidied away we pushed forward into the darkness, careful to keep one eye on the neighbourhood weta as we did so. The ground was rough and uneven, and we walked with our harnesses clipped onto a rope set into the wall, just in case of sudden movement underfoot. I concentrated on placing one foot firmly ahead of the other, ensuring that my footing was firm before moving forward. My thighs were beginning to burn from the unaccustomed exercise.

St. Benedict's was only about four hundred feet in length, but the loose, uneven flooring made for slow progress. A glance down revealed streaks of light brown mud across my boots and legs, illuminated in the stark white glow from my helmet. My hands were covered too, from groping for the walls as I stumbled forward one step at a time. I could see why the overalls were so essential.

There were occasional dark streaks in the lighter mud of the walls, and as I struggled over a particularly large boulder I asked Robbie what they were.

'All this rock used to be under the sea once, it's mainly limestone and sandstone laid down on the seabed. Those streaks are seaweed deposits, where it's been compressed over the centuries along with the rock. Give me a second and I'll show you a shell too.'

He pushed forward ahead of me, and I realised for the first time that he'd been holding back to allow me to keep up. My body already felt as if it had been through a tough workout, and I marvelled at how fit he must be to clamber through these caves twice a day. Caving wasn't just about adrenaline after all.

I hurried after him and eventually caught up further along the same passage, where he was shining his light on the wall. Sure enough there was a shell, fossilised and remarkably well preserved in the layers of mud.

'That's a scallop shell. They're thicker than most shellfish, which is why they tend to survive down here better. Most of the others will have been crushed to a fine powder, but the scallops were fossilised instead. It's pretty easy to find them along here if you know what you're looking for.'

He continued to talk as we walked through the passage but my attention was elsewhere. My body was feeling tired now that the adrenaline was ebbing away, and I had to concentrate on where I was placing each step. The last thing I wanted to do was twist my ankle a hundred feet below the surface.

After a few minutes we finally emerged into a wider space, and I was glad to see that the cavern floor was considerably flatter than the passage we'd just passed through. It was also breathtakingly beautiful, stalagmites soaring up from the drab grey rock in spectacular formations, while the stalactites inched downwards with excruciating slowness. This was how I'd expected a cave to look, and it put the paving stones and handrails of the Glowworm Caves to shame. The fact that we had this underground grotto to ourselves only added to its majesty.

'This cave was only discovered fairly recently,' Robbie told me, his voice echoing slightly in the crisp air. 'The whole area was deforested in the Sixties and Seventies, and they uncovered lots of caves before they were finished. This one actually sits in local farmland, and we pay the farmer for access. It's one of the reasons that it still looks so unspoiled, there hasn't been enough time for visitors to ruin it yet. Hopefully, now that they keep an eye on these things, it'll stay this way forever.'

Suddenly there was a clattering of falling stones ahead, and Paerau appeared around the corner carrying an icebox in one hand.

'I thought you fellas could probably use some refreshment by now, since you've been doing all the work.'

We hunkered down for five minutes by a few suitably large rocks while I attempted to get some sugar back into my bloodstream. It had been a challenging trek so far, but my exertion had been rewarded. To see the cave formations so close to their natural state was a rare privilege, even if my leg muscles were begin to cramp with the effort.

Robbie and Paerau had a surprise waiting for me once our break was over. Our new home might look untouched by human hands, but they were used to bringing groups down here on a daily basis, and lacking the near-death experience of black-water rafting to spice things up they had decided to conjure up their own adrenaline sport. The main cavern dipped down in the centre, and across this slight depression was stretched what the Kiwis like to call a Flying Fox, although I knew as the Death Slide. A rope led from one side to the other on a slight incline, and the aim was to slide down it using a special harness. They'd added their own unique twist to it too. They wanted us to do it in pitch darkness.

Paerau went first to show me how it was done, although the lack of light meant that I only heard the vaguest impression of his descent. He gave a whoop when he reached the far side and we all switched our helmet lights back on. I was glad to see that he was still in one piece, even if I was no wiser as to how he'd got there, and Robbie assured me that there was nothing to worry about. Once the harness had been winched back across to our side he strapped me in. I muttered 'when in Rome' over and over to myself like a traveller's mantra as I stepped forward to the edge.

We switched our lights off together on the count of three, plunging the cave into impenetrable darkness. I held my hand an inch or two in front of my eyes as a test, but no matter how hard I tried I couldn't pierce the blackness. I took a slow, ragged breath and stepped forward into the dark.

Without warning the ground suddenly disappeared beneath me. I might have screamed, although I can't be sure. If I did, it was with an equal mix of fear and delight. Only the air rushing past me and the whirring of the harness above my head gave any clue as to how fast I was moving, and as soon as I felt myself slowing down I reached up and flicked my light back on. I still had a few feet to travel but the Flying Fox was gradually coming to a stop. Paerau grinned at me from the makeshift platform.

'See, told you it was fun. You'll never have done anything like that before I bet.'

I hadn't, and I didn't have the heart to tell him that, given the choice, I probably wouldn't do it again. At least it meant that we had a few less boulders to clamber over, although my legs were shaking enough to make walking a challenge.

As it turned out, St. Benedict's had one more surprise left in store. A few minutes after dicing with the Death Slide we emerged into the main cave of the complex, a large cavern that the small lights on our helmets struggled to penetrate. Huge stalagmites cast shadows on the walls behind them, adding to the impression of impenetrable depths. The formations here looked fluid, as if someone had poured quick-setting concrete over the rock and left it to dry where it lay, and it was amazing to think that these organic shapes had formed over thousands of years.

Robbie took me for a close-up inspection of one of the stalactites, showing me the narrow straw that sat at its centre, but it didn't take long for him to move on to less scientific pursuits. At his suggestion we started naming the formations, pointing out spurious resemblances to Papa Smurf's house or the Clinton family. Once this was exhausted, our tired minds having constructed elaborate fantasies around most of the random shapes that the cave had to offer, we walked up a set of rough steps to the exit door. It was small and round, designed to look like the hobbit holes in *Lord Of The Rings*, but my brain was too fatigued to make more than a passing note of this structural joke. As we emerged into the light, squinting like moles returning to the surface, I found myself breathing a sigh of relief. It had been a fascinating experience, but one that was far beyond my normal comfort zone. I brushed some dried mud from my sleeves, and luxuriated for a moment in the warmth of the sun. I was definitely a surface-dweller.

For most of the journey back I sat in stunned silence in the rear of the minibus, playing over what I'd seen time and time again in my head. It was only when Robbie mentioned rugby that I tuned in to the conversation. His belief in the ability of the All Blacks was overwhelming and occasionally overbearing, and eventually I felt the urge to step in and point out that they hadn't won a World Cup since 1987.

'Yeah, but England just won it with Jonny Wilkinson's boot. Any chance you had, you just passed the ball to him, and he kicked it over for the points. That's not rugby.'

I pointed out that in the strictest sense it was, actually, and that England's Martin Johnson had easily been the best captain on display during the competition.

'I'll give you that, but Johnson's a Kiwi anyway. He learnt everything he knew from his time in New Zealand. He doesn't really count.'

There seemed to be little arguing with such nationalistic fervour, so instead I asked him what he felt had kept the All Blacks from fulfilling their potential. The answer was one that I'd met before: there was more money abroad, and their best players left the country to play club rugby overseas. As a small nation they already had a limited pool to select from, but if they continued to lose players to other countries they'd be severely restricted in the future. I was reminded of the Vinnie Anderson controversy that I'd heard on the radio. It seemed that he had a point.

By the time I returned to my motel room, having scraped most of the mud from my hands in the car as I drove back, my body was starting to shut down. My feet felt heavy and slow, as if my shoes were filled with cave mud, and my muscles throbbed with a slow ache. Every so often I'd smell a salty tang, a reminder that the mud had once been part of the seabed.

My time on the North Island was rapidly drawing to a close, but I still had one more stop before I turned my sights southwards, to the scenery and the sights that I'd heard so much about on my travels. It was time to return to Wellington.

* * *

Something had happened to me since landing on New Zealand soil. It might have been an airborne virus, or perhaps a toxin in the water supply. It could even have been something I'd eaten. Whatever it was, something had caused a change. I'd started saying 'neat' a lot more, only rarely using it as an expression of tidiness. I sighed wistfully whenever I saw a mountain in the distance, or an untended field, and I sometimes felt an uncontrollable urge to walk through the countryside for several hours. I even seemed to be enjoying the painful cramping that was now seizing my limbs every time I moved.

I had plenty of time to consider this unexpected transformation as I drove down the west coast towards Wellington. The route was different from the one I'd taken before, straying to the west of Lake Taupo and picturesque Mount Ruapehu, and managing to avoid the meteorological abnormalities of the Desert Road. When I finally reached the intersection at Hunterville, a little past the halfway mark, I felt as if I was returning home. I was disappointed to see that someone had removed the 'Hooterville' graffiti, and if I'd had a spray can or a Sharpie in the trunk I'd have been tempted to stop and rectify it myself. I departed on the road to Bulls, consoling myself with the knowledge that it would forever remain as Hooterville in my mind.

I pulled up outside Ian and Heather's house a little before eight that evening, and I realised for the second time that I didn't have a gift to offer them. On this occasion, however, the thought was pushed immediately from my mind. As I shrugged my bag onto my back from the open trunk I could already see their daughters, Kate and Olivia, waving from the front porch. The gift was a formality that they didn't expect from me. I was among family.

As we said our goodbyes at Wellington airport the following morning I felt a pang of nostalgia for the North Island. I'd seen some spectacular scenery during my time there, and had discovered a lot about Maori culture along the way. I'd drunk wine within sight of the vines that gave birth to it, I'd eaten from a traditional Maori *hangi*, I'd even abseiled a hundred feet into a cave, only to be confronted by an insect that had survived since the age of the dinosaurs.

Most importantly, however, once all these adventures had receded into the distant past, I'd made some lifelong friends. As my newly-adopted Kiwi family slapped me on the back and shook my hand, wishing me all the best for the rest of my trip and entreating me to visit them on the return leg, I almost felt a tear welling in the corner of my eye. They'd shown me more hospitality than I'd dared to hope for. Wellington had almost started to feel like home.

It was this thought that finally propelled me through the departure gate, desperately telling myself not to look back as I handed my boarding card to the attendant. I'd seen most of the North Island now, and in my time here I'd gained a good grasp of its culture and atmosphere. Now it was time to step outside of my comfort zone again, to travel beyond that horizon.

It was time to go exploring.

11
Otautahi *(Christchurch)*

I'd already heard enough about the South Island to form a mental picture long before landing, although my experiences further north had taught me that my preconceptions were only there to be proved wrong. The scenery had a reputation for being even more spectacular than on the North Island, and much of the *Lord Of The Rings* trilogy was filmed among its plains and valleys. I'd found the north sparsely populated, but the south was even less developed, a vast expanse of empty space punctuated by the occasional town or city. In between these points of reference stood the mountains, the fjords, and the sheep. Apparently there were a lot of sheep.

I'd also heard from various sources that there were far fewer Maori on the South Island than on the North, and some of the rumours I'd encountered suggested that there was hardly a Maori presence at all. I had a suspicion that this was a rewritten version of the island's history, though, and hardly a true representation of the facts. When Europeans first began to settle on the South Island it was convenient to deny the Maori presence, for without their prior claim to the land it was open to free settlement, and the Waitangi Tribunal listed a catalogue of errors made by the Crown in purchasing land on the South Island, ranging from the purchase of land without proper consent to the failure to protect access to Maori food resources. The region's heavy deposits of greenstone lent it a huge cultural significance for all New Zealand Maori, and when an apology was finally received from the Crown after seven years of negotiations many of these lands were returned. There would be fewer Maori here than in the north as there were fewer people in general, but I found it hard to believe that they had vanished altogether.

As my taxi driver negotiated her way through the grid-like streets of central Christchurch I peered through the window at the storefronts and passers-by, trying to pick out the noticeable differences from the Kiwis I'd met in Auckland and Wellington. The streets here were wide and straight, and from time to time our wheels would jolt against the rails that were set into the surface as part of the city's tram network. The regular grid of the roads and the smart dress of the businesspeople we passed suggested a conservative, ordered social structure, more so than the chaotic jumble of central Wellington. Christchurch seemed quiet and functional in comparison, a tame English village after the capital's vivacious creativity.

It came as little surprise that Christchurch possessed such a conservative streak when you considered the history of the settlement. The clue, after all, was in the name. The first Europeans to settle on the Canterbury plains were Scottish brothers William and John Deans, in 1843, but the true origin of the region lay in the formation of the Canterbury Association six years later. This group was the work of Irishman Robert Godley, and, as his name might suggest, it was remarkably clear in its aims. The early years of European settlement had been marred by bands of seamen, seal hunters, and escaped Australian convicts setting up camp on the fringes of the new society, determined to turn the period of unrest to their financial advantage. The South Island had largely been overlooked, and was relatively free from their influence. It was here that Godley saw his chance to found a utopian Anglican society in the virgin territory, a settlement that would actively promote proper Christian living and divine worship. And so Christchurch was born.

The marks of this unusual genesis were still plain to see as we drove through the city centre, *en route* to my motel. It was hard to miss the cathedral that sat in the middle of the city's grid-like road system, its gothic spire stretching high above the surrounding buildings. Christchurch was still a relatively low-rise city, and the cathedral was placed in the perfect centre of the settlement, a giant spoke for this Anglican society to revolve around and a constant reminder of the reason for its existence. Christianity would bring reason and order to this new, untamed land. At least that was the idea.

By the time I reached my motel, having negotiated three sides of the centre's complex one-way system, I was keen to get outside and experience this utopian settlement for myself. I paused only to fling my bag on the bed and freshen up in the bathroom before heading out again. The sky was hazy but clear, and given the rumours I'd heard about the South Island's climate it was surprisingly warm. God, it seemed, was smiling on Christchurch.

Every guidebook I'd read had compared the city to a large English town, and the local planners had gone out of their way to reinforce this impression: you only had to glance at the street names to see the source of their inspiration, as Durham Street carried me into Cambridge Terrace, winding along the banks of the River Avon. Such rampant anglophilia put the early settlements of convict Australia to shame, and reminded even the casual visitor of the high-minded aims of the city's founding fathers. With its rigid social structure, religious conservatism, and well-tended flowerbeds, this could almost be small-town England. They probably shipped in scones and cream by the ton.

At the Arts Centre I bought myself a bag of handmade fudge and wandered through the old university buildings, a cluster of creepy-looking replicas of the ancient edifices of British learning. It felt like a theme park of English clichés, boasting a surface resemblance to both Oxford and Cambridge that was rendered shallow and unconvincing by the lack of history. Only the Lebanese lamb kebab that I bought from a stall next to the quad hinted at the modern, multicultural society that had settled in this curious miniature England. Even the goat's milk soap on sale at one of the stalls was finished with a neatly tied tartan ribbon. My granny would have been proud.

My feeling of unease increased as I sauntered back to my room, and as I navigated through the streets it occurred to me that the grid layout undermined any impression of Englishness that they'd strived to create. Real English towns were chaotic, organic webs, growing slowly over the centuries, adapting and changing as they went. Christchurch was too planned, too ordered, an unrealistic idea of England imprinted onto a sterile grid of wide boulevards that betrayed its modernity. Even the tram only managed a tired circuit of the central blocks, saving you no more than a few minutes' walk, even if you travelled from corner to corner. It was about as functional as a rollercoaster.

Clearly I'd been foolish to think that Christchurch could replicate centuries of English development and eccentricity. The Canterbury Association had been doomed to failure from its inception, entertaining a dream of an English utopia that could never be realised. As I readied myself to go out that evening I wondered what else they'd got wrong. I'd hardly scratched the surface, and already their veneer was flaking. I was eager to discover what lay beneath.

* * *

As intriguing as Christchurch's history was, it wasn't my real reason for visiting the city. When I'd gone online to buy tickets for the Wellington Sevens a month earlier I'd noticed that there was a Super Rugby match at the Jade Stadium shortly after my arrival on the South Island. Beer would undoubtedly be involved, and I was sure that more than my fair share of pies would be consumed. With that on offer, how on earth could I resist?

The Super Rugby competition was conceived in 1996, boasting teams from New Zealand, Australia, and South Africa, the three great southern hemisphere superpowers of the sport. It was played according to the standard Rugby Union rules, although the emphasis was placed on fast-paced offensives rather than the slow, defensive game that I was used to seeing in European competitions. The speed at which it was played, combined with the inclusion of some of the biggest names in the sport, had earned it considerable popularity across the globe.

Tonight's match was a local derby against the Waikato Chiefs, and I tucked my ticket into my back pocket as I headed out the door of my motel room. It promised to be a hard-fought competition, if a little one-sided. Local team the Canterbury Crusaders had become one of the sport's most successful franchises in recent years, and they were expected to win at a canter, but the Chiefs wouldn't go down without a fight, especially in a North-South encounter. The Crusaders had already won more of the previous Super Rugby tournaments than any other team, however, and they were favourites to win again. Nothing short of a miracle could secure a win for the Chiefs tonight. Mind you, miracles had been known to happen, especially in sport.

I'd been worried about finding the stadium, but as soon as I reached the outskirts of town all the traffic was flowing in one direction, making my navigation simple, if a little inevitable. Christchurch only had a population of a little over 300,000 people, and the Jade Stadium held a capacity crowd of 36,500. It didn't take a mathematical genius to work out that more than ten percent of the local population could fit into the stadium if the match was a sell-out, and it appeared that tonight that might happen. The sidewalks were a sea of red and black shirts, the Crusaders' colours, with the occasional flash of the Chiefs' blue and yellow almost lost in the torrent. Cars hooted their horns as they sped past, scarves streaming from half-open windows. If I'd still entertained any doubts about the Kiwis' commitment to rugby they were quashed within seconds of joining this mile-long scrimmage. There couldn't be any more exciting place to be in New Zealand tonight.

As the stadium came into sight, looming over the nearby businesses like a land-locked concrete cargo ship, I saw a giant inflatable knight above the heads of the crowd, his large rubber sword lifted high in the pale evening sky. The Crusaders were renowned for putting on a pre-match show that rivalled the action on the pitch, and our inflatable protector was hopefully indicative of what was to come. My head was buzzing with anticipation, although it might just have been the chatter of excitement that surrounded me as I was borne along by the red and black tsunami. This was almost as exciting as caving.

It took me nearly ten minutes to find my seat once I was through the turnstiles, having been distracted by the pie stand and the beer tent on the way. As I settled into my spot on the worn wooden benches, a touchingly sentimental feature in this age of massive concrete stadiums, I couldn't help hearing the conversation between the two fans on my right. Usually ability to recognise accents was poor, but having spent a couple of months in New Zealand I'd slowly grown accustomed to their nasal intonations. If I hadn't known better, I could have sworn that my neighbours were Australian.

At the next pause in their conversation I artfully butted in, my confidence bolstered by a few sips from a bottle. I was curious to know what had brought two Aussies to a match between rival Kiwi teams.

'Well, Super Rugby's massive, isn't it,' came the reply from Andrew, the closest of the two. 'We're here helping to set up a new store in Riccarton, so we had to come to the match. I wouldn't miss this for the world.'

So who were they supporting, I asked?

'It'll have to be the Crusaders, since they're the local team. Plus they have those great foam swords, and I really wanna get one. They look seriously cool.'

It seemed that the power of the Crusaders franchise had won yet another set of fans, but before we had a chance to debate the merits of the rest of their merchandise there was a burst of light and a sudden roaring off to my left. That corner of the ground was occupied by an unlikely-looking medieval keep, and the braziers on either side of the gate had started to erupt with billowing tongues of flame. Although this had caught my eye the true spectacle was yet to come, as the gates slowly swung open and seven knights rode through on horseback, waving their swords in circles above their heads as if they were warding off an aggressive pack of crows. They galloped a full circuit of the field while I stared open-mouthed, my beer forgotten by my side. I'd seen the occasional kilted bagpiper when Scotland played at home, but nothing on this scale, and certainly not for a regional competition. When they finally vanished back through the gate, the braziers flaming again to usher them off, I found that my mouth was still open in astonishment.

Andrew leant across to me, a smile on his lips.

'You don't see that every day, do you.'

You certainly didn't, and I marvelled again at the Kiwi enthusiasm for rugby, which they managed to muster even for a one-sided game between two local teams. The Jade Stadium was filled almost to capacity, entire families waving red and black foam swords enthusiastically above their heads as the players ran onto the turf. Enthusiasm didn't seem to do them justice: this was an almost religious fervour. Perhaps Christchurch had achieved its utopia after all.

It was easy to get carried away by the enthusiasm of the home crowd, and by the second half even the two Aussies next to me were cheering every point and shouting abuse at the referee. This kind of sporting fanaticism wasn't a new phenomenon in New Zealand: when the first All Blacks team toured Great Britain in 1905, under the less catchy title 'The Originals', premier Richard Seddon interrupted parliament to announce the latest scores cabled to him by the High Commissioner in London. The touring side won all their matches, apart from a controversial confrontation with Wales in Cardiff, where a disallowed Kiwi try allowed the home team to sneak to victory. The whitewash was considered a patriotic triumph for the emerging nation and marked the start of the All Blacks legend. It was fair to say that they'd never looked back since.

When the final whistle blew I elbowed my way out through the turnstiles and walked back to my motel, the crowds slowly dissipating as I moved further away from the stadium, the jubilant Crusaders fans spreading out across the city as each headed for their favourite watering hole. It was as I sauntered down Manchester Street that I saw my first crack in Christchurch's utopian veneer, and my first hint of the extremes that existed side by side in this modern city. I'd already passed this way earlier in the evening, and apart from the large wooden church that graced one end of the street, and the scattering of industrial warehouses that littered the other, it looked like a standard residential road, the houses neat and well-tended, their gardens separated from the street by waist-high brick walls and wooden fences.

Manchester Street had been almost empty when I'd walked down its length earlier, and it was almost empty now. Almost, but not quite. In the distance I could see a few solitary figures standing by the curb or leaning against the brick walls, as if they were waiting to hail cabs from the roadside. It didn't take me long to realise that they had a different kind of ride in mind. As I approached the first of them I noticed that she was wearing a tight leather mini-skirt and a lacy bodice, a black fleece jacket her only concession to the chill that had crept into the air since the sun went down. The jacket didn't even come close to matching the rest of her sultry attire, but I figured that this was still New Zealand – fleeces were something of a national obsession here, and were worn by everyone from shop attendants to businessmen. Working girls were apparently no exception.

She tried to smile suggestively as I hurried past, but my eyes were fixed firmly on the paving stones at my feet. There had been nothing earlier to warn me of this nocturnal activity, and my previous impressions of the city were rapidly dissipating in the cool night breeze. After dark, it seemed, Christchurch was a different place.

There was still a chance that I'd been wrong about her intentions, but after passing a few more of these lone curb-walkers I knew that I hadn't made an error of judgement. Two of them attempted overfriendly greetings as I hurried by, while the others obviously took note of my averted eyes and decided that I wasn't worth the bother. As a solitary man in this one-street red light district I felt oddly exposed and uncomfortable, as if someone I knew might see me here and immediately leap to a naturally sordid conclusion. The thought made me walk even faster.

As I walked I noticed a car pull in and park in front of me, its driver a barely-visible young male hunched over the steering wheel. Once I'd passed him, keeping my head low as my feet pounded the sidewalk, he pulled out from the curb and drove a few yards further down the street, parking just in front of me again. This happened five or six times as I walked, the car leapfrogging ahead of me every time I managed to sneak in front, and it eventually occurred to me that the driver must be a pimp, or a rent-boy trawling for business. The fact that he'd followed my progress for the entire length of the street did nothing to relieve my discomfort, and when he finally executed a u-turn and roared off in the opposite direction I found that my heart was beating faster than normal, my pulse racing. I was glad when I finally reached the security of my motel room and clicked the deadlock into place.

The following morning the plot thickened. Despite the shock of the previous night I headed for Manchester Street again, as it was the quickest route between my motel and the centre. At least it would have been, if the entire road hadn't been cordoned off with yellow Police tape. Being of a curious nature I stood for a few minutes at the tape, surreptitiously peering at the activity beyond its borders, and trying to piece together some idea of what had happened. I'd seen enough episodes of *CSI* to know that the small, numbered markers dotted across the pavement and the nearby church's lawn indicated the locations of various pieces of evidence, and that there were enough of them to suggest a trail of blood. The wooden church with its freestanding bell tower no longer looked quite so innocent and provincial. Dreams of a Christian utopia had passed overnight.

Newspapers later identified the victim as Maru George, a local man who appeared to have fallen foul of the area's nocturnal industry. It was reported that he'd stopped to talk to two prostitutes, and had fallen into an argument with their pimp that eventually came to blows. The pimp was carrying a knife, and Mr. George had been discovered behind the church in the small hours of the morning, having bled to death on the lawn. Two knives were discovered on the church lawn, one of them stuck into the ground. Rather worryingly, it later emerged that neither of these was the murder weapon. Manchester Street was starting to feel more and more like Brooklyn.

I began to notice other signs of this seedy underbelly, too. As I walked through the Christchurch suburbs many of the yards were untended, old couches and fridges left in the long grass to slowly decompose over the next few millennia. In the city centre there were stores with boards advertising the sale of 'party pills', herbal uppers and downers that were legal to buy over the counter. There were an unusually high number of strip joints and massage parlours near Cathedral Square, too, and street racers revved their engines in the middle of the night. The cathedral was looking very lonely.

Strangely, though, I found myself liking Christchurch more and more. My initial impression of the city as a large-scale copy of a quaint English town had been pretty but soulless, less like a city and more like a theme park. The hookers, the party pills, and the street racers were ugly, but at least they showed that the place had a pulse. Christchurch could feel gritty and seedy at times, with an air of menace in certain areas after the sun went down, but at least it felt real. I remembered Ian's friend Dave telling me that it was a 'shithole', with only a few decent streets in the centre, and at last I could see what he'd meant. To my surprise, however, it turned out that I liked shitholes more than I'd thought. The city's founders could keep their utopian plan, their perfect Christian community. I liked life to be a little rougher around the edges.

In spite of my newfound dark side, however, I still decided to give Manchester Street a wide berth after nightfall. Some places were just a little too exciting.

12
Hakaroa *(Akaroa)* –
Te Whakatakaka O Te Ngarehu O Ahi Tamatea
(Hanmer Springs)

My first day out of Christchurch was to mark the beginning of a new journal, a thick, black volume with a built-in strap that I'd purchased before leaving the city. Perhaps it's one of the foibles of the travelling writer, but I'd grown remarkably attached to the notebooks I scribbled in as I journeyed, and even the sight of their plain covers would sometimes transport me back to a specific time and place. This new volume was slightly larger than normal, as big as a paperback novel and impressively thick. I had no doubt that I'd fill it long before my travels were over.

If I'd arranged things better I might have started a new journal on my arrival in the South Island, but in retrospect it was fitting that things should start afresh after Christchurch. The city had been large enough to still feel like civilization, but the rest of the South Island was notoriously open and wild, an entirely different landscape to the one I'd travelled through so far. It seemed apt to start on a clean page as I passed beyond the city's borders, to open a new book for this part of my trip. This would be my wilderness journal.

It wasn't just my stationery that was changing. I'd handed back the rental car when I flew out of Wellington, and after my brief stay in Christchurch it was time to get myself a new set of wheels. A taxi ferried me from my motel to the rental offices just outside the airport, dropping me unceremoniously on the sidewalk with my bags at my feet. If this was to be a genuine wilderness trip then I'd need more than just a regular car. New Zealand's South Island was, after all, the spiritual home of the camper van.

When it first occurred to me that the only way to appreciate the island's rugged scenery was from the back of a van I'd taken a glance at what was on offer, only to find myself overwhelmed by the options. Vehicles ranged from adapted Transits – fitted out with kitchens and hand-painted with funky designs – to mobile homes the size of a truck. Did I want a bed that pulled down, or that folded away? Did I want a shower? And what about a toilet? There was even an upmarket camper with a swivel-mounted TV/DVD player, although they'd been so busy fitting it out with the latest technology that they'd failed to notice the severe lack of space once all the hi-tech gadgetry was in place. Then, of course, there was the option of camping: I could just as easily rent a car and a tent as a van, although there was a nip in the air that discouraged me from being quite so adventurous so late in the season.

Once I'd battled my way into the crowded rental office I discovered that I had to wait several hours for my van to be ready, and although they offered complementary coffee I was almost tempted to upgrade (or downgrade) if it meant that I'd finally get to leave Christchurch. It was gone lunchtime by the time my van was cleaned and parked in front of the building, and even then it had to undergo several inspections before I could sign for it and clamber inexpertly aboard.

My final decision had been a tough one, and not without its share of mental wrangling. While the idea of having a toilet and shower appealed to me, ensuring that I wouldn't be forced to traipse through a cold, wet campsite in the middle of the night should I be caught short, the pros were outweighed by the cons. The only vans large enough to accommodate bathroom facilities were wide and cumbersome, and I didn't fancy my chances at manoeuvring one down New Zealand's narrow back lanes. Besides, all that human waste wouldn't just disappear, and I didn't want the job of having to empty it at one of the campsites' communal dump stations. I'd heard that most sites here boasted excellent bathroom facilities, so in the end the toilet went out the van's back window. I'd just have to make sure that I parked close to the nearest cubicles.

As consolation for having to wait the rental agent gave me a bottle of red wine to drown my sorrows, and a little after three o'clock I climbed clumsily into the back of the van, clutching this much-needed tonic firmly in one fist. After many hours of deliberation I'd finally opted for a Toyota Hi-top, a small two-berth van with an ugly roof extension that allowed a modicum of headroom inside. I'd also booked it through an agency that specialised in older, cheaper models. At the time I'd reasoned that a van was a van, and since all rentals came complete with full breakdown insurance the vehicle's age had seemed immaterial. The several hours I'd spent sipping cups of weak coffee in their waiting room was the unwelcome fruit of my frugality, but at least I was now ready to hit the road. All that caffeine meant that there was little chance of me falling asleep behind the wheel, too.

The van was destined to be my home for the next four weeks, and it seemed prudent to take a few minutes to look it over before I left the agency compound. The exterior was a dirty shade of white, the twin stripes of pink and lilac that the rental company had added doing nothing to alleviate the overwhelming sense of decrepitude. There were small patches of rust dotted across the bodywork, gathering in small clusters about the wheel arches and doors. Bolted to the front was an imposingly solid metal grille, probably intended as a bug screen but looking tough enough to take on the occasional bird, possum or rental agency employee that I might decide to mow down on my trip. It, too, was rusting. It might once have been black.

If the outside fared badly in the initial inspection, however, the interior was a pleasant surprise. Everything looked slightly worn and faded, from the patterned seat cushions to the plastic-backed curtains, but it was clean and surprisingly intact. Despite being a little over six feet tall I could stand up comfortably in the middle of the living area, although doing star jumps might prove to be a challenge. It smelled a little musty, but not as damp as I'd feared. Either the last owner had been remarkably keen on personal hygiene or they really had just spent the last four hours cleaning it.

Above the driver's compartment was a convenient niche where I slung my bag. Beneath it sat a small but functional sink, complete with complementary unbranded dish detergent. Turning clockwise my gaze passed over a small cabinet, home to my crockery, cutlery and the world's tiniest wardrobe, before coming to the cooking area. The two gas rings looked newer than the rest of the van, and the microwave beneath them was definitely a recent addition. At the back of the van was the seating area, comprising a slightly wobbly wooden table and thinly padded benches to either side: this was also my bed for the night. The agent had given me a demonstration of how to assemble it before scuttling back to her coffee machine, but after half a day of mind-numbing boredom in the waiting room I hadn't really taken it in. I was sure that I'd be able to work it out for myself. A cursory examination of the storage space over the back of the table uncovered my bedding and a pair of towels, inexplicably sealed in cling wrap. Somewhere at the back of my mind lurked the knowledge that a bucket and a hose were located under one of the benches, for when I needed to empty the sink or refill the water tank. It was unclear where or how this could be achieved.

And that was it. This was where I would live for the next month, a mobile home in the truest sense. It was less than half the size of most of the motel rooms I'd stayed in, but I didn't foresee that being a problem. After all, it just meant there was less space to heat.

Manoeuvring the van out of the parking space and through the gates proved to be a challenge, and by the time I finally turned onto the main road I was thankful that I'd decided against the larger models. My escape from Christchurch wasn't quite complete, as my route took me back through the city centre again, allowing me one last look at the party pill stores and the cathedral. My time there had done nothing to unravel this contrast, or to acclimatise me to the sight of garish posters advertising legalised drugs. The time had come to accept this schizophrenia and move on.

My first overnight stop would be in Akaroa, the main settlement on the Banks Peninsula and only a short drive out from the city. Like so many other areas in New Zealand the peninsula was formed as the result of volcanic activity, and the beautiful semi-circular harbour at Akaroa sat in the crater created by the explosion. As I drove out of Christchurch the plains gradually swelled into gently rolling hills, then craggy outcrops could be seen rising from the lush grass, the result of this geological inheritance. The road wound through the hills, slowly gaining altitude as it did so, until, shortly after passing through Little River, I finally reached its high point and could look down across the peninsula to the sea. This small patch of land, a pimple on the side of the South Island, looked more like England's Lake District than the plains I'd just left behind, the craggy hilltops nestling around the brilliant blue water of the harbour. After the city it looked wild and uninhabited, a far cry from the crowds that had thronged to Jade Stadium. I was back on the open road.

When the peninsula was first sighted by Captain Cook in 1769 he'd named it after his ship's botanist, Joseph Banks. Unfortunately history wasn't kind to Cook on this occasion, as he rushed into naming the newly sighted land 'Banks Island', having failed to check whether the land he'd sighted was connected to the mainland. The name stood for forty years, until Captain Stewart of the Pegasus corrected it in 1809 and the Banks Peninsula was christened. Ironically those forty years weren't the only time that this land had been an island: at the time of the volcanic explosions it had been separate from the mainland, but alluvial deposits from the mountains had eventually linked the two together over the intervening centuries. A more generous man might give Cook some credit in the light of these facts, even if he was several millennia too late, but unfortunately I was inclined to attribute the error to his egotistical mania for naming everything that drifted into sight. Given the social and ecological damage caused by the first waves of European settlers, Captain Cook had a lot to answer for.

While the Banks Peninsula derived its name from this European mania for discovery, however, Akaroa boasted a different origin that exploded the many myths I'd heard about the South Island. The Maori word 'hakaroa' meant 'long harbour', and it was the local name for the area long before Cook's voyage around the coast. It appeared that there had been Maori tribes living down here after all, and in large enough numbers for the European settlers to adopt their place names. They might have dropped the 'h' from the Maori spelling, but in essence the name remained to this day. Akaroa was Maori land.

The history of the settlement also differed from those I'd visited so far, as its cultural roots lay not in Britain, but somewhere marginally further east. In 1835 French whaler Jean Langlois founded a whaling station at what was now known as French Bay, and three years later he returned home to arrange colonization of this new plot of land. His timing was impeccably bad. By the time the party of colonists left French shores it was already too late: the Treaty of Waitangi had been signed thirteen days earlier, and New Zealand was now under British sovereignty. Of course, Langlois knew none of this when his ship sailed. It was only when he arrived on the shores of his new home that he discovered what had happened, and by then it was too late to return to France. Eventually he accepted the new situation and Akaroa became one of the first truly cosmopolitan European settlements in New Zealand, although he didn't formally sell the land to the British-funded New Zealand Company until 1849.

The town still bore the imprint of these Gallic origins, and today it traded upon its pseudo-French status, using the unusual cultural mix to sell itself to the tourist market. After spending time in Wellington and Christchurch the town centre felt laughably small, and I parked my van in the first parking space I could find, choosing to see the rest of it on foot. The town of Akaroa sat curled around the shore of the harbour, so I made my way down to the wharf, turning left along the Rue Jolie and past *L'Hotel*, a small, homely-looking motel and restaurant. The fact that their menu was largely Italian didn't deter them from claiming a spurious French connection. If it was in Akaroa then it must, by definition, be French.

The waterfront did have a surprisingly continental feel, though, the sidewalk dotted with café tables that bore the remains of several croissants for the seagulls to peck over, and I found it hard to sustain any ill will towards such a charming little town. A faded signpost directed me inland towards the French Cemetery, and out of curiosity I decided to follow it, keen to discover how a French graveyard would differ from the morbid rows of headstones that the rest of us made do with. Hopefully it would prove to be more French than their Italian restaurant.

It was a short walk through some sparse woodland to the cemetery, a narrow dirt track winding lazily up the hillside above the town. In the end I almost missed the cemetery itself, the single obelisk hardly demanding my attention. It was painted white and mounted on a small tiled plinth, black and green damp streaks staining the sides and top. Only the plaque on the side facing the path gave any suggestion that this was a monument, or, indeed, the focus of all those signs. The original cemetery, I discovered, had been dug up in 1925, as part of the restoration and renovation of the hillside. It had been the first consecrated ground in Canterbury, with its earliest recorded burial in 1842, but by the time the new works were undertaken there were only eighteen discernable names among the headstones. These were the lucky souls whose names now adorned this rather sad monument. Mrs. Watkins and Mr. Peter Walter didn't sound terribly French, and on closer analysis I could only make out nine names that were discernibly Gallic in origin. This suggested that roughly half the original settlement had been French, hardly the petit-Paris that I'd expected. Akaroa was starting to look about as French as Christchurch had English.

Only the trees hinted at what might once have been, a small grove of weeping willows that surrounded this functional and slightly tawdry monument. The willows were introduced by Francois Le Lievre upon his arrival in 1837, and local legend had it that the cuttings had been taken from the trees at Napoleon's grave in St Helena. I'd seen more of these trees lining the River Avon in Christchurch, although the ones that surrounded this lost cemetery predated even those. As invasions went this was a subtle one, but there were indisputably French roots growing in this alien soil. The toilet-block aesthetics of the obelisk faded into insignificance.

Despite the disappointment of the cemetery the town was still pleasant enough, and as I wandered back down the hillside I found myself enjoying the change of pace. The sun dipped low over the harbour, gleaming off the surface of the water as if it was polished silver, and now that the day-trippers from Christchurch had departed the only sound was the cry of the seagulls as they searched for the last few elusive crumbs of croissant. As I wandered back along the Rue Jolie I felt myself relax into Akaroa's faux-French ambience.

My first night in the van was spent in a picturesque campground perched on one of the hills overlooking the harbour. I managed an unambitious tea of baked beans on toast for my inaugural meal, burning the toast on the grill and filling the van with the smell of charred bread in the process. When I tried to put the bucket under the external waste pipe, in preparation for the dishwashing, a family of mallard ducks appeared from nowhere and repeatedly pecked at the red plastic, pushing it out from under the pipe. I suspected that they were used to being fed, but my paltry store cupboard only contained dried pasta and more tins of baked beans, neither of which looked terribly appetizing to me, never mind my new avian neighbours. Eventually they abandoned their attacks on the bucket, obviously calculating that I had nothing worthwhile to offer them, and I was able to place it back under the pipe.

It was only as I flicked the cap off the complementary dish detergent that I realised that I didn't have a sponge, cloth or any other cleaning implement to wipe the dirty crockery with. A quick search of my bag only turned up a pair of balled socks, and although they would have done the job I didn't fancy finding an errant baked bean tucked between my toes in the days to come. Instead I piled the dirty utensils in the sink and brought the bucket back inside, just in case the ducks were preparing to launch a second wave of attacks. The dishes would have to wait until tomorrow.

By the time I'd worked out how to assemble the bed my eyelids were heavy, and I was glad to discover that despite appearances to the contrary the thin foam mattress was remarkably comfy. As I drifted off to sleep I heard the sound of quacking outside, the local gang returning to inspect this strange new arrival. If I hadn't known better, I could have sworn they were laughing.

* * *

I found myself back in town remarkably early the following morning, having risen when the sunlight first began to filter through the gaps in the curtains. As the skies had remained clear I booked myself onto a tour of the harbour, and since I had an hour to kill before the boat set off I secured myself an outdoor seat at one of the local cafes, breakfasting on a cup of coffee and a surprisingly buttery croissant. Apart from the fact that the croissant was almost as large as the plate, I could easily have been sitting somewhere on the French Riviera, and it helped to take my mind off the dirty crockery from last night, sitting strewn across the van's sink after being shaken around on the drive back down the hill. I really had to get myself some dishwashing sponges.

Our boat's captain introduced himself as Terry as I scrambled clumsily aboard from the town's jetty, and his short stature made me wonder if he'd appeared as one of the hobbits in *Lord Of The Rings*. Fortunately a moment of rare good sense kept this thought firmly inside my own head, having rightly decided that he might not appreciate the question. I still kept an eye out for unusually hairy feet, though.

As we steered slowly away from the jetty I noticed that Terry was wandering among the passengers, chatting to his guests and pointing out notable landmarks on the seafront. For a few seconds I wondered who was steering the boat, then I noticed the bulky black controller pressed between his palms, like the remote control for a child's toy blown up to three times the size. A pair of cables trailed back to the upper deck, and I realised that he was keeping an eye on our course as he made small talk with the paying customers. I wasn't sure if I felt more or less secure in this knowledge, but at least it gave me something to keep my mind off the gentle rocking in the swell.

We followed the eastern side of the harbour on our way out to the open sea, with Terry pointing out local features from time to time over the P.A. The cliffs were sheer and dark, the black volcanic rock layered in places with thick bands of grey, reminders of the ash that had fallen here during those formative eruptions. Occasionally there would be openings in the cliffs where a gully slid inland, the stream at its base nourishing a separate ecosystem within those black walls. There were palm tress growing here and there, and Terry informed me that this was one of the most southerly places in the world that they could be seen growing in the wild. At times they'd been known to have palm tress, snow, and penguins all resting within the same gully. What had once felt like the English countryside now looked like the Lost World.

It was at the point where the calm waters of the harbour met the rougher waves of the open ocean that we first saw the dolphins. Akaroa boasted three families of Hector's dolphins, the world's smallest and rarest dolphin breed, and after a few patient minutes of waiting, all eyes scanning the waves for signs of movement, our boat was approached by the pod. They swam up to the hull, rolling over on their sides to see us, and once again their curiosity fascinated me. They couldn't have been more than five feet long, their flanks shiny and sleek in the swelling waves. As we watched them they peered back, inspecting this newest batch of visitors to their back yard, and I was reminded of my similar encounter in Bay Of Islands. It has become a cliché in recent years, but there was a noticeable sense of intelligence emanating from these beautiful, inquisitive creatures. They probably wondered why we'd travelled so far just to stare at them.

As it turned out, they weren't the only denizens of this stretch of coastline that we would encounter on our trip. As Terry showed us the unique rock formations of Scenery Nook, ragged red-brown stacks that looked like crumbling piles of cocoa powder, I saw a movement on the rocks at the water's edge. It took a few seconds for my eyes to separate the seal from the rock, its fur perfectly camouflaged against the grey background. Unlike the dolphins it seemed utterly uninterested in our presence, and while it flopped across the outcrop I counted another three in the group, two of them asleep on the flattest rocks at the water's edge. They looked completely relaxed this close to human intrusion, and untroubled by the world in general. By the time Terry restarted the engine, having given us ample opportunity for photographs, they'd moved no further than a few feet.

The dolphins made a final appearance on our way back to shore, darting through the waves off to our left as we re-entered the calmer waters of the harbour. With this convoy guiding us back in to dry land I couldn't help feeling that Akaroa harbour looked more lively than the town.

Before leaving the Banks Peninsula for good I took a ten-minute detour around the east coast of the harbour, searching for something I'd spied from the boat. Onuku was only the smallest of settlements, a few houses gathered around a bend in the road, but their church had caught my eye from the water. Perched on the cliff top above the harbour, it was small enough to be a private house, only the extravagant porch and tiny bell tower giving away its true purpose. As I drew near, however, it became clear that this was no normal church. The slatted walls were painted white on the outside, but the main decoration was around the doorway, a terracotta-painted arch carved with traditional Maori designs, bringing to mind the *wharenui* I'd seen at

Rotorua and Waitangi. To the left of the doorway was a freestanding carved figure, keeping guard over God's house. Not only was it beautifully picturesque, but the unusual combination of Christian and Maori designs also presented a unique mix that piqued my interest. I couldn't resist parking up and wandering inside.

A commemorative plaque informed me that the foundation stone of the building was laid in 1876, with the cost of construction being raised by public prescription. Cemented into this foundation was a sealed bottle, containing a half sovereign and a piece of *pounamu*, the greenstone that was found in New Zealand's South Island and which held deep cultural significance for the Maori. The bottle was intended as a statement of intent, a symbol of the two cultures uniting under God's roof, and this unity and freedom of expression had continued through to the present day. When it opened in 1878 it was the first non-denominational church in the country, and their first service concluded with the *hongi*, the ceremonial Maori pressing-together of noses. This was more than just a church: it was a symbol of coexistence.

I spent some time examining the carved font before returning to the van, intrigued by this discovery among the hills of the Banks Peninsula. It appeared not only that there were significant Maori communities on the South Island, but that they had achieved some degree of equilibrium with the European settlers, as early as the end of the nineteenth century. This contradicted what I'd heard when I was on the North Island, and as I drove back through Akaroa I began to re-examine some of my preconceptions of the cultural divide. My visit to the South Island might turn out to be more eye opening than I'd imagined.

For the evening I stopped in Waipara, where their small campground proved to be rundown but more than adequate. Fortunately I'd remembered to buy some dishwashing sponges before the stores closed, and more importantly I'd also recalled that the Waipara was a recognised wine region. A quick visit to local winery *Pegasus Bay* meant that I could stock up on a few bottles of Sauvignon Blanc, although they didn't produce anything that could compare with the vineyards of Martinborough or Hawkes Bay. Nevertheless, as I sat hunched over my dinner in the back of the van, my head resting against the flimsy curtain rail, I was glad of the small glass of wine that I'd allowed myself. It didn't look like much, swilling around the bottom of a cheap cut-glass beaker, but at least I could pretend that I was enjoying a night of luxury.

* * *

The following day my course swerved inland to Hanmer Springs, only a little over an hour from Waipara. As soon as the road turned away from the coast the mountains began to rise, growing from the undulating foothills that flanked me, and shortly before reaching Hanmer I was greeted with the sight of a cloud sitting halfway down the mountainside, the peak jutting above it like a giant hat. This was the scenery I was used to seeing in the brochures, the landscape that had wowed worldwide audiences when the *Lord Of The Rings* films were first released. For once the rumours I'd heard on the North Island rang true: the views here really did take your breath away.

A quick meal in one of Hanmer's many cafes filled the ache in my stomach, then it was time to check out the town's main attraction. The European settlers first discovered the thermal springs in 1859, and by the early twentieth century hotels and other facilities were starting to appear around the site. While this marked the first European incursion into the springs, however, it came as no surprise to discover that the Maori had known about the site and its properties for several centuries. Their name for it was Te Whakatakaka O Te Ngarehu O Ahi Tamatea, and as was often the case with Maori place names this unwieldy title situated the area firmly within the structure of their cultural history and mythology. Legend had it that Tamatea was one of the original Maori explorers who came to New Zealand as part of the Great Migration, having left his homeland of Hawaiki for these alien shores. The place name translated roughly as 'where the ashes of Tamatea's fire lay', and referred to a specific incident from the stories concerning his exploration of their new home. Tamatea's canoe had been wrecked off the coast of the South Island, and in order to save his party from freezing he'd called on the Ariki of the Northern volcanoes for help. They had sent volcanic flames down the Wanganui River and across the Cook Strait, and when they reached Nelson the flames rose into the air, flying airborne the rest of the way to where Tamatea's canoe had run aground. On the way they dropped a piece of volcanic flame on the mountainside, creating the thermal springs.

As I gathered my swim shorts and a towel from the back of the van I considered the meaning of this legend, and its use of mythology as an explanation for the island's geological features. In some ways it was similar to the manner in which the Aborigines had mapped out vast tracts of the Australian outback, linking features together with a story framework that could be passed down from generation to generation, a kind of oral map that would be learnt by all tribesmen when they were children. If you knew the story then you would be able to navigate from location to location using the geographical markers mentioned in the legend. It seemed to me that the Maori had done something similar when they first reached Aotearoa's shores, simultaneously mapping out the landscape and identifying themselves with the geographical features on a cultural level. Taken at face value, the legend told us that the thermal springs only existed thanks to the arrival of the first Maori settlers from Hawaiki. Tales of the great explorers were really a statement of belonging and possession.

Having spent this time ruminating on the stuff of legends I was slightly disappointed when I paid my entry fee and walked through into the thermal springs enclosure. I'd been expecting bubbling natural pools emerging from the rocks of the mountainside, but although that might once have been the case more than a century of European intervention had sterilised the natural feature for mass consumption. There were several pools dotted about the complex, each one looking as manufactured and fake as a resort on the Costa Del Sol. The largest even had swimming lanes marked on the bottom, rendering it as picturesque as a public swimming pool. Only the eggy smell of sulphur hinted that these perfectly groomed water features were actually a naturally occurring spring.

Since I'd already paid my money I decided to make the most of it, so I swiftly changed into my shorts in the depressingly clinical changing rooms and stepped outside. The cool New Zealand breeze raised goose bumps on my arms within seconds of emerging from the changing block, and I could suddenly see the appeal of the springs. Dipping swiftly into one of the mildest pools, where the water was maintained at a comfortable 90°, I luxuriated for a few minutes before my curious nature got the better of me. Just how hot did these pools get?

A nearby map marked out two small pools at the rear of the complex as the hottest of the bunch, so with a little hopping and skipping across the cold tiles I scurried over to their corner. The sulphur hung heavy in the air here, the chemical smell singeing the back of my throat, and I wondered at the fact that people actually came here to relax. As aromatherapy went it was about as relaxing as a pig farm. In the name of exploration, however, I stepped forward and took the plunge.

At first the pool felt comfortably warm, and I wondered if my map reading had let me down. In less than a minute the beads of perspiration were starting to dot my forehead, however, and my body felt flushed. It felt less like a spa and more like an endurance test. The nearby plaque informed me that the water was kept at a steady 105°, and I recalled reading somewhere that this was the maximum safe temperature for bathing without running the risk of scalding. I just hoped that their thermostat was working.

It took me a couple of minutes to notice the local inhabitants who shared my hot tub. They registered first as a movement on the edge of my vision, a swiftly moving black blob that was barely glimpsed before it vanished, and I wondered if the combination of extreme heat and sulphurous gases was causing me to hallucinate. A sudden buzzing by my ear soon identified the intruder as a honeybee, however, and before long I saw another two drifting by the edge of the pool. I wasn't sure if it was the heat or the sulphur, but something made this spot particularly attractive for the native bees. If I hadn't already been dripping sweat into the water and gagging at the fumes their presence might have disturbed my relaxation; as it was, their sudden interest in this red-faced foreign body was enough for me to call a halt to my experiment. Checking my watch I realised that I'd stayed in the pool for a little under five minutes. It was no wonder that the bees were the only occupants of these two cooking-pots.

A quick dip in the milder pool restored my body to a reasonable temperature, and after a cool shower I dressed and headed back to where I'd parked. I could see why the springs had fascinated early visitors to the site, but I failed to understand the attraction for the modern tourist. My skin still felt uncomfortably flushed after the various shocks that I'd subjected it to, and checking my watch I discovered that the strap was encrusted with unidentifiable yellow deposits. I felt like I'd been the subject of a giant chemistry experiment.

I spent the evening in a quiet little caravan park on the edge of town, preparing a marginally more ambitious tea of mushroom omelette and salad. It was starting to feel surprisingly homely in the van, so I was slightly distressed when I noticed a couple of small flies on the inside of the window. I crushed these with the back of my nail, only to see them replaced tenfold within a few minutes. Soon there were flies on every surface, mostly crawling but a few beginning to test the joys of flight, and I was forced to take refuge outside. I guessed that something must have laid eggs in the van, possibly in the plastic bag that contained the last two days' trash.

Fortunately the campsite office was able to lend me a can of fly spray, and after emptying half of it through a crack in the door I went for a short walk, allowing time for my miniature genocide to take effect. When I returned I cleared the carcasses out the door with a brush, searching for any straggling survivors on the windowpane. The spray had left an unpleasant chemical odour in the back of the van, and if it had been a few degrees warmer I could easily have believed that I was back in the spa pool again.

Instead I retired to bed early with a headache, probably caused by the many noxious chemicals that were now eating into my brain, and dreamt disturbing dreams about being chased by swarms of bees. Tomorrow I would head back down to the coast – hopefully there I could catch a breath of fresh air.

Ka Mate

13
Kaikoura

As morning broke I woke to the sound of rain drumming against the roof, the acoustics of the van turning it into a giant kettledrum on wheels. While I disconnected the power supply and packed the red bucket away my clothes were systematically drenched by the downpour, until I finally clambered into the front seat soaked through to the skin. Since even changing my top would involve stepping outside again I resigned myself to my condition. I was cold, wet, and gradually seeping into the upholstery beneath me. I was beginning to see the appeal of motels.

Fortunately the grey skies cleared as I drove down the mountainside, and by the time I hit the coast the morning's downpour was almost forgotten. Overhead all had returned to a brilliant blue, interrupted only by a few wispy clouds drifting slowly towards the horizon. My clothes were still sticking to my back – when they weren't clinging to the equally wet cushion beneath them – but they were the only reminder of the storm I'd left behind me in Hanmer.

Kaikoura proved to be a surprisingly small cluster of residential streets radiating out from the main road, and I promised myself that I'd soon stop being shocked by the reduced scale of things on the South Island. Given its meagre population, small towns like these were to be expected – large cities would be the exceptions here. I found myself a welcomingly warm bar where they served an excellent seafood chowder, and I set about drying myself out in front of the open fire.

If the size of Kaikoura should have been expected, then its Maori origins will surely come as no surprise either. Kaikoura means 'to eat crayfish', an oblique reference to the excellent sea fishing available here, the contents of which I was proceeding to spoon down my throat as steam rose from my sodden jeans. The entire peninsula also had an added significance for the Maori, as it was *Taumanu O Te Waka A Maui*, the seat of Maui's canoe. According to legend it was here that the great Maui sat when he fished up the North Island from the depths of the ocean, and as such it was a place of special significance. The blending of historical fact and mythological tale in Maori legend made for a cultural complexity that was alien to my rational European upbringing, and I wasn't sure how to take the Maui legend, especially when it sat alongside the more realistic stories of the Great Migration. It seemed to require a leap of faith that I wasn't yet ready to make.

As in Christchurch, the first European settler in Kaikoura was a Scot, this time a whaler by the name of Robert Fyffe. He'd arrived in 1842, when much of the South Island still lay undiscovered by the new wave of settlers, and had set up a whaling station that stayed open until 1922. The station had enjoyed a particularly high degree of success, due in part to the exceptional geographical advantages that Kaikoura offered. The sea off this stretch of the coast teemed with marine life.

This maritime abundance was due to the presence of the continental shelf, which passed unusually close to the mainland just off the Kaikoura shoreline. The shelf was in fact a gigantic underwater cliff, the shallows that surrounded the continent suddenly dropping away to incredible depths. At its deepest the canyon was over three thousand feet down, a depth roughly equal to four times the height of Auckland's

Sky Tower, and it acted as an ideal habitat for many kinds of marine life. From the tiny organisms that lived in its depths to the whales that came here to hunt, the continental shelf attracted creatures from all levels of the food chain, eager to eat at such a well-stocked natural buffet. It was for this reason that a pod of sperm whales had made their home a few miles off the Kaikoura coast, putting this small town on the map in the process.

After lunch I walked through town to the Whalewatch operation on the outskirts of the settlement, the new eco-friendly business that had taken over from the former whaling station. After the station closed in 1922 the area was left without a principal industry, and the local population had suffered from a chronic shortage of work. In 1987 Whalewatch was founded as an attempt to combat this unemployment. Even today, more than fifteen years later, a proportion of the company's profits was fed back into the community, a worthy attempt to improve the local standard of living. They also contributed to whale and dolphin research projects, ensuring that the tourist dollar was used to further our understanding of these unique creatures, not just to line the pockets of venture capitalists. As businesses went, it was a fine example of how tourism could have a positive effect on an area. It didn't always have to mean fast food franchises and cheap hotels.

This didn't stop them from trying to grab every cent from my wallet during the course of the afternoon, although at least I knew that this daylight robbery was undertaken in a worthy cause. Once I'd checked in for the afternoon's trip I had half an hour to kill before the bus came to collect our group, and as there was nothing I could walk to nearby I was left stranded in the gift shop. The displays boasted whale key rings, whale erasers, whale t-shirts: if there was enough space to print on it, then they'd stamped it with a picture of a whale. Only the motion sickness pills were spared this rampant branding, so I bought a small blister pack of them just in case, popping one in my mouth as the bus pulled up outside. I didn't usually suffer from seasickness, but the storm this morning felt like a premonition of what was to come.

Before we even left the harbour I could feel the swell rocking our boat from side to side, the deck rolling beneath my feet with every step, and I knew that the pills had been a wise idea. With the canyon running so deep beneath the surface of the water the swell was sure to increase as we moved further out to sea, and I didn't fancy seeing my seafood chowder again. I was sure that it wouldn't taste quite so appetizing the second time around.

Our ship was named *Aoraki*, meaning 'cloud piercer', and once we were clear of the harbour we sped out to sea at an impressive pace. An electronic gauge at the front of the vessel showed the current water depth, which quickly settled at about five hundred feet. After almost ten minutes the waters began to grow visibly choppier, *Aoraki* riding across the swell like a toy boat in a child's bathtub, and even with the stabilizing effect of the seasickness pills I could feel my lunch beginning to swill around inside me. Suddenly the depth gauge began to drop, the numbers ticking down at an alarming rate. When they finally stabilised the gauge registered a depth of twenty-one hundred feet, over four times the depth that we'd sat in only a minute earlier. We had travelled over the edge of the canyon.

Now that we were here it didn't take long for us to make our first sighting. The pod that lived in this section of the canyon consisted of four bachelors, the females and their young spending the majority of their year in the warmer waters of the equator. The sperm whale's principal prey was arrow squid, and as the canyon harboured hundreds of these giant fish there was a good reason for the bachelors to endure its colder waters, in return for an almost unending supply of food. Add the local seal population into the equation, and Kaikoura offered a veritable feast.

Ka Mate

When the news that a whale had been sighted went out over the P.A. system I hurried outside onto the observation deck, my unstable staggering sending me bouncing off the fifty other people who were struggling to find a suitable viewpoint. The waves here were the highest I'd seen so far on my travels, and the boat would sometimes pitch suddenly to one side, sending the passengers clambering for a handhold. It was tough trying to see anything in these conditions, never mind a whale. The sperm whale might be the world's largest predator, but as it only ever showed about ten percent of its body above the waterline they weren't always easy to spot. I tried to swallow back the rising nausea and scanned the horizon for a sign.

Before long it came, a tiny blur above the surface of the waves, the signal of a whale clearing its blowhole. It was only the faintest cloud of spray, but it was enough for our captain to change his course. Slowly we edged forward, careful not to stray too close to our target: we were only here to observe after all, not to hunt. With their emphasis firmly on eco-tourism the Whalewatch crew were keen to follow the latest regulations to the letter.

I'd been expecting a moment of inter-species communion similar to that which I'd experienced with the dolphins, but as we drew closer it became clear that I was to be disappointed. Despite having been christened Little Nick by the local crews our new friend was anything but little, and his tendency to remain largely underwater meant that we could only see the crest of his back, his eyes and other features remaining hidden beneath the waves. It was only as we slowed to a stop at the limits of the safe observation area, the boat still pitching wildly in the rough sea, that I realised just how big he was. Little Nick might not possess the inquisitive charisma of the Hector's dolphins, but he still made an impression with his bulk alone.

By now two other boats had arrived on the scene, hanging back like us to watch Nick from a distance. It was a measure of the area's recent success as a tourist destination that there were so many of us spying on this giant denizen of its waters, and it was encouraging that all three boats were following the correct protocol and maintaining a comfortable distance. Whale tourism would only continue to thrive as long as the whales were comfortable here, and that meant not interfering with their natural environment.

On average sperm whales only spent about three minutes at a time on the surface, coming up for air before diving to hunt for food once again, and as Little Nick's allotted dive time approached several cameras were unsheathed and held at the ready. With predictable regularity his body slowly disappeared back beneath the waves, and as he dived headfirst into the canyon his tail was raised out of the water, a final slow wave goodbye before he vanished from sight. This was the image I'd seen on the postcards in the gift store, the raised tail having turned into an icon to attract the visiting whale watchers, and I heard shutters clicking on both sides as the tips of Nick's tail slid back into the water. I'd have had my own camera out too, if I hadn't been so worried about losing it over the side. The boat was still rocking with each wave that we hit, sometimes leaning over so far that I felt sure we'd capsize, and I was glad to be able to return inside to my seat. A couple of deep breaths restored some kind of equilibrium, but I still didn't feel entirely settled.

The sperm whale's ability to dive was a miracle of nature, and one that wasn't entirely understood by modern science. A third of the sperm whale's body weight rests in its head, with much of this mass taken up by a substance known as spermaceti. (When early whalers cut into their catches they mistakenly thought that the viscous liquid inside was sperm; obviously no one saw fit to question why the whale stored this in its head.) There was a theory that the spermaceti could be solidified by taking in cold water through the blowhole, enabling the whale to plummet straight down to the ocean floor by effectively turning its own head into a diving weight. When it needed to rise, the spermaceti could be returned to a liquid state once again, the added buoyancy making their quick ascent to the surface possible.

It was only a theory, but it went some way towards explaining the sperm whale's fascinating and unusual behaviour. It was known that the whales descended almost straight down in a vertical line, their massive heads pointing at the ocean floor. Exactly what they did down there was still a matter for conjecture, however, as they swam deeper than we'd been able to send a camera. They regularly dived almost a mile beneath the ocean's surface, to depths that even submarines couldn't achieve until the 1950s. The pressures at such depths were enormous, and yet for the whales this was their normal hunting ground. The giant squid that whalers used to cut from their stomachs were the only indication of what took place in those unplumbed depths.

Their behaviour on the surface was easier to observe. They would stay down in the canyon for half an hour at a time, resurfacing for about three minutes twice an hour to breathe fresh air and clear their blowholes. It meant that there was only a brief window of opportunity for us to observe these fascinating sea mammals, and to aid us a small plane circled overhead, watching for the surfacing males. If we wanted to see them during their three minutes of exposure, then we'd need as much help as we could get.

It took almost twenty minutes for our crew to sight another whale, so I remained sitting in the cabin, desperately trying to convince my body that the slow rocking motion didn't mean that it had to reject my lunch. When the call went out over the P.A. that another whale had been sighted I staggered out to the viewing decks again, clinging on to every solid object that I passed along the way. If I'd had any doubts before, then it was rapidly becoming clear that I wasn't cut out for a life on the ocean waves. Not if I wanted my stomach to digest anything, anyway.

It didn't take long for our captain to identify the new whale as Te Aki, 'The Protector' or 'The Chief'. He'd earned this title a few years earlier, when the whale had driven a pod of Orcas out of the area, saving the local seal population in the process. Given that sperm whales had been known to snack on seals when squid weren't available, this wasn't the charitable act that his name might suggest, and it was more likely that he didn't fancy sharing his after-dinner nibbles. Whatever his motivation for repelling this invasion, though, the name had stuck.

After a couple of minutes drifting on the waves and spouting bursts of mist-like water droplets into the air his head ducked beneath the surface again, and this time I was ready for the money shot. As his tail rose above the water, fanning out behind him to align his body ready for the descent, I gently squeezed down on the shutter release button, joining the chorus of clicks that surrounded me on every side. It would be another half an hour or so before he resurfaced, by which time we'd be heading back to the harbour. Now at least we all had our memento to take home with us.

On our way back to Kaikoura we returned to the spot where we'd seen Little Nick earlier, and with remarkable regularity he resurfaced again, in almost exactly the same place that he'd left half an hour earlier. By this stage, though, my discomfort was turning into full-blown queasiness, and I found that I preferred watching from my seat next to the window. A few deep breaths from time to time kept the cold sweats at bay, but I didn't fancy my chances if I stood up. After Nick's second departure we stopped again to watch a pod of dolphins playing in the surf, and I found myself checking my watch in the lull between waves. By now I had only one thing on my mind. The whales had been fascinating, but I was beginning to feel as if someone had just put me through a washing machine's spin cycle: I wanted dry land.

It was with some relief that I staggered down the ramp onto the rough concrete of the harbour twenty minutes later, my legs wobbling as they readjusted to solid ground. The fact that my stomach contents had returned intact was almost certainly due to those deceptively small pills that I'd purchased at the Whalewatch gift shop. I definitely didn't feel well, and as I walked shakily back to the van I swore that the pavement rippled beneath my feet on several occasions, my balance skewed after just two hours out on the boat.

Even as I sat down to a crude dinner in the back of the van later that evening, having parked in a nearby campsite, my stomach felt queasy and unsettled. Kaikoura might mean 'to eat crayfish' in the Maori, but right now that sounded just a little too rich to handle. Beans on toast suited me just fine.

* * *

Fortunately my equilibrium righted itself at some point during the night, and I woke to find clear skies overhead and a fresh salt tang on the breeze. Yesterday's experiences had quelled any desire that I might have had to take another boat trip, but it seemed a shame to spend such a fine day inside the van so I drove down to the far end of the town, where I'd heard that a walking track led around the tip of the peninsula. The sperm whales weren't the only sea mammals that claimed Kaikoura as their home, and thanks to Te Aki's run-in with the Orcas there was also a large seal colony based on these shores.

I parked in the large paved area that marked the end of the Kaikoura road, and read the warning signs carefully before starting off along the shoreline. Seals were territorial animals, and we were warned not to approach within thirty feet of any we should see on the trail. It sounded a little overcautious, but rumour had it that these weighty mammals could lunge at a frightening pace when provoked, and I'd heard that there were a number of fatalities each year from seal attacks, often caused by the infections that set in after being bitten. If the bite itself didn't kill you, then their poor dental hygiene just might. A thirty-foot exclusion zone seemed a small price to pay when it came to death by gangrene.

As soon as I stepped out of the parking lot, however, I was faced with a dilemma. A short wall separated the road from the rocks along the shore, and lazing in the shade afforded by this wall was a large female seal, her eyes closed as she slept within a few feet of man's intrusion. To step down onto the rocks, and onto the trail that led around the end of the peninsula, I'd have to walk within touching distance of her head. At the furthest point I'd still be passing within about ten feet of her. So much for that safety zone.

After a few nervous glances in her direction I lowered myself down onto the rocks, and I was pleased to note that she remained slumbering, either blissfully unaware of my presence or completely untroubled by it. I just hoped that I wouldn't run into any more of the local inhabitants on the path, especially if they were a little more alert to my intrusion: I wanted to get close enough to them to observe, but I didn't want to get into a territorial war. I didn't rate my chances against a mouthful of nature's own chemical weapons.

The rock formations near the parking lot were an attraction in their own right, and once I'd negotiated my way past the sleeping guard I spent a few minutes clambering among their crags and pools. There were several families here too, the children searching the pools for crabs and trying to pry unwilling molluscs off the rocks with bits of driftwood, but once I started along the coastal path these beachcombers suddenly vanished and I found myself alone on the track. In the distance I could just make out a couple clambering over a pile of rocks, but otherwise there wasn't a soul to be seen. I hoped they hadn't all been put off by the stories of fatal seal attacks. Maybe another Whalewatch tour wasn't such an unappealing option after all.

The rock formations along the coast hinted once again at the area's volcanic past, and observing their unusual shapes kept me occupied as I followed the hardly distinguishable path around the shoreline. Some of the rock layers had remained parallel with the ground while others had been thrust upwards, creating strange landscapes of shelves and crenulated outcrops in the process. This geological upheaval was so fascinating that I almost lost the path on several occasions, but since it trailed along the shoreline it didn't take me long to find it again. Sometimes it petered out among the loose stones of the beach only to re-emerge several feet further along, a barely visible track of trodden-down earth. After a while I stopped trying and simply followed the coast.

It was as I rounded one of the crenulated outcrops that I saw a small group of people gathered on the nearby rocks, all of them staring at a point a few feet from where they stood. These were the first walkers I'd come across since leaving the rock pools by the parking lot, and I couldn't help being curious at what had caused them to stop here, some distance from the main path and less than halfway along the peninsula walk. Hopefully it meant the seals were nearby.

As I drew closer my curiosity was answered, the sea breeze carrying an unpleasantly strong odour to my nostrils. It reminded me of wet dog mixed with rotting fish, and it didn't take me long to work out that this distinctive perfume must belong to the local seals. Sure enough, as I approached the group of walkers I glimpsed a dark shape reclining on one of the flatter rocks, nestled into a slight crack beneath an overhanging ledge. I counted five seals in total, sprawled across the rocks on either side of a small inlet. They appeared to be sleeping, but as one of the walkers edged forward with his camera, eager to steal the perfect close-up, the largest of the five lunged forward in a sudden explosion of movement and noise. His bark sounded more like a loud sneeze but there was no mistaking his intentions as he chased the cheeky intruder back to where his friends were standing, now clutching their cameras nervously at this sign of aggression. The seals were happy to be watched but there were clear lines that they didn't want crossed. They obviously knew the thirty-foot rule as well.

I nodded a brief greeting to the group as they consoled their friend, then I headed back to the path, eager to get going before they decided to leave the seals to their siesta. I'd enjoyed having the path to myself, and I felt certain that there would be other seals further along the trail. I definitely didn't want to be there if they tried to ambush them again.

Soon afterwards a branch of the path cut off to my right, leading a zigzag route up the side of the cliff to the fields above, but I decided to stay with the shore path. Although I'd already had a couple of seal encounters I was still keen for more. My persistence paid off as I rounded the next corner and smelled a familiar fishy odour on the breeze. I was prepared to hunt out the source of the smell, but it soon became clear that no searching would be necessary as I passed an outcrop and was greeted by the sight of twenty seals lying across the stones of the next beach, a few jostling to find a more comfortable spot, but most of them dozing in the sunshine. Fortunately none had decided to bed down too close to the path, but I still trod carefully and quietly as I passed them, in case they should take offence at this clumsy land-locked intruder. Their bodies lay to either side as I tiptoed through the makeshift dormitory, the stench of rotting fish occasionally making me gag as the breeze blew it inland from the beach. It was little wonder that the peninsula had acquired such a reputation among amateur naturalists. I couldn't recall ever being this close to seals in the wild before.

It was about a mile further down the path that I ran into my first real dilemma. The trail ended at an outcrop of densely layered rock, and I could see that the path started again on the far side. Across the rock, however, lay two large seals, their fur dark and sleek as if they'd just emerged from the water. To reach the other side I had no choice but to pass within a few feet of them. I held my breath as I tiptoed across the rock, stepping gingerly from ledge to ledge as I kept one eye on their slowly rising flanks. I'd already seen how fast they could move if provoked, and their bite was definitely worse than their bark.

The situation worsened once I'd passed these first two sentinels. The path started again once the rock ended, but it wound through a small gap in the promontory on the other side of the bay, a space that was only about ten feet across at its widest. Sprawled in this opening were the dark shapes of four sleeping seals. In order to pass them I'd need to step within inches of their heads, a manoeuvre that would be as foolhardy as it was intrusive. To go back, though, meant passing the other seals again, and it was quite a distance to return to the cliff path. After due consideration pushing forward still felt like the best option, and as I followed the path around the curve of the bay I could feel my body growing tense, my hands twitchy and nervous. If it wasn't for the pervasive odour of sweat and fish you probably could have smelled my fear.

I tried edging slowly towards them at first, but the largest of the four, presumably the male of the group, raised his head from the rock and let out a loud, rasping bark in my direction. I took a step back and he lowered his head onto the rock again. So much for stealth. Instead I looked for an alternative route, and I found one in a large ledge that stretched along the cliff face, passing through the gap about four feet above the heads of the sleeping seals. Getting onto it would involve approaching the large male again, but as long as I took a quick step up before he lunged I'd be out of his limited reach. It wasn't ideal, but it was the only option if I wanted to keep moving forward.

Gathering my wits I paused for a moment to take a slow breath, then in one quick movement I stepped forward and onto the rock ledge, my legs carrying me as swiftly and as confidently as I could manage. There was a loud bark beneath me and I could see the male lunging forward again, but by the time he'd moved I was already making my way along the natural shelf in the cliff side, far enough above them to be out of reach. I knew that I'd just shown a blatant disregard for the thirty-foot rule, but I couldn't help smiling at my success. My heart was still racing as my feet touched down on the path on the far side of the pass.

Several dark clouds were beginning to gather on the horizon, and now that I was past the promontory I started to increase my pace. The last thing I wanted was to get caught in a sudden storm. It looked as if there were fewer seals on the rocks here too, although I wasn't sure if this was a good omen or not. Perhaps they'd all taken to the sea before the impending deluge arrived.

The Kaikoura peninsula had one last surprise to offer me as I rounded the final bend in the path. There was a large rocky plateau here that stretched out into the sea, waves sending up fans of spray as they broke across its tip. Strewn across it were about thirty seals, visible from a distance as dark shapes against the lighter grey of the rock. Perhaps it was the storm brewing out at sea, perhaps it was just the time of day, but the seals here were livelier than those I'd seen earlier. Those closest to me still reclined lazily in patches of seaweed, but further out on the rock there was a surprising amount of activity. As I stood watching two large males reared up at each other out on the very tip of the plateau, their bodies crashing against each other with terrifying force as the sea threw up a cloud of spray behind them. Even at a distance the force of the impacts was terrifying. My risk-taking back at the gap in the promontory suddenly seemed remarkably foolhardy.

And then the rain started. It came down gently at first, small droplets spattering my shoulders and wetting my hair. As I stopped to dig a waterproof out of my rucksack it grew heavier, and by the time I had the hood up it was beginning to approach torrential. When the wind started to blow in off the sea too, swirling the sheets of rain around in the air and ensuring that even single inch of me was damp, I decided that it was time to pick up my pace. My van was now several miles away, with no shelter between us. It looked like I was destined to get wet.

I walked back along the cliff top, the coastline looking less appealing now that the wind was driving the waves hard at the shore. Compared with the coastal walk, though, the cliffs were remarkably uneventful, and I wondered who could possibly choose to walk this well-defined but dull path when there were such adventures waiting at sea level. Perhaps the views might have been more spectacular on a clearer day, but it was all I could do to trudge onwards with my eyes directed at the path ahead, alert for the crusty brown mines that the local herds had planted in the long grass. There was less chance of dying from a germ-laden seal bite here, but boredom was becoming a real threat.

The rains finally cleared as I drew close to the parking lot, slowing to a nagging drizzle then stopping altogether. It was as I pulled my hood down that I caught sight of an unusual conical hill sitting half a mile inland, its sides stepped in what remained of a series of terraces. This was a Maori *pa*, one of the fortified villages that had protected them so well during their occasional battles with the European settlers, and with each other. The local tribes had steepened the natural hill by scooping earth from the sides, ensuring that they enjoyed a height advantage when under attack. During the years prior to European settlement, when this was a fully functioning *pa*, the most important buildings would have sat on the flat surface at the crest of the hill, while the terraces below would have provided space for other buildings and open areas for communal activities. At certain times of the year it would have stood empty, only being used for important gatherings or in times of trouble. Today it was nothing more than a shadow on the hillside, a ghost in the landscape.

The presence of a *pa* on the South Island was important for me as it confirmed the suspicions that I'd developed over the previous week. There were a total of fourteen Maori archaeological sites on the Kaikoura peninsula, including two of New Zealand's oldest archaeological finds. In addition to the *pa*s a human skeleton had been uncovered at Avoca Point, clutching onto a fossilised egg of the now-extinct moa, and ancient middens had been discovered at the mouth of the Clarence River. There was good reason to believe that the abundance of marine life caused by the proximity of the continental shelf had provided the mainstay of these early communities, and current studies suggested that Aotearoa's seal population might have been hunted close to extinction in the early years of Maori settlement. There hadn't been just an isolated settlement here, but a thriving community. The presence of the moa egg helped us to date it too, right back to the first settlement during the Great Migration. The Maori were on the South Island from the outset, and in significant numbers. The myths I'd heard of their absence in the South were rapidly collapsing.

As I stood looking at the *pa* from a distance, trying to make out the shadows of its fences and trenches in the short grass that now covered its slopes, the rain started up again. There were a few droplets by way of a warning and then the heavens opened, large drops plummeting heavily to earth in a steady curtain of water. After five minutes of sliding through the mud of the hilltop I finally saw the parking lot below me, and I ran down the wide steps cut into the slope, keen to reach the security of the van. It might only be an oversized tin can on wheels, but at least it was dry.

Once I was back inside, the rain drumming loudly on the roof above me, I turned the heating up to full and sat with my hair in the hot airstream, trying vainly to ward off the chills. I was glad that I hadn't been out on the Whalewatch tour today. The stories I'd heard about the lack of a Maori presence on the South Island might have turned out to be false, but the rumours concerning its weather systems were proving to be all too accurate.

14
Wairau *(Blenheim)* – **Whakatū** *(Nelson)*

Driving north from Kaikoura the following morning I had no option but to pass through one of the best known wine regions in the southern hemisphere. While there weren't many people back home who could claim to have heard of Blenheim – Marlborough's main city – the region it served had achieved an impressive degree of fame over the past few years. With the words 'Sauvignon Blanc' and 'Marlborough' now intrinsically linked, it would have been rude for me not to make a brief stop at one or two of their cellar doors.

Despite the quality of their output, however, it soon became apparent that the region could never attract a tourist industry to rival the vineyards of Tuscany or the Napa Valley. As I drove through Blenheim I passed one concrete monstrosity after another, enduring a parade of ugliness that was strangely impressive in its lack of commitment to the principles of aesthetics and general good taste. The outskirts were ramshackle and rundown, concrete buildings left to crumble to dust next to untended parking lots, and by the time I emerged from the centre my mood had plummeted. It was little wonder that alcohol provided such a thriving industry in this part of the world.

A brief stop at the Visitor's Centre suggested that a walk around the Wairau lagoons might be a more picturesque option than spending another minute in the city centre, so I drove out of town in search of their relative tranquillity. The lagoons here had gained international significance with the unearthing of an archaeological site on their seaward side that dated back over a thousand years, to the age of the original moa-hunting Maori settlers, and it seemed that the more I travelled, the more I discovered that the South Island was teeming with Maori history. The archaeological discoveries in this area would have been enough to draw me here in their own right, even if the sea breeze hadn't seemed like a good tonic for the concrete relics of Blenheim.

My hopes of breathing lungfuls of restorative sea air were dashed as soon as I parked at the end of the dirt track and opened my van door. At first I thought it was my imagination, but as the breeze gusted past my nose I caught a whiff of something decidedly unsavoury. I sniffed again, only to regret my decision a second later as the smell settled at the back of my nostrils and began to inch its way down towards my taste buds. There was no mistaking it, no matter how hard I tried to convince myself. The lagoons smelled, rather strongly, of shit.

Of the many offensive smells on the planet human excrement is quite possibly one of the worst, and it was almost enough to make me seal myself back into my tin can and head back down that dirt track. I held my breath as I read a large sign at the end of the track, which informed me unsurprisingly that the lagoons were located on the edge of the local sewage treatment plant. The information did nothing to lessen my gag reflexes every time I breathed in the noxious stench, but at least it meant that the path was leading away from the offending pools. I'd come too far to turn back now.

A sign at the start of the path warned that it was dangerous to touch standing water this close to the sewage works, but since the track led through a vast, shallow puddle at the outset it appeared that I had no choice. I was reminded of the thirty-foot rule on the coastal path in Kaikoura as I tiptoed gingerly through the marshy ground, trying to use patches of dry land as stepping stones wherever possible, and I found myself wishing that the Kiwis weren't so keen on highlighting unavoidable risks. I couldn't follow the path without touching standing water, so I'd much rather have been ignorant of its dangers. Where would this trend end? Hazard signs by the roadside warning that crossing could result in death? Warnings on food packaging informing us that eating might lead to a fatal choking incident? Sometimes it was better simply not to know.

After five minutes the waterlogging cleared and I was finally able to walk freely along the designated path. The land here was flat and covered with a strange spongy grass that would have looked perfectly at home on a *Star Trek* set, its worm-like tubes striped in various shades of grey, pink and orange. I was just starting to enjoy my stroll, the sea breeze blowing all offending smells back inland, when the ground began to squelch underfoot again. A glance ahead revealed that the entire path vanished into a seemingly endless puddle, with no dry patches rising out of its placid surface to act as stepping-stones. I took a deep breath of the fresh air, desperately trying to hold some of it in my lungs before I turned around and headed back to the van. Without a pair of gumboots the archaeological secrets of the Wairau lagoons were decidedly out of bounds.

When I returned to the van I rinsed the soles of my shoes with some clean water, just in case the warning signs had contained a grain of truth, then I drove back into Blenheim. It hadn't improved at all in my absence, and I was distressed to find that my caravan park was thronging with screaming children hurling themselves under the wheels of passing vans, and exhausted parents watching hopefully from the limited comforts of matching foldaway chairs. I'd forgotten that this was the Easter weekend, and it appeared that half the South Island had left their picturesque homes behind for the concrete marvels of downtown Blenheim. I only hoped that they were buying enough crates of wine while they were here to make it all worthwhile.

Fortunately a bottle of Sauvignon Blanc from the nearby Villa Maria vineyard helped to deaden the sound of children kicking empty soda cans across the pavement outside, and I eventually drifted off into a relatively untroubled sleep.

* * *

Determined to learn from my mistakes I began the following day by booking myself onto a wine tour of the Marlborough vineyards: I assumed that a local would know how to avoid the sewage works, at least.

When the minibus pulled up outside the campground to collect me, however, I was surprised to note that our host had an English accent. It quickly emerged that Barry was originally from Kent, but had been tempted out here by the casual lifestyle and the flourishing wine industry. He was part of the latest wave of European settlers to arrive on the shores of Aotearoa, often spurred on, as the original settlers had been, by visions of the country as an unspoiled wilderness, offering a host of natural wonders alongside a simple, old-fashioned way of life. It must have sickened him that he'd ended up in Blenheim.

He filled us in on some of the details of the area as we drove to the Hunter's Winery, our first vineyard of the day. Sauvignon Blanc accounted for approximately half the grape planting in the Marlborough region, which made sense given their worldwide reputation, with Chardonnay and Pinot Noir accounting for almost all the rest. Their Pinot production was on the increase, though, and for the first time in the region's history it was expected to exceed the Chardonnay output later this year. Marlborough might have had an international name to uphold, but the vineyards were still finding their feet in such young territory.

Hunter's was established in 1979, making it one of the oldest vineyards in the region, another legacy of New Zealand's prohibition movement. If their story was typical of the country as a whole, however, then their output was quintessentially Marlborough. At the cellar door they offered five different Sauvignon Blancs for tasting, along with a Sauvignon/Chardonnay blend, the one concession they made to the alternative white grape. It was their Rosé that caught my attention, though, and it came as little surprise to hear that it had won eight consecutive prizes at the Air New Zealand wine awards. A bottle quickly opened my collection for the day, and Barry lent me a box to house my purchases as we drove from vineyard to vineyard. He could obviously sense that I was along for more than just free nibbles.

As we drove to our next destination I stared out the minibus window at the ordered ranks of vines, all running away to an unseen meeting point somewhere in the distance under the shadow of the surrounding hills. The soil was almost as gravely here as it had been in Hawkes Bay, the old riverbed deposits leaving large, visible stones scattered among the topsoil, and I marvelled at the way in which the vines' struggle against adverse conditions could produce such exquisite and palatable results. No matter how much sunlight and water the plants received, without this constant desire to draw nutrients from the thin, stony soil the end result would be watery and weak. As I stared out of the minibus window at the Marlborough plains it occurred to me that this was the perfect metaphor for life – although that might just have been the five Sauvignon Blancs that were slowly working their way through my bloodstream.

Forest Estate was even younger than Hunter's, having been founded in 1988 by a husband-and-wife team when they retired from their lucrative careers in the medical profession. It sounded like a dream come true, but as we were shown around the vines it became clear that hundreds of hours of hard graft were put into every year's output, and that owning a vineyard was anything but an easy retirement option. On average they could make only three bottles of wine from each individual vine, and while about sixty percent of their grapes were picked by machine the remaining forty percent were still collected by hand. This was largely due to the way the machines went about their work, shaking the vines and collecting the falling fruit in large baskets. The procedure was designed to be kind to the fruit, saving it from bruising or splitting, but it was still traumatic for the vine itself. Younger vines had to be harvested by hand, in case the machine accidentally shook their roots clear of the ground. Since the vines improved with age their future had to be protected at all costs, even if it meant spending hours plucking their fruit.

We were allowed to taste some of the grapes straight from the vine, and I was surprised at how greatly they differed from the regular household fruit. Small, dark and remarkably thick-skinned, they burst in your mouth with a unique intensity of flavour, the large pips sticking awkwardly between your teeth as your taste buds struggled to cope with the sudden influx of sensory data. This was the result of forcing the plants to struggle against the gravely soil, and also a consequence of their leaves being trimmed back to a bare minimum. The plant was forced to concentrate its efforts on growing fruit, but with the small number of nutrients available it produced tiny, intensely flavoured grapes instead of the large, watery fruit we were used to buying in the supermarkets. Intensely flavoured grapes made for intensely flavoured wine, and they provided plenty of natural sugar for the fermentation process to turn into alcohol. I suspected that any wine produced from commercial grapes would taste no better than watered-down cider.

The temperature was beginning to rise as the sun climbed in the sky, so after our stroll through the vines we retired inside to sample some of the finished product. Once again the Rosé was outstanding, the extracted juice having been reintroduced to the coloured skins for about three days before being finished off as a white wine, and I added a bottle to my distinctly pink collection in the back of the minibus. I also bought a bottle of dessert wine, an unusual choice that was prompted by its lightness and delicacy of flavour when compared with the bolder, sweeter 'stickies' that I'd tasted before. I noticed that Barry bought himself a bottle too, and as we drove back up the driveway I sat smugly nestling my purchases against my side. It seemed that I had better taste than I'd thought.

While we enjoyed a platter of sun dried tomatoes and cured meats at the Highfield winery I asked Barry how these vineyards compared with the nearby giants like Montana. We had passed their superstore on our travels, and it dwarfed even the largest of the boutique Marlborough wineries.

'Well, if you look at the figures then Montana produced about thirty-five thousand tons of grapes last year. Most of the wineries we'll see today managed around one or two thousand tons. So they're, what, twenty or thirty times bigger? A lot of that's in overseas sales, though. You'll find bottles of Forest Estate in restaurants and bars around New Zealand, but I doubt anyone's even heard of them back in the US. Whereas Montana are everywhere now.'

I pondered this as I finished my lunch, and came to the conclusion that the international dominance of the large wineries like Montana wasn't entirely a bad thing. It had put New Zealand wines on the map, and with limited distribution deals for the smaller vineyards it meant that we at least had a chance to taste some of Marlborough's sunshine on the other side of the world, even if it was the sanitised, corporate version. I still wouldn't be buying a t-shirt, though.

Once lunch was over we trudged lethargically back to the minibus and Barry drove us to the Drylands cellar door, our final stop for the day. I was distressed to discover that the vineyard was owned by Nobilo, the other large New Zealand winery that sat wedged between Montana and Villa Maria in the rankings. To make matters even worse it emerged that they were part of the same group that owned Hardys and Banrock Station in Australia, who between them had a stranglehold on the market in this part of the world, aimed at the cheaper, mass-produced end of the shopping scale. Maybe I'd been spoilt earlier in the day, but I found my nose turning up at the consistently unadventurous samples on offer. If I was to buy anything from their well-stocked shop then I might have been tempted by the Australian Banrock Station Reserve Shiraz, as my mini-cellar was lacking a drinkable red, but since this might be a hanging offence in Marlborough I decided against such a treasonable act. I was secretly rather glad when we waved goodbye to their ranks of McWine and headed back to the bus for the last time. A day of food, wine and sunshine was starting to take its toll, and I was struggling to keep my eyes open.

* * *

'So have you folks been having a great time in New Zealand?'

Sue turned her head to face us as she spoke, almost crashing the tightly packed minibus in the process. We were on our way to Grape Escape, a small shopping complex that consisted of a craft shop, a cellar door, and a local liqueur producer, and Sue had already nearly crashed the van a couple of times as she gossiped with the day's crop of tourists. I could tell that it was going to be an entertaining afternoon. When I told her that I'd been to the Crusaders' match earlier in the month she almost crashed for the second time, narrowly missing a turning car as her head whipped around to carry on the conversation.

'I'm so jealous, they're my home team you know. I've been up here for a few years now but I'm still a Canterbury girl at heart. Best team in the country, and given how good the rest of our boys are that's saying something. You'll have seen Dan Carter too. We like Dan Carter.'

I wasn't sure if she was expressing a personal preference or simply reflecting on the nationwide Carter-mania that I'd seen pasted across the sides of buses on both islands, but fortunately she moved on to interrogate three cowering Norwegian girls, and I was able to look out the window at the passing scenery. It was another hot, dry day on the northern end of the South Island and I'd heard that the wine region here, on the outskirts of Nelson, boasted over two thousand hours of sunshine a year. While the road ahead looked dry and dusty, however, the fields surrounding us were green with clinical rows of vines. Nelson might be one of New Zealand's smallest wine regions, but Marlborough had taught me that bigger didn't necessarily mean better.

Unfortunately it didn't take long for Sue to work her way through the other occupants of the minibus, her loud nasal tones cutting through us like a road accident, and she found her way back to me despite my best attempts to curl into my seat.

'Now, the place we're going to first is a great little store, they sell all sorts of stuff there, not just wines, but all sorts of great Kiwi products. They've got that and the cellar door all in one place, so you can shop till you drop, as we like to say. That sound good, Dan?'

She drew my name out so that it sounded like a tortured whine, and I resisted the temptation to cover my ears. I'd hardly begun to express my pleasure at the fact that we were nearly there before she butted in again.

'Well you know, we've always been ahead of the times here in New Zealand. You'll see when we're at the shop that us Kiwis are an inventive bunch, always looking for a better way to do something or something new to try. I hear you guys are getting chip and PIN credit cards now, but we've had them here for about twenty years. That's just Kiwi ingenuity for you, always there first.'

I wasn't entirely sure that the technology required for chip and PIN was even possible in the late Eighties, but I bit my tongue and nodded my head. We were still hurtling along the tiny back streets at remarkable speeds, and the last thing I wanted was to provide yet another reason for Sue to take her eyes off the road.

When we finally stopped at Grape Escape, the minibus leaving a haze of raised dust in its wake, I was pleased to discover that our guide's enthusiasm hadn't been misplaced. Two local producers were represented at the cellar door, Te Mania and Richmond Plains, and both held up well against the multinationals just along the road in Marlborough. In particular their reds were unusually bold and robust for New Zealand, and I decided that it was about time that I weaned myself off the Sauvignon Blanc, at least for a day or two. I liked the heaviness of the Richmond Plains Escapade Red despite the drinking notes, which described it as carrying 'hints of tar, liquorice, tobacco, leather and some gamey spicy notes'. The blend of six different grapes lent it a complexity that their comparisons had struggled to capture. There was room for at least another six bottles in my van, but I limited myself to a single purchase this early in the day: who knew what else the tour would offer.

Before we left Grape Escape I also paid a visit to the Prenzels store, which sold a bizarre combination of locally made liqueurs, flavoured oils, and tacky gift items. I was curious about their name, but before the shop assistant had a chance to reply to my discreetly asked question Sue popped up from behind a display of butterscotch schnapps, an empty glass clutched in her hand.

'There's a story behind that you know. They're a local company and they wanted something memorable for their name, so they thought of the word pretzel. Only they weren't allowed to use that, so they inserted an 'nz' into the middle for New Zealand. I told you us Kiwis were an ingenious bunch, didn't I?'

I couldn't help wondering if the Kiwi character wasn't also overly inclined towards rampant exaggeration, but despite her overbearing personality and eardrum-piercing voice I was beginning to like our tour guide. She might have been loud and ridiculously opinionated, but there was an honesty and enthusiasm about her that was hard to resist after a while. Either that, or the Escapade Red was stronger than I'd thought.

Our next stop was the Waimea Estate, and while we snacked on a lunch platter we sampled a few of their wines. I was particularly impressed by their 'Spinyback' range, named after the local spinyback lizard, as a proportion of the sales went to the local Maori tribe for the use of their ancestral lands and their imagery. It was a small gesture, but a worthy one, and typical of the spirit of coexistence that I'd seen across both islands. As always there were complex issues attached to it, particularly as this kind of fixed 'free' income was sometimes seen to promote idleness in the Maori communities, but it certainly felt like a step in the right direction. It was hard to imagine such a spirit of co-dependence occurring in apartheid South Africa, or even in the current political climate in Australia. In New Zealand at least the Maori still maintained the rights over their cultural heritage.

As we drove to our next stop the minibus was unusually silent, all of us beginning to feel the effects of so many consecutive tastings, and I pondered the appeal of these wine tasting tours. I'd taken enough of them now to feel like something of an expert, even if I still felt amateurish alongside the tasters who hosted our visits. What struck me most about the tours was that it wasn't just the wine that made them appealing. I could easily have bought several bottles of wine myself for less than the price of the tour, and enjoyed more than a thimble-sized slurp of each one, but somehow that wasn't the point. It was the promise of social interaction that made these trips so enticing, and I realised through my tipsy haze that travelling was a lonely occupation. On the tours we ate, we drank, we made merry: it was the perfect blueprint for a happy life. It was no wonder that their buses were always packed like sardine tins.

For all my flippant remarks about drinking free booze, my understanding of the winemaking process had also increased dramatically over the last couple of months. On a blind tasting I could just about distinguish a Riesling from a Chardonnay now, and I could even guess at the blends that were used to produce the cheaper reds. I knew the difference between household grapes and winemaking fruit, I could detect the difference that the oaking process made on a white wine, I even knew how egg white fining worked. Most importantly, however, I was also beginning to understand my own tastes a little better. My palate was best suited to dry whites with a hint of citrus, a light blend of fruitiness and acidity; when it came to reds the heavier berry flavours were the thing, perhaps even with hints of vanilla, but certainly without the peppery spiciness that some vineyards seemed to favour. I could now walk into a wine store and select a bottle I'd enjoy from the description on the label, which was no mean feat.

Our final stop of the day was at Redwood Cellars for a taste of something slightly out of the ordinary, even to this hardened wine tour veteran. Redwood produced mainly fruit wines, along with a selection of spirits and liqueurs, and as we filed through the doorway I felt my wine-fortified heart sink. I'd tried someone's homemade apple wine when I was at University, sipping the tasteless clear liquid politely from a coffee mug as three of us crouched on the edge of a bed. It was only when I stood up afterwards that I felt my legs fade out of focus, as if someone had poured Jell-o into them while my attention was distracted. I'd only supped about a third of a bottle and yet I was inexplicably drunk. I could only assume that the flavourless liquid we'd all imbibed was dangerously close to neat alcohol.

When it came to tasting the produce at Redwood, then, I was understandably a little wary. When I spotted their kiwi fruit wine on the counter I knew that I had to sample some, but it took me a couple of minutes to ask for a small taster, as my mind wrangled with the memories of that apple-fuelled night. I noticed that it was a golden yellow colour as the shop assistant poured it, more yellow even than the heavily oaked Chardonnays, but I was pleased to discover upon the first sip that its sweetness was balanced by a sharp, sour acidity. I found myself enjoying it, and I only refrained from buying a bottle because I could already feel my lips beginning to pucker with the sourness. After half a bottle I'd probably look as if I'd opted for Botox injections.

I didn't buy anything at Redwood in the end, and when I returned to the campsite the bag at my side was surprisingly light. Maybe Sue's choice of venues had been a little too eclectic for my taste, but I liked to think that my purchasing restraint signalled a new refinement in my wine-drinking tastes. During the day only two wines had passed my stringent requirements, and I told myself that those two were, if not the finest we'd sampled, then certainly the most suited to my own palate. Either that or I was already growing sick of New Zealand's wines – and somehow, that didn't seem likely.

Ka Mate

15
Te Tai Tapu *(Abel Tasman)*

Abel Tasman was one of history's accidental over-achievers. Born in Holland in the early years of the seventeenth century, he joined the East India Company in his late twenties, having already been made a widower, and having remarried at the age of twenty-eight. Within a few years he was given a ship of his own to captain, and so began the first of his many voyages of discovery. On November 24, 1642, he sighted the southern tip of what is now Tasmania, and in a moment of generosity that would put Captain Cook to shame he named it Van Diemen's Land, after the governor-general of the Dutch Indies. Having skirted the Tasmanian coast he then intended to turn northwards, but the prevailing winds carried him east, across what is now known as the Tasman Sea, commonly referred to as 'the ditch' in Australia and New Zealand's beer-fuelled Cold War. On December 13, Tasman sighted land again, what turned out to be the northwest tip of New Zealand's South Island. He was the first European to do so, and he came across it by chance.

By this stage the Maori had been living along this stretch of coast for over five hundred years, slowly developing a culture that relied on the sea and the land in equal measure. Five days after this initial sighting, on December 18, 1642, exactly one week before Christmas Day, Abel Tasman anchored his ships near what is now

Golden Bay, known to the Maori as Mohua. When he and a handful of crew members came ashore they were the first Europeans to set foot on Aotearoa, over a hundred and twenty-five years before Cook would 'discover' the landmass for the second time. First contact with the natives ended in a skirmish, during which four of Tasman's crewmen were killed. History began as it intended to continue.

This northwest corner of the South Island was now the Abel Tasman National Park, created on the three hundredth anniversary of that first fateful meeting. As I drove from Nelson the following morning the skies were still clear, lending the sea a brilliant blue-green glow as I followed the erratic curve of the coast around Tasman Bay. I planned to stop at Kaiteriteri before taking one of the convenient water taxis further round the coast to a suitable drop-off point within the National Park, at which point I'd turn around and walk back to my van. It seemed a typically Kiwi thing to do: walking in the open countryside simply for the hell of it, indulging in the pure pleasure of fresh air and grass beneath your feet. I remained aware, though, that this was also a well-trodden tourist path. Abel Tasman's Coastal Track was the most visited walking trail in the country, to the extent that the footfall was beginning to have a detrimental impact on the area. They estimated that a hundred and sixty thousand people walked the track in a year, around a sixth of the entire population of the South Island; the more I looked at the figures, the more this unspoiled wilderness was beginning to sound like a tourist conveyor belt.

Kaiteriteri consisted of little more than a sprawling caravan park and a few scattered shops and kiosks, so I checked in as quickly as possible and parked close to the park's facilities, in the hope that I could get underway without delay. The caravan park was a small village in itself, with its own shop and numerous concrete bunkers housing the facilities, and it took me a couple of minutes to walk back to the shoreline. It was eerily quiet, and I guessed that many of the van owners were already roaming the National Park that sat on its doorstep, leaving their homes and their belongings sitting vacant. Several of the vans were propped up on piles of bricks, however, and one had tufted green moss-like growths sprouting from its roof. They clearly hadn't been moved in weeks, and in some cases years. Perhaps some of those hundred and sixty thousand walkers never came back.

When I reached the beach some of the kiosks were now open for business, offering taxi services along the length of the National Park's scenic coastline, and I began to consider my plans. I didn't like the thought of my home-on-wheels slowly rusting away next to the moss-covered vans in the park, so in the end I played it safe, planning a four mile walk along the central stretch of Abel Tasman's coastline that seemed perfectly manageable in what remained of the day.

'Now, your return boat leaves at half three,' the swarthy gentleman in the taxi kiosk warned me, a furry black fleece looking out of place next to his knee-length shorts. 'If you miss it then there's not another one, you'll just have to wait for the first boat the following morning. I've had that happen to a few folks before, so make sure it doesn't happen to you.' That explained the abandoned motor homes, then. He pointed to a bowl that sat on the end of his desk. 'Take an apple if you want. You'll need some food if you get stuck out there tonight.' As understatements went, it was almost heroic in its magnitude.

My taxi wouldn't leave for another thirty minutes, so I spent the time back at the van, preparing for what might turn out to be an unintentionally long trip. I made sure that I had plenty of water, aware that the air was now warming up as the sun climbed high in the sky, and I packed a thick sweater down in the bottom of my daypack. I wouldn't need it during daylight hours, but it seemed best to be prepared. I dropped my apple in last of all, like a good luck charm. Hopefully I'd be eating it in the warmth and security of the van later that evening, not hunkered down by the roots of a large tree, desperately looking for shelter. It might be warm now, but I knew that temperatures could drop dramatically at night.

When I returned to the shoreline my water taxi was already waiting for me. A hinged gangplank linked the back of the boat to Kaiteriteri's narrow stretch of beach, the long metal contraption looking as if it might unbalance the entire vessel and drag its keel beneath the waves. I'd been expecting water taxis like those I'd witnessed in Fiji: small, simple boats that you had to wade through the shallows to reach, your pants rolled up past your knees if you were foolish enough not to have brought a pair of shorts. They'd had nothing like this military-looking vessel, with its mechanical arm reaching out across the shallows. I guessed that a hundred and sixty thousand people was a lot of bodies to transport in and out of the Park's boundaries, and they had to ship us around in bulk. It was somewhat lacking in picturesque qualities, though.

Once I was aboard the boat the natural Kiwi quirkiness began to reassert itself, however, and I was pleased to note that the enterprise wasn't as slick as I'd initially thought. The boat's skipper hardly spoke to us, his eyes fixed firmly on the open sea as he pined in a way that us landlubbers could only guess at, but out host for the trip was the kiosk operator, the generous contributor of the apple that now sat in my pack. When he saw me again he nodded and held his hand out to be shaken, his palm course and dry as if there were grains of sand embedded in the skin.

'Good to see you again, mate. I'm Peter, I'll be giving you some commentary on the way up the coast. You still got your apple with you?' I smiled and gestured to my pack. 'Glad to hear it. Plenty of water too? It's going to get hot out there today, even though we're heading into autumn.'

I had a two-litre bottle that I'd filled from the drinking station at the caravan park, as well as a small bottle that I could carry in my hand. After all the wine I'd drunk in the last few days, hydration was foremost in my mind.

'Good stuff. I think we're all here then, so we'll get going. Grab yourself a seat and we'll be off.'

It took almost a minute for the gangplank to slowly fold itself back into the boat, and I used the opportunity to examine a rudimentary map of the Park. It looked as if the path would be simple to follow, its wobbly blue line only occasionally deviating from the coast and rarely branching off in other directions. Most of the people who came to Abel Tasman were here for the hiking, which meant that there were none of the complications you'd usually see on tracks in rural areas: farms, villages, archaic rights of way. That, I supposed, was part of the joy of the National Parks. Without the complexity of civilization, life was rendered simple.

Our journey up the coast was pleasant enough, although I was becoming used to hearing the regurgitated facts that tour guides fed us concerning the local wildlife, or the Kiwi propensity for finding unorthodox solutions. At Towers Bay we stopped to look at Split Apple Rock, two other boat companies bobbing alongside us in the mild swell, and I dutifully unpacked my camera for the compulsory photo. The rock itself was a curious oddity of nature, an almost perfect sphere that had been split down the middle and now lay gaping in the waters of the bay, but I found the constant parade of tourists irritating, as if it cheapened what should have been an intriguing personal discovery. Fortunately Peter quickly pointed out the red staining around the base of the rock, an effect caused by the oxidization of the high iron content in the local stone, and then we moved on. This kind of geological freakshow wasn't what I'd come to Abel Tasman for.

A short while later we passed Torrent Bay, the pick-up point that I'd arranged with Peter back at the kiosk, and over the drone of the engine he pointed it out to me for future reference. There were several holiday homes set back from the beach, although many of them looked ramshackle to the point of collapsing and I found it hard to believe that anyone still holidayed there. Scattered among them, however, were a number of new houses, their carefully preened balconies looking out over the waters of the bay. Over the steady background noise Peter told us that many people were buying the old houses and then demolishing them, using the land to build more desirable properties. The Department of Conservation was trying to reduce the number of buildings in the Park and they weren't granting any new plots of land, but it was perfectly legal to buy a rundown cottage and level it, raising any concrete monstrosity you desired in its place. Some of the ramshackle old homes were selling for over a million dollars, the land around here was in such demand. A holiday home in Abel Tasman could set you back several million by the time it was completed.

We also passed Bark Bay as we headed up the coast, my starting point on the coastal path, but Peter had already explained to me that they'd take me to the furthest extent of their route first so that I had a chance to see the rest of the Park, dropping me off on the way back. It meant that I was still onboard as we passed Tonga Island, where we paused briefly to watch the seals playing among the rocks. The area had recently been declared a Marine Reserve, with fishing bans extending for some distance out into the open sea, and a variety of marine life was beginning to return to the region. I'd already nearly tripped over a colony of seals in Kaikoura, so the sight of their dark bodies among the rocks was nothing new, but I was pleased to see that there were several cubs living with this group, playing among themselves in a shallow pool near the island's edge. Watching them diving in and out of the shallow swell they looked remarkably sleek and graceful, and it was hard to believe that before long they would turn into the bulky, stinking hulks that I'd encountered on the east coast. Once they were in the water even the adults had a certain grace about them, though, and I reminded myself that when I'd stumbled across them they'd been out of their element. Here they were entrancing as they slid swiftly through the waves.

The taxi continued around the coast as far as Totaranui, and once there we drifted ashore to drop off a handful of passengers, while the rest of us took a ten-minute break and made use of the facilities. The campground was desolate and undeveloped, little more than a clearing among the trees with a small log cabin housing the primitive toilets. Somehow its appeal was increased by this isolation, though, and I found myself wishing that I'd had the courage, and the know-how, to stay out here, rather than in the ramshackle village of Kaiteriteri. I couldn't help being envious of the campers at Totaranui, with their peaceful isolation and wide expanses of open beach, only populated by a few scattered seagulls jabbing their beaks into the wet sand. It wasn't a typical view of paradise, but it came surprisingly close.

Once the gangplank had slowly retracted back into the boat we retraced our course, heading back down to Bark Bay, where I was to be dropped off. As it turned out the beach there was little more than a narrow stretch of sand, and once the few of us who were walking this section of the path were safely ashore our taxi headed slowly back out to sea. I checked my watch and found that I had two and a half hours to complete the four-mile walk back to Torrent Bay, a simple task in such clement conditions. There was only one track leading away from the landing point, so before the other walkers had gathered their wits I headed off, keen to get a jump on the rest of the group. If I was lucky I might get a chance to sample the true solitude of Abel Tasman.

On my map the track had seemed to hug the coastline, but I soon discovered that the forest growth along this section often hid the open sea from view. Light green mosses hung from the trees as if they'd been draped there by a passing fashion designer, and the light filtering through them was gentle and subdued, only slightly warming the damp air. I wasn't sure if the others had stopped already to eat their sack lunches, but after a few minutes my own clumsy footsteps were the only noise. It lacked the beaches and the ocean view of Totaranui's campsite, but it brought its own form of tranquillity beneath its spreading branches. If Totaranui was a paradise of isolation then the coastal track hinted at a long-lost Eden.

I ate as I walked, keen to preserve my solitude, and aware of the several pairs of feet that were already following mine. I encountered a few other walkers on my way, but we exchanged little more than muffled welcomes or silent nods, all of us keen to preserve the natural calm that Abel Tasman offered. Silence tended to beget silence.

At Falls River I crossed the suspension bridge warily, treading the broken boards as carefully as possible while it rocked gently from side to side. At the midway point I found myself clutching the ropes tightly in clenched fists as it swayed, and despite the fact that I felt as if I could be upended into the water at any moment I made it safely to the other side. As if this Indiana Jones-style crossing wasn't enough, there was a swarm of wasps waiting for me on the far bank, emerging four or five at a time from small holes in the clay of the path. I walked through them as quickly as I could manage, and was surprised to emerge unscathed a few feet further down the path, where the air finally cleared. It was a timely reminder that there was more to paradise than isolated beaches and shaded groves.

Then, before I knew it, I was at Torrent Bay. I thought that I might have misread the sign, but the track soon emerged onto a seaweed-strewn stretch of beach, complete with a scattering of benches and a familiar log cabin housing the toilets. Checking my watch I was distressed to discover that I still had another hour and a quarter until I was due to be picked up by the water taxi, and this tiny neglected stretch of sand didn't make for an inspirational stopping point. I'd been so busy walking that I'd completely forgotten to pace myself.

Fortunately I was soon rescued by the timely appearance of an unlikely guardian angel. As I sat on a log by the water's edge, the wood worn smooth by the sea and bleached almost-white by the sun, Peter appeared from out of the trees, his fleece now wrapped around his waist as a minor concession to the midday heat. He waved when he saw me and strolled over.

'You're here a bit early aren't you? I thought we weren't picking you up for a good while yet.'

I explained my predicament and he nodded sagely, as if this happened to him all the time.

'I thought it was a pretty short walk for a young guy like you. If you want to walk further there's another stop round the coast at Anchorage. It only takes about an hour from here, so we can add you to our pick-up there if you like. It's up to you, but there's not much here to entertain you for an hour. Not unless you're a big fan of driftwood.'

It sounded like a plan, so we arranged that I'd join the quarter-to-four collection at Anchorage and I set off into the trees again, rejoining the path where it branched away from Torrent Bay's limited facilities. From here the path hugged the coast more closely, at times trailing along the top of shallow cliffs that dropped straight down to the sea below, and I was pleased to be on the move again. I hadn't been savouring the idea of spending an hour among the seaweed and bleached driftwood of Torrent Bay, and this new stretch of track was closer to how I'd imagined the coastal path would be.

This time I made a point of keeping an eye on the time, and now that I'd eaten most of my primitive lunch the apple that Peter had given me was looking lonely and insubstantial in my pack. By three-thirty I was starting to worry. The track seemed to be heading for the coast for a short stretch, and I'd just convinced myself that Anchorage was around the corner when it suddenly twisted inland again, climbing to slightly higher ground where the sea felt uncomfortably distant. This happened four or five times, and each time I convinced myself that I was finally there before the path turned inland. With only five minutes to go until my allotted pick-up time I was beginning to panic. What if I'd missed the turning? What if Peter had underestimated the length of this stretch of path? Or overestimated my fitness? I hadn't thought to ask him how far Anchorage was, and had taken his estimate at face value. What if he was used to a brisker pace than me, and I was still a mile away from the pick-up point?

I could feel the pack starting to stick to my back as I hurried along the path, but I was also becoming increasingly aware of how it no longer dragged down on my shoulders like it used to. It now contained only my sweater and the apple, the fruit having already forsaken its right to be thought of as a good luck talisman. In this perfectly preserved slice of Eden I should have known better than to accept an apple from a stranger.

And then, suddenly, I was there.

I'd thought that the sea was still some distance away, but without warning the path pushed through a line of dense undergrowth to my left and emerged on a tiny crescent of sand, only a little larger than a child's sandpit. There were two couples already seated on the tiny beach, both of whom I recognised from the boat earlier. They nodded a silent greeting as I checked the face of my watch. Three forty-five exactly. Miraculously my timing was spot-on.

Unfortunately the same couldn't be said for my ride home. It was nearly four o'clock by the time the boat appeared around the curve of the headland, its gangplank sitting cocked in the back like a miniature crane. It took them a couple of minutes to steer into the bay, the water sitting shallow over the surface of the sand, and once we were all aboard Peter apologised for the late departure.

'We were waiting for another three pick-ups at Bark Bay, but they didn't show up so we've come along for you guys first. I'm afraid we'll have to head back for them now though, we don't want to leave them stranded out here tonight. We like to joke about it, but we're not complete bastards.'

As I tucked my bag beneath my seat I felt the apple roll around inside, and after a moment's deliberation I took it out and bit into it. It appeared that I wouldn't be needing my emergency rations after all.

16
Kaiteriteri – Māwhera *(Greymouth)*

During my time in the van the quality of campground facilities had become a major issue. Often they were clean and cosy, three or four showers sitting alongside a few toilets and a urinal, with sinks lined up along a mirrored wall. Some expected you to mop the floor after use, but despite this DIY ethic almost all were relatively clean and hygienic. If cleanliness wasn't a problem, however, then overcrowding could be. If the campground was nearing full capacity then there were often queues for the showers in the morning, a line of bleary-eyed travellers clutching towels to their chests, winding their way past those of us trying to shave in front of the steamed-up mirrors.

There were various solutions to this problem, although they rarely proved to be effective. Some sites plastered signs across every available surface asking users to be considerate during busy periods, but as this relied on everyone practicing patience and understanding it was doomed to failure from the outset. Many of these signs consisted of handwritten scrawlings on scraps of notepaper, which didn't help. It also appeared that people had differing views on what constituted a reasonable length of time for a shower, and some campgrounds posted up suggested time limits, ranging from a couple of minutes to a ridiculously generous five or six. Neither made any difference to the length of the queues.

Some of the larger caravan parks even boasted coin-operated showers, and as I shuffled into the facilities at Kaiteriteri the following morning I discovered that this was the case here. It meant that I had to walk back across the park in my grubby t-shirt and pyjama bottoms to fetch some change. Fortunately I found a couple of fifty-cent pieces tucked into my jeans pocket, which meant that I wouldn't have to make the walk of shame to the main office to change a note, and I hurried back to the facilities before a queue formed. After a few days of travelling I'd learned to hold onto a reservoir of small change for just such a situation, avoiding the embarrassment of having to deal with the park authorities in your pjs. The Kiwis might have invented chip and PIN, but their campsites still ran on hard currency.

On returning to the shower block I was pleased to discover that there were still several vacant cubicles, but now a new challenge presented itself. The coin-operated machines that controlled the flow of hot water were usually situated inside each cubicle, often as part of the shower mechanism itself, but here they all seemed to run off a single box bolted to the wall in the main washing area, just opposite the urinals. Fifty cents bought me three minutes of hot water, but if I wasn't finished by the time the clock was up then I'd be forced to scurry back out into the washrooms to top up again, my thin travel towel wrapped around me for a modicum of privacy. Three minutes sounded like a reasonable amount of time, but I knew from previous experience that it was difficult to wash and rinse from head to toe in such a short period. In the past I'd simply been able to slot another coin into the machine, but today it wouldn't be so simple.

I carefully balanced the coin on the rim of the slot and readied myself for the race to the cubicle. As it slipped through the mechanism with a metallic clink I was already striding purposefully toward my designated shower, clicking the lock into place and depositing my clothes quickly on the bench. Luckily the water ran hot from the start, and I'd learned from my previous experiences that it was best to wash my hair first, as that was the most time consuming task and the toughest to rinse out. I was counting down from a hundred and eighty as I washed, my crude stopwatch hopefully keeping me within the designated limits. When I reached thirty I began to hurry, immersing myself in the flow of water in an attempt to rinse every inch of my body simultaneously, and as the last of the suds swirled into the communal drain the water cut out, leaving me standing in the brisk morning air. I smiled as I towelled myself down and pulled some clothes on, trying to keep my pants out of the puddles that had pooled on the floor. At it turned out, three minutes was exactly how long it took me to shower. Maybe I'd adapted to life on the road better than I'd realised.

I walked back to the van with a slight swagger in my step, pleased with my success in the morning's race against the clock, and disproportionately happy to have saved my second fifty-cent piece. Hopefully it boded well for the day ahead.

For the first half hour of driving I was forced to retrace my route back to Nelson, passing through several fruit farms on the way, before Highway Six veered off to the west. The landscape here was similar to the route I'd driven between Wellington and Martinborough, the road rising into a low range of pine-topped mountains before dipping occasionally into a lush green valley, and despite the inevitable drop in temperature I was looking forward to heading south again. I still had so much to see.

At lunchtime I allowed myself a brief detour to Buller Gorge, which I'd heard boasted the longest swingbridge in New Zealand. In most countries this would sound a fairly hollow claim, but I was certain that the Kiwis must have built some fairly long bridges in their time, and if my experiences in Abel Tasman were anything to go by then swingbridges were still very much in vogue. The original Buller Bridge had been constructed in 1974, but it had to be rebuilt in 1988 after floods washed it away, a fact that didn't fill me with confidence. Their leaflet informed me that the new bridge spanned a distance of five hundred and twenty-five feet from anchor to anchor, and three hundred and sixty feet between the two gantries. That was over three hundred feet of unsupported bridge, hanging between the two gantries like a giant skipping rope. I was beginning to see where the swing came into it.

Once I'd parked at the visitor's centre I was allowed a breathtaking glimpse of the river as it sparkled through the trees, and I felt a certain calm settle upon me. The Buller was the largest river system in New Zealand that didn't have a hydroelectric power station on it, and the air of peaceful seclusion was a welcome surprise. Even the wilds of Abel Tasman began to look overcrowded in comparison.

As I emerged from the visitor's centre, however, the feeling of calm suddenly drained away. The bridge hung in front of me with the river rushing swiftly beneath it, its walkway suspended from two overhead cables and two floor level ones, the centre dipping several feet below the level of the gantries. As I set my first foot on the boards I felt them sway in that direction, then as I took my second step they realigned themselves, the ground beneath me rocking gently. The further I progressed, the more this effect was magnified, and as I approached the middle I could feel the entire bridge swaying from side to side. I gripped the handrail in two fists, desperate to avoid the apparently inevitable dunking in the river. Once the centre had passed I was able to tear my eyes away from the floorboards and look at the scenery again, but I still felt my heart pounding in my chest. I was glad when my toes finally touched solid ground – until I realised that the bridge was also the only way back.

Fortunately there was a short walk marked through the trees on the far bank, so I followed it for a few minutes as a way of avoiding the inevitable return leg. This area had suffered a major earthquake in 1929, measuring 7.8 on the Richter scale, and for a short distance the path followed the fault line through the woods. One side of the line had been raised about fifteen feet above the other, creating a sudden cliff in the heart of the forest, and my path wound slowly up the side of it, sometimes using protruding tree roots as steps. It was yet another reminder of the precarious nature of New Zealand's landscape, and of the fact that the entire nation was built on fault lines and active volcanic fields. The Kiwis obviously had a liking for danger even before the invention of adrenaline sports.

The return trip over the bridge wasn't as bad as I'd feared, although seeing the effects of the 1929 earthquake had done nothing to boost my confidence, and I was secretly relieved when I reached the visitor's centre again. The attendant lifted his hand from the acoustic guitar he was aimlessly strumming to wave goodbye, and on a whim I stopped to ask his advice. I knew that I wanted to head south, but beyond that I wasn't even sure of what my options were.

'If you're heading that way then I'd do the drive from Westport down to Greymouth,' he told me, still clinging to his beat-up guitar as he scratched his head through a thick woollen hat, 'the scenery down the coast there's totally rad. Visit the brewery at Greymouth too, best beer you'll get in New Zealand.'

He looked like he knew a thing or two about beer, so I nodded my thanks and returned to the van, checking his proposed route on the map. It looked like a couple of hours' drive to Greymouth once I hit the coast, so without further ado I strapped myself back into the driver's seat and set off down the road. If another earthquake decided to hit the Buller River then I wanted to be long gone.

Ka Mate

* * *

The 'Caution' sign at the side of the road warned me that there might be penguins for the next ten kilometres, forcing me to re-read it in case my eyes had deceived me. It was the first sign of its kind that I'd seen, and a sure indication that I was slowly heading southwards into chillier climes. I kept one eye on the road while I scanned the nearby bushes, eager to catch a glimpse of its reclusive occupants, but there was no flash of black and white through their green foliage. Maybe it was still too warm for them, with autumn only just kicking in.

I was glad that the wannabe musician at Buller Gorge had sent me along the coastal route, though, and not just for the quirky road signs. Australia's Great Ocean Road, running west from Melbourne on its way towards Adelaide, was often cited as the best coastal drive in this part of the world, but New Zealand's southwest coast easily challenged it for the top position. Craggy headlands jutted out into the swell, occasionally leaving pillars behind as they eroded and fell, rugged towers that sent up waves of spray when the tide rushed in. It was as if an ancient civilization had left behind the remains of a city, half buried underwater as the sea rose to swallow it. Maybe I was being hopelessly romantic, but it was breathtaking scenery.

It also had another advantage over the Great Ocean Road. Inland the landscape rose into the foothills of yet another mountain range, their pale grey peaks rising mysteriously in the distance, and while Victoria offered flat, dusty highways and an occasional gum tree, New Zealand was displayed here in all its finery, from the peaks that soared off to my left to the lush greenery clinging onto the crumbling cliffs on my right. There were even a few seals visible on the rocks below, occasionally dipping into the water where they suddenly soared with a grace that was unimaginable on land. All it needed was the penguins to finish the picture off.

It even had a geological attraction to rival Australia's Twelve Apostles. As the road passed near Punakaiki it suddenly opened up into a vast coach park and visitors' complex, and I found myself being sucked into their concrete walkways and well-tended flowerbeds. This was the site of the Pancake Rocks, one of the most common landmarks that I'd seen gracing picture postcards on my trip, and as such it seemed as good a place as any to stop for a breath of west coast air.

The 'pancaking' of the rocks was a geological anomaly, caused by the fact that sediment had been laid down over the millennia in alternating layers of limestone and mudstone. The mudstone weathered more quickly than the limestone, causing it to erode away between the flat layers of rock: the limestone formed the 'pancakes', while the mudstone was relegated to the tiny pats of butter in between. It was a striking geological oddity, and the mainstay of the tourist trade along this stretch of coast.

The wide paths that led from the parking lot to the rocks were testament to the money that the feature had brought to the local community, and they were easily the best-kept tracks that I'd encountered so far on the South Island. Once I reached the cliff face it was simple to see why such a volume of tourists passed through here. The paths wound through a complex web of arches, bridges and blowholes, offering every possible angle to view the abnormal rock face. Natural limestone structures rose out of the cliffs like abstract sculptures, turning this stretch of coast into a surrealist art gallery, while the sea boomed through gaps in the cliff, sending its spray fizzing into the air like an erratic fountain. As I crossed a natural bridge between the cliff and one of the many outlying pillars I peered cautiously over the edge, watching the surf surge beneath my feet before it was sucked back with the tide. The pancake comparison didn't really do it justice. This was a rock garden the like of which I'd never seen.

The arrival of a new coach party soon prompted me to move on, and I snapped a couple of photos before following the tarmac back to where my van was parked. My pictures couldn't do justice to the overwhelming scale of this unique feature, but at least they would give me a chance to examine some of nature's eccentric sculptures later that evening. I could have sworn that I'd seen the outline of a face in one of them.

* * *

It wasn't just the incessant rain that persuaded me to leave Greymouth early the next morning, although it helped. A quick stroll through town revealed that there was little of interest, and when I saw the Kiwi Experience bus parked outside a rundown bar I made the instant decision that Greymouth was not for me. It wasn't simply that it looked dirty and dull, as if it had been abandoned several years ago without anyone bothering to tell the local residents, but it was also the lack of historical interest, and the obvious dearth of any attractive feature to hang the tourist trade on. It was no surprise that the Kiwi Experience bus was parked outside a bar. They must have been wondering where else they could take their fee-paying cargo.

Fortunately I remembered my friend at Buller Gorge, and a quick visit to the Information Centre on the way out of town pointed me in the right direction for the Monteith's Brewery. The solid brick building looked unassuming from the street, but I figured that nothing could be more boring than Greymouth's town centre, and I stepped eagerly inside. I was told that the next tour left in a few minutes, so I settled down to wait.

The story of Monteith's was a triumph of local passion and expertise over the slowly sprawling reach of the multinationals. The brewery at Greymouth only employed ten full-time staff, but with an average length of service of seventeen years they boasted more brewing know-how than Budweiser must have in their entire worldwide operation. Even this small outpost wasn't immune from the spread of globalisation, however, and a few years ago DB Breweries, the largest beer manufacturer in New Zealand, had bought them out. DB had intended to relocate the Monteith's production line to Auckland, where the majority of their bottling plants and other facilities were located, but when a Greymouth journalist found out about their plans he went national with the information, causing an unprecedented public outcry. Petitions were signed on the streets of New Zealand, demonstrations were held in bars, and the Kiwi public were actively discouraged from buying any DB products. After five days the company backed down, promising to keep Monteith's on its original site on the west coast. It was a triumph for the small company over the multinational, and for the voice of the individual over the powerful dollars of big business. It also seemed to me to be a typically Kiwi reaction. Who else would instigate public demonstrations over a beer?

Once a small group had gathered on the worn carpet tiles of the brewery's foyer we headed off into the works of the factory, capably led by our Canadian tour guide Anne. The irony of having a foreigner tell us that Monteith's was a national institution and a proud Kiwi brand seemed to be lost on most of my tourmates, but that didn't stop me from chuckling to myself as we walked around the brewery's towering vats. Maybe my good cheer was a side effect of all that evaporated alcohol.

The escaped fumes might also have explained my lack of interest as we sauntered through the bottling and kegging plants, while Anne bombarded us with a stream of facts and figures that sailed clear over my head. It was only when she showed us their depalleting machine – a curious turnstile of robotic arms designed to break down the pallets of empty bottles when they entered the factory – that I tuned back in to what she was saying.

'When DB Breweries took us over we requested a new depalleter from them,' she told us with a glint in her eye, 'and they quoted us a price of a quarter of a million dollars. There's no way we could afford to pay that, so our master engineer had a look at it for us, and instead of buying their machine he built one himself, from scratch. The total cost for this machine was around eighteen thousand dollars, just a fraction of the price we were being charged by DB. That's New Zealand ingenuity for you folks. If there's a quicker, easier way of doing something, then the Kiwis will find it.'

I was reminded of Sue's nationalistic boasts on the wine tour in Nelson, although somehow this felt like a more believable fairytale than her yarns about credit cards and pretzels. There was certainly a spirit of hands-on innovation that seemed to exemplify the down-to-earth Kiwi character.

It was only when we reached the last stage of the tour that the group finally came alive. Anne led us into a small bar area for a complementary taste of their products, and a crackle of anticipation passed like static electricity through the room. I found myself sitting at a table with a young couple, and after our brief introductions I asked where they were from. I was pretty sure that I'd grown used to the New Zealand accent, and to me they sounded more like Eastern Europeans.

'We're from the Czech Republic,' replied my new friend Havel, pushing his long, straight hair behind his ears in an attempt to keep it out of his face. 'You know our country at all?'

I said that I'd been to Prague, mainly attracted by their excellent cheap beer, but also because of the magnificent architecture in the old part of the city. It was when I mentioned my trip out to Marienbad, however, that his eyes widened and he broke into a grin.

'Mariánské Lázně? It's a beautiful town, such a lovely place to visit. You go to the spa baths there?'

I'd walked around them, although I hadn't ventured inside, but as soon as I mentioned the spectacular fountains in front of the main building he nodded and laughed.

'The tourists always take photos of the fountains, I have a photo of them myself. It's a good place for Czech people to go on holiday, but not many foreigners go there. It's good that you know it.'

He appeared to be impressed by my knowledge of his home country, but I was equally stunned by the appearance of a pair of young Czechs on the southwest coast of New Zealand. Most of the backpackers I'd seen had been either British or American, with the occasional neighbourly Aussie thrown in for good measure. There were a few German and French accents around, but this was the first time I'd heard the clipped sound of an Eastern European voice.

'We spend most of our time travelling,' Havel replied when I pointed out their uniqueness, 'we love to travel. We have another month in New Zealand, then we go back home for three or four months. After that we're going off to the UK, perhaps to Scotland. We can earn more while we're away than we can at home, so we just take bar work, or anything that will pay for our travels. Right now I'm a pizza chef.'

He laughed again, but before I had the chance to enquire further into this strangely modern take on the nomadic lifestyle Anne began to call us forward for our samples. The brewery produced six main beers, with a seventh specialty brew sold as a limited edition during the summer months. Beer by beer we were treated to a small taster of each brew from the range, while Anne desperately encouraged us to swill the beer around our mouths and savour the nuances of each mouthful, rather than simply necking it. I particularly liked the Radler, a light, zesty, German-style beer that was originally intended as a refreshing alternative for passing cyclists, although its sweetness did stray a little too close to British lager and lime. Unsurprisingly my new Czech friends preferred the Pilsner, declaring it to be almost as good as the beer back home. It was said in such a way that I assumed they meant it as a compliment.

Once we'd sampled our way through the entire range Anne left us to help ourselves for a few minutes, and in between visits to the bar I probed the Czechs for information. They'd already stopped in Queenstown and were now heading northwards, our paths happening to cross within the drab confines of Greymouth entirely by chance. Neither they nor I fancied staying a second night in its concrete wasteland. When we finally spilled out into the greyness again, the cool breeze blowing off the sea sobering everyone up, I thanked my new friends for their camaraderie and we parted ways. I'd been cautious in my own excesses and felt just about capable of driving out of town, but I feared that they might be stranded in Greymouth for a second night. At least the drab concrete housing might look slightly more appealing after a few beers.

It was only when I reached my van that I realised that I hadn't asked either of them for a contact number or email. I turned around but they were already out of sight, slowly trekking their way back to the Czech Republic. Another brief friendship was over, as we all obeyed the urge to hit the road: my route lay southwards, while theirs lay to the north.

I pulled an extra sweater on before I set off, contorting my body to squeeze into it within the confines of the van. The mountains were waiting.

17
Ka Roimata o Hine-Hukatere *(Franz Josef)*

As I drove into Franz Josef the next morning I heard the chattering of a helicopter circling above my head, the offending vehicle flying low enough to cause a stir in the treetops, and while I parked outside a pleasant-looking motel I watched it land in a field only a couple of blocks away. After a few minutes spent gathering my belongings I stepped outside, and was almost run down by a 4x4 as it sped around the corner, its back seat piled high with bulky khaki bags. It felt like I'd stumbled into a war zone, but fortunately this frenzied activity was due to the area's local attraction, the Teutonically-named Franz Josef glacier. As attractions went, it felt unusually hostile.

It soon became clear that the town of Franz Josef only existed to serve the nearby glacier, and the main road was lined with tour operators, helicopter sightseeing companies and 'outdoor wear specialists', these outlets worryingly free of the frivolous gadgets and trends that filled camping shops back home. Instead their displays were stacked with climbing ropes and spiked poles, as well as a variety of solid clasps and buckles whose purpose eluded me. It seemed that the military comparison wasn't entirely redundant after all. Climbing the glacier was potentially fatal.

All of which made me reconsider what I was doing in Franz Josef. The bulk of the people around me were kitted out in robust boots and thick socks rolled up over the bottom of their pants, their heads poking out from brightly-coloured quilted jackets. I was clothed in an old, grey sweatshirt and a pair of jeans, and the top half of my sneakers was beginning to pull away from the sole in two or three places. My inadequate attire made me feel strangely exposed, as if I'd forgotten to dress this morning and was walking naked through a strange town. As I crossed the road to the largest of the tour operators I thought I could feel several pairs of eyes following me. I was hardly well dressed enough to go shopping, never mind scale the foot of a glacier.

Fortunately the girl at the ticket desk assured me that they could provide everything I needed, although with the considerable amount of money that was changing hands I suspected she'd say whatever I wanted her to. Once my wallet had been lightened she pointed me in the direction of the waiting room, where I was told that I could pick up a kit bag and watch a video about the glacier, until the bus collected us on the half hour.

In recent years New Zealand's two most popular glaciers, Franz Josef and Fox, had become an essential stop on the tour trail, their popularity boosted by their proximity to the extreme sports playground of Queenstown. During peak season the guide company employed over fifty staff, facilitating a flow of tourist dollars that far exceeded the flow of the ice itself. As I joined the queue for my kit bag I couldn't help feeling that I was back on the South Island conveyor belt, but the opportunity to walk on a glacier was too enticing to miss. At least there wasn't a Kiwi Experience bus parked outside.

One of the company's unfeasibly fit employees gave me a warm smile as I shuffled forward to the front of the line.

'Okay, I need your ticket and your shoe size, then I'll grab you some gear. Have you got a waterproof with you, or shall I get you one of those too?'

I muttered that I had a waterproof jacket packed away somewhere in the van, but she shrugged and pulled a shapeless blue bundle from the shelf behind.

'I'll give you one anyway, you'll be up there for a while and it looks like you'll need it today. Now, here are your boots,' they thudded unceremoniously onto the wooden bar, 'and your spikes are in the bag. Just carry them with you for now, and they'll show you how to put them on when you need to. Once you've got your boots on bring your shoes over here, and we'll keep them safe for you while you're up on the ice. Any questions?'

I was tempted to ask whether she'd had any training with the Marines, but I thought better of it and found myself a seat to change into my new gear. The boots looked almost as battered as my sneakers, but at least they were intact and dry, and robust enough to withstand the addition of spikes once we reached the ice plain. The waterproof was slightly on the large side and remarkably shapeless, but once again its plain functionality won out over any vestige of fashion sense.

Their orientation video showed sweeping shots of ice plains glowing pale blue in the brilliant sunshine, suggesting that the camera crew had spent a few weeks on the glacier waiting for such perfect conditions, but I was more interested in the history of this mammoth attraction. The Maori might not have ventured onto the ice as frequently as this current wave of European explorers, but they had certainly known of its existence. They named it Ka Roimata O Hine-Hukatere, or the 'Tears Of The Avalanche Girl', and their legends told of an adventurous Maori girl, Hine-Hukatere, who loved mountaineering. She persuaded her lover Tawe to climb the mountains near Franz Josef with her, but he slipped near the top and plunged several hundred feet to his death. The gods froze her tears as a memorial to her grief, and so a glacier formed in the valley. It was a strong fable about knowing one's limits, and the limits of those around you, but it didn't bode well for my journey up onto the ice shelf. I found myself empathizing with Tawe more than Hine-Hukatere, and I couldn't help seeing the story as a warning to unskilled climbers like myself about the dangers of amateur mountaineering.

Fortunately the bus arrived before I had a chance to dwell on this cautionary tale, and we filed into its rickety, damp-smelling interior. The seat beneath me was still wet from the previous occupant, feeling slightly cold and moist to the touch, and the air smelled musty and stale, as if the entire bus was slowly rotting away in this atmosphere of persistent drizzle. The girl at the counter had been right about my need for a waterproof, and I shrugged it on as we drove the short distance to the foot of the glacier. If nothing else, at least it would protect me from the sodden upholstery.

I had little idea of what to expect when we arrived at the valley, but somehow the dirty blue-black wall of ice felt like a letdown. The photos I'd seen of glaciers in the past had always been taken from above, looking down on the vast, slow-moving river of ice. I was beginning to see why they avoided photographing the foot of the ice flow, carrying as it did the dirt and debris that the glacier had scraped from the valley sides on its slow journey downhill. I'd been expecting a field of pure, crisp snow, but had been given a pile of slush and churned up mud.

It didn't help that the clouds had settled on the mountaintops, the day's drizzle turning gradually into steady rain. With the blue hood of my borrowed anorak pulled forward over my face I struggled to hear our guide's gems of wisdom before they were washed away by the downpour. Our party trudged sullenly across the floor of the valley, picking its way through rocks and boulders tinged red with algae, the first sign of life reasserting itself in the wake of the glacier's retreat. Over hundreds of years this primitive growth would be replaced with plants, then shrubs, then trees, until this area was finally clothed only again with a leafy canopy. Today it was still open to the elements, though, every surface stained and slippery under the relentless deluge. I kept the promise of future foliage to myself.

As we neared the foot of the glacier its true scale became apparent, impressing us with its magnitude despite the lack of picturesque qualities, but before we drew too close our guide led us up the side of the valley, scrabbling over loose scree and wet rocks in an attempt to gain the altitude that we needed if we were to make it onto the ice shelf. With every step I felt myself slide half a stride back down the slope, as the Herculean effort of climbing the valley sides made my thigh muscles burn with exertion. I wondered briefly why I was torturing myself in this way, but the vast off-white mass to my left silently answered that question whenever it surfaced. The Franz Josef glacier was massive, imposing, and hostile to human intrusion. Every bone in my body wanted to master it.

There was a moment's respite when we finally reached the path that ran along the slope of the valley, a brief pause to fit our crampons onto our boots and change guides, our original leader obviously being blessed with a sense of self-preservation that kept her from venturing onto the ice. The glacier was almost close enough to touch, the ice a pure, crystalline blue beneath the surface dirt. It seemed to glow slightly as if lit from within, a block of blue sky frozen and fallen to earth on this grey afternoon. It was easy to see why the Maori had detected the handiwork of the gods.

As I searched for somewhere to sit while I rearranged my gear I began chatting with the only other solo adventurer in our party, a Welshman who introduced himself as Gwil. Having checked the spelling of his name several times over I asked him what he'd made of the trip so far, and what he thought of the glacier.

'It's not the best day for it really, is it? Part of me wishes I'd stayed back down in the town, with one of those huge bowls of coffee they serve up here. I've only got a day here, though, so I didn't have much choice if I wanted to see the ice. It's now or never.'

I found myself sympathizing with his plight, especially when he mentioned the coffee. As I buckled the spikes onto my boots, the metal prongs screeching against the wet stones, I tried imagining a bowl of latte cupped between my hands, its steam rising to warm my face. It was remarkably evocative, and I found myself pining for the warmth and security of my van. Without realizing it my tin can on wheels had started to feel like home.

Our new guide was called Billy, although I struggled to make out what he looked like through the various layers of clothing that shrouded his face. His voice carried well in the damp conditions, though, as if he was used to talking in such heavy downpours, and even in such inhospitable surroundings his enthusiasm and energy shone through. By the time we set off for the ice, our spikes clanging and screeching like an army of robots, I was almost feeling upbeat again.

'This glacier was sighted by both Abel Tasman and James Cook,' Billy told us as he chipped away at a set of crude steps carved into the ice, 'but it was first explored in 1865, by the Austrian explorer Julius von Haast. He named the glacier after Emperor Franz Josef of Austria, which probably answers some of your questions about the name, but if you're thinking this was a remarkably selfless gesture then take a look at a map when you get back to camp. The area you've just walked through is called the Haast schist, and there are several Haast rivers in the nearby area. He was probably under instructions to name the glacier after the Emperor, but after that it was hubris all the way.'

I struggled to follow Billy as he led the way up the makeshift staircase, my boots repeatedly slipping on the slick surface like skates. It was only with a little practice that I learned to scuff them into the ice, allowing the spikes to grip into the dusting of softer snow on the top. Once my technique was established I had to hurry forward to catch up.

'The first tours of the glacier began in 1906, and were run by the Graham brothers, a pair of local entrepreneurs,' Billy continued. 'They had none of our technology in those days, so they used to wear a pair of socks over their boots to try and give themselves some purchase on the ice. This glacier has actually been advancing since the day it was first explored by von Haast, and it's now about three kilometres closer to the coast than it was in 1865. That makes it pretty rare among the world's glaciers. The river that runs out from the base of the glacier, through the valley where you walked today, is at times the fastest flowing river in the southern hemisphere, and on average the base of the glacier is moving at about a meter a day. The third icefall, further up, is moving at about five meters a day at the moment. That's ten times the speed of the glaciers in Swiss Alps. Forget global warming – you're standing on a steadily expanding ice age.'

It sounded as if the locals were fairly proud of their glacier, and with good reason too. When I finally had a moment to pause and survey my surroundings the scale of it was almost too much to take in, a vast sheet of ice stretched between the dark valley walls. In the distance, further up the valley, I could see the first of several icefalls, the point where hundreds of tons of packed ice suddenly collapsed under their own weight, creating teetering towers the size of skyscrapers that occasionally fell with a rumble like thunder. It might have been dirty in places, but the reality of Franz Josef was far more impressive than the image I'd had of a large frozen river. This was geography on a mammoth scale.

While we paused to catch our breath I asked Billy about the steps we'd just come up. He'd had to chip at them with his pickaxe as we walked, but they seemed to be permanently carved into the side of the glacier.

'We cut those this morning. It might not look like it, but the ice is moving and changing so quickly that they'd only last for a day or two if left alone. Every day we come out here before the tours to cut a path, and we have to keep fixing them as the day goes on. Nothing's very permanent up on the ice.'

So had it changed at all during the time that he'd been working here? Or was the movement too small to register on a daily level?

'Well, a few years ago the ice plain was pretty flat, but now you can feel a definite slope to it. That's due to the ice higher up the valley piling into it, pushing the back of the plain up with the pressure. It's noticeably different to how it was even a few months ago. It really is that fast.'

He obviously decided that we should get moving again before we were swept away by this movement, and he signalled for us to follow him through a shallow fissure. The ice plain was crisscrossed with these fissures, many of which were hidden from view by the drifts of snow, so I was careful to follow his footsteps as precisely as possible. I'd seen *Cliffhanger* enough times to know what happened when you fell down a fissure.

I was still concentrating on the path ahead of me, this time following Gwil's feet, when a high-pitched cry pierced the dampness. Given that this was *Lord Of The Rings* country I almost expected a horde of Orcs to come pouring over the edge of the valley, but then Billy pointed to a dark dot moving across the surface of the ice. It was a kea, a large alpine parrot that was now on the protected species list, and I'd already heard stories about its ability to tear windscreen wipers from cars, or steal food through open windows. Even at a distance I could see the wicked hook at the end of its beak, although the icy backdrop didn't offer much indication of scale. I knew they were large, though, albeit non-aggressive. This was a mischievous sprite rather than a dangerous predator.

Billy grinned as the tour party started to break out their cameras, although I could see that he looked a little restless. I wasn't sure whether he was more concerned about us falling down a crevasse or being ambushed by keas.

'They're cheeky buggers, the ones around here, they learn pretty quickly. I've had food stolen by them before, and they've been known to open the zips on people's bags to get to what's inside. You'd better make sure you don't leave anything unattended, or they'll snap it up. They're worse than magpies for that.'

Fortunately it didn't take long for our avian visitor to realise that we'd been warned of his banditry, and with a blood-curdling shriek he disappeared off into the trees at the glacier's edge. Billy checked his watch, rolling up several sleeves to get to it.

'We've still got about ten minutes left before I need to take you back down to solid ground. You fancy seeing an ice cave?'

This was obviously a rhetorical question, and he led us along a ready-prepared path that ran beside another shallow fissure, on several occasions ascending a carefully carved staircase. The cave was too small for us to do anything other than peer into it, and was perched on the side of the glacier in such a way that only two of us could reach it at any given time. When my turn finally came I stomped up the stairs, careful to dig my toes into the ice and avoid a *Candid Camera* moment. So far a few people had slipped, but there hadn't been any major accidents.

The same blue glow that I'd noticed at the foot of the glacier bathed the cave in otherworldly light, and I had to steady myself on my makeshift perch as its beauty literally took my breath away. Not much wider than a person, it descended several meters on a slight incline before turning a corner and disappearing, the sense of icy purity seeping into the air and making me shiver despite my many layers. The sight was made all the more spectacular by the knowledge that the cave would soon collapse under the weight of its own roof, burying this frigid grotto forever.

We stopped at the same resting place on the way down the glacier to remove our crampons, finally defeating the clanking, screeching army of robots that we seemed to have brought up with us, then we slid slowly back down the loose scree to the valley floor. I found myself walking beside Gwil again, so I asked him where his next stop would be.

'I'm not sure to be honest. I'd like to have a look at Fox Glacier, but I'm not sure I'll have the time. In the real world I work in an office in London, but I've taken six months off to travel. I think I need to be in Queenstown in a couple of days if I'm to stay on schedule.'

I was about to offer him the passenger seat in my camper van when he uttered those fatal words.

'I'm on the Kiwi Experience bus, actually.'

Ah, the Fuck Truck.

He laughed, almost slipping off the mountainside in the process. 'Yes, I think it does get called that. It's full of eighteen year olds mostly, just wanting to get drunk and be ferried to the next bar. You can probably tell that, by the fact that none of them are here. Unfortunately it was just the cheapest way for me to get around, so I figured I could put up with the hungover teenagers. Most of them sleep half the time anyway.'

Once we were back in Franz Josef we swapped numbers, just in case our paths should cross again, then he headed back to the rest of the Kiwi Experience tour. It was as I returned to where I'd left the van, having unloaded my rented gear and recovered my own battered sneakers, that I saw one of the coffee shops still open for business. The image of that steaming cup of latte sprang unbidden back into my thoughts, and I couldn't resist the draw of their comfy chairs and a warm cup clasped between my hands. I might have emerged alive from my glacial expedition, but my extremities were still numb from the cold, my hair plastered to my forehead by the rain. A few creature comforts were due before I retired to the back of the van.

* * *

On my way out of town the following morning I found time for a detour to visit the foot of the region's other icy attraction, the Fox glacier. It only took about half an hour from Franz Josef, and once I'd parked it was an easy walk through the valley floor to the glacier itself. Thankfully the rain had dried up today, and my beaten-up footwear was just about up to the task. I reminded myself to visit a shoe store as soon as I was back in civilization again. Whenever that might be.

The glacier was originally called the Victoria Glacier, but in 1872 it was renamed to commemorate a visit by New Zealand Premier Sir William Fox. The ice here looked less steep than that at Franz Josef, but as I neared the foot of the glacier itself, where a torrent of clear, cold water raged out of a naturally formed cave, I realised that the face was even sheerer than that which we'd faced yesterday. The public barriers were set further back, too, and a large warning sign alerted us to the potential dangers of straying past them. In addition to falling ice there was a risk of the glacier dropping rocks it had picked up from the valley sides, and the river sometimes surged and burst its banks as water was released from beneath the ice. All in all in wasn't a safe place to be, and I felt no urge to cross the barriers and experience this natural minefield for myself. There were already plenty of ways to die in New Zealand, without adding another three to the list.

Ka Mate

As I contemplated the vast ice wall in front of me – its muddy, blackened surface occasionally allowing glimpses of the blue compacted ice within – I noticed a group of walkers climbing over the barriers to my right. I almost shouted a warning to them, worried that they hadn't seen the large, obvious sign informing us of their impending death and dismemberment, but then I realised that they were following a professional guide, identifiable by his utterly unsuitable knee-length shorts and sturdy walking boots. No one else would be masochistic enough to expose their legs to such chilling temperatures, and I breathed a small sigh of relief. At least if they died they were doing it under supervision.

In reality part of me was jealous as I headed back in the opposite direction, away from the ice. Yesterday's experience had been a unique one, and surprisingly fulfilling, allowing a brief glimpse of natural wonders that I'd only previously seen in photo books and magazines. My thighs were still stiff from the walk up the valley sides, though, and my grey sweatshirt was hanging from the curtain pole in the back of the van, in the desperate hope that it might dry out during the day. For the time being my memories would have to suffice.

As if on cue I felt a raindrop hit my cheek, and before I had the chance to pick up my pace the heavens opened, pelting the valley with cold droplets the size of pebbles. I pulled my waterproof around me and scurried as fast as my aching thighs could manage, but by the time I reached the safety of the van I was drenched through, my jeans sticking heavily to my legs as I scrambled inside. A glance back up the valley showed that the clouds had descended again, and the Fox Glacier was hidden from view behind a grey veil. I turned the heating on and directed the fans at my legs, which were now beginning to shiver as the wet cotton clung tight, but almost an hour later, passing through the village of Haast, I patted my thighs again and found that they were still damp. I could only assume that when Julius von Haast passed this way in the late nineteenth century, naming everything that crossed his path, he brought some heavy-duty waterproofs with him.

The wet and wild west coast was living up to its reputation, but thankfully the time had come for me to turn inland again. Among the mountains sat the playground of Queenstown, home to the rich and famous, and holiday destination for thrill-seekers the world over. I could feel my adrenaline start to pump as the sea retreated in the rearview mirror, the van's rusted hood pointing to higher ground. Extreme sports, here I come.

18
Tahuna *(Queenstown)*

As I stood on the grassy slopes of Bob's Peak the following afternoon I tried not to think about what we were preparing to do. Luckily the streets of Queenstown were hidden from view, although the tiny dots of the boats out on the crystal blue lake didn't fill me with confidence. Pius, my large and over-friendly Italian guide, only checked my straps briefly, apparently trusting my clumsy attempts at fastening the harness. If I'd known that his checks would be so perfunctory I'd have taken a bit more time over them myself.

'Are we ready?'

His accent made him difficult to understand, and with the alpine wind whistling about my ears it took me a few moments to translate his thick vowels. Before I had a chance to answer him he had positioned himself behind me, and I felt his hand tap my shoulder.

'Run.'

It would have been easy at that moment to sit back down on the grass and call it a day. Somehow, though, my instincts for self-preservation had been temporarily silenced. This was Queenstown, after all. I began pumping my legs, my feet hitting the turf hard as I struggled against the machinery – and the large Italian – strapped to my back. At first it felt as if someone had tied me to a car as a prank, and I almost turned around to check that everything was as it should be. Then the thought of Pius's withering look made me pound my feet even harder. We were nearing the edge of the cliff now, and with it a sixteen hundred foot drop down to the town below. My mind flitted back to those straps again. I really should have spent more time tightening them.

And then something changed behind me. Where there had been resistance before there was now a slight tug, as if Pius had sprouted a pair of wings and was trying to pull me off my feet. It was an odd sensation, simultaneously lifting me up and dragging me back, and I was almost too busy marvelling at it to notice that I was suddenly a few inches off the ground. I may have been lifted off my feet but we were still travelling forward at some speed, the cliff edge disappearing beneath us as Queenstown came into view, the houses looking no larger than Monopoly pieces. After a few seconds I remembered to stop wiggling my legs, and I pulled down self-consciously on my helmet strap, trusting it to see me safely home. Sixteen hundred feet looked an awfully long way to fall.

At the start of the day I hadn't intended to end up nearly half a mile above the ground with a large Italian strapped to my back. My plan had been to bungee jump at the site of the very first bungee, Queenstown's Kawarau Bridge, and I'd driven there in the van, filled with an irrational desire to throw myself from it.

If the story of commercial bungee jumps started at a rather rickety bridge just outside of Queenstown, though, the true origin of the semi-suicidal sport lay further north. As part of the harvest ritual on the Vanuatu Islands the young men used to build a tower of lashed-together branches, which they would then tie themselves to with long vines before throwing themselves off. If they were lucky they'd have cut the vine to almost exactly the correct length, and it'd pull them up just as they hit the ground, lessening the blow and simultaneously wrenching their legs out of their sockets. If they were unlucky they'd cut it too long, the results of which you can imagine for yourself. As harvest festivals go, it was a pretty messy one.

Fortunately for adrenaline addicts the world over, a documentary on these rituals happened to be watched by some members of the Oxford University Dangerous Sports Club during the Seventies, and they decided to stage some attempted jumps of their own. Their equipment was still primitive, but it provided them all with a bit of a giggle in between lectures, and nothing more was thought of it.

Until Kiwi entrepreneur A J Hackett happened upon a video of the Dangerous Sports Club in action, that is. While others might have wondered why these English intellectuals were throwing themselves off things with such gay abandon, Hackett immediately saw the dollar signs flashing before his eyes. Enlisting the help of friend and fellow speed-skier Henry van Asch, he began to pioneer what became the modern bungee cord. Their first tests were undertaken at the Ponts de la Caille near Annecy in eastern France, and once the equipment was ready they decided to launch their new adrenaline-sport in the most high-profile manner possible. In June 1987, A J Hackett threw himself off the Eiffel Tower.

The stunt resulted in his immediate arrest by some stereotypically dour-faced gendarmes, but he was released a few minutes later into a blaze of media attention. The following year the Kawarau Bridge bungee opened, and since then over 500,000 people had thrown themselves into space above the torrents of the Kawarau River while attached to a large piece of elastic. A J Hackett was now a very rich man.

When I pulled into the Kawarau parking lot my eyes weren't drawn to the bridge itself, however: I was too busy looking at the crowd. Some of the revenue from the bungee had been poured back into developing their facilities, which now included a space-age visitors' centre and a large wooden viewing balcony. It was here that I joined the gathered masses to worship at the altar of Hackett, fifty of us jostling for elbow-room as we waited for the poor fools on the bridge to jump. It might have resembled a public execution, but the $140 price tag told the true story. At least you got the hangman's noose for free.

The first jumper was obviously a regular visitor, as he hardly needed any encouragement to throw himself off their slightly ramshackle platform into the crisp New Zealand air. I watched as he hung for a second in midair, before gravity reasserted itself and he plummeted towards the river below. They'd set the bungee slightly longer than normal, and his head dipped in the water before the cord pulled him up again, dragging an arc of spray behind him. He bounced a couple of times, the cord jerking him from side to side, then they launched their small yellow dinghy and gathered him safely in. The whole experience took a little under three minutes, including the time it took to return him to dry land. I'd expected the bungee to be thrilling, but I'd never expected it to be so brief.

As I stood watching the conveyor belt of jumpers I decided not to bother signing up for it myself. I knew that I'd be berated for it when I returned home, but the hefty price tag had sapped any desire that I might have had to throw myself from this particular bridge. Outside of Las Vegas there couldn't be a quicker way to lose $140, and I didn't exactly have the spare cash to throw into this churning river. Besides, Queenstown was reputedly the adrenaline sports capital of the world. Surely there must be something more satisfying to spend my few spare dollars on?

A quick examination of the map showed me that the Shotover Jet was located nearby, so I decided to give that a look instead. I knew very little about jetboats, apart from the fact that one of them had ruined my attempts at photography at Taupo's Huka Falls. I figured that I should keep an open mind, though, and this particular company had been recommended to me by a couple in Fiji. Their literature told me that they'd ferried over two million passengers down the Shotover River, which by my calculations made them at least four times as popular as the Kawarau Bridge bungee. With figures like that behind them I had to see what all the fuss was about.

In a nutshell, jetboating was exactly as it sounded. The hi-tech boats had an internal propeller that sucked water in through the hull, then drove it out again through jet nozzles at the rear. Not only did this unique propulsion device allow them to reach speeds of forty-five miles an hour in the Shotover River's narrow canyons, it also offered them a flexibility of movement that was unknown in regular craft. Here at Shotover the boats had two engines and two nozzles, allowing them to turn sharply, brake, and even send the boat into a three-sixty degree spin. It put Hackett's little yellow dinghy to shame.

Once I'd been suited up in a full-length waterproof and scarlet lifejacket we were herded onto our boat, the crew ushering us through the iron gates like cattle. With the sun sparkling off the surface of the river it all looked remarkably tranquil, and I wondered if Shotover's reputation had been exaggerated. Apart from anything else, it looked like quite a nice spot for a picnic.

I didn't have to wonder for long. Once our pilot was in place he checked that we were all securely fastened, then the boat roared into life. I'm not a huge fan of rollercoasters, and I generally believe that anything worth seeing is worth seeing slowly, but I couldn't keep myself from grinning as we hurtled away, my back pressed firmly into the seat. Taking the bends we were flung viciously from side to side, and even in my nervous state I marvelled at the company's excellent safety record. Perhaps it only felt like I was about to be flung into the icy waters of the river.

The experience was over all too soon, although a quick glance at my watch told me that it had taken just over twenty minutes. My legs were a little shaky once I stepped onto solid ground again, but I couldn't keep an idiotic smile from spreading across my face. To my great surprise, jetboating had turned out to be fun.

It took a few sips of water back at the van to restore a degree of calm to my battered nervous system, then I began to consult the map again. My day of adrenaline sports in Queenstown was only half over. Now that I had the bit between my teeth, I wanted to make the most of it. It occurred to me that I'd experienced extreme speed – what I needed next was extreme height. The bungee still looked too expensive, and it finished far too quickly for my liking, which sent me back to the drawing board. Where else could I experience the thrills of extreme heights without having to dunk my head in a river? What else was there in Queenstown to jump off, apart from the bridge?

This might go some way towards explaining how I came to be strapped to an overweight Italian sixteen hundred feet off the ground, the houses of the town laid out beneath me like a Lego set. I shuffled my butt back in the harness, just to make sure that there was no chance of falling out. On the way up I'd heard stories about a tourist whose equipment had failed, sending him plummeting into the backyard of an unexpecting resident, breaking almost every bone in his body in the process. At the time I'd written it off as an urban myth, but it now felt worryingly feasible. I tugged on my helmet strap again, just to be sure.

Suddenly there was a ringing sound behind me, and for a fraction of a second I thought that it might be some kind of alarm, warning us of our impending death in an old lady's flowerbed. Fortunately Pius's laughter set me at ease.

'Sorry, that's my cell phone. It seems someone wants to talk to me. They always call at the worst time, eh?'

I managed to stutter a cursory yes, trying to drag my eyes away from a particularly solid-looking paved garden.

'Too damn right. You feeling okay?'

I wasn't sure that he'd heard my last outburst, so this time I gave him the thumbs-up.

'You fancy doing some acrobatics before we land?'

To be frankly honest, part of me wanted to say no. No matter how hard that part screamed in my head, though – while pointing out the very solid ground that lay almost a thousand feet below us – I still managed to give him the thumbs-up again. I figured I might as well live a little, even if it wasn't for very long.

'Hold on tight then.'

At first I barely noticed the change in direction, but then the ground slid away, our bodies spinning in a tight spiral that sent the world reeling past my left ear. Then Pius span us the other way, and I tried to imagine the s-shaped trajectory that we were following through the sky, if only to take my mind off the fact that the earth kept moving beneath us, and that I was rapidly losing any sense of up or down.

After a couple of minutes we resumed a steady course, and I felt a hand tap me on the shoulder.

'That was good, eh?'

I swallowed against the dryness in my throat and managed to prize my hand off the strap long enough give a final thumbs-up. It had been good, if incredibly unnerving. The bungee wasn't looking quite so daring after all.

Once we were back on the ground, having crash-landed clumsily in the sports field of the local school, Pius set about folding away the parachute while I unbuckled myself from the rigging. He grinned as I stepped shakily out of the harness, my feet remarkably glad to feel the reassurance of firm ground again, but still a little unsure of its solidity.

'Not bad for two heavy pricks, eh?'

I couldn't help smiling and nodding in agreement. We'd drifted over the houses of Queenstown for a little over ten minutes, rising at first as a thermal took hold of us before slowly cruising back to terra firma. Not bad at all, really. A quick glance at my watch told me that I still had a couple of hours to spare before the sun went down, but I'd already had enough excitement for one day. What little adrenaline I had left would be just enough to propel me back to my camper van, then I intended to sit very still for at least half an hour while my equilibrium restored itself. With my feet firmly planted on the floor, of course.

* * *

That evening I received an unexpected phonecall from Gwil, the Welshman I'd met on the Franz Josef Glacier climb. He was in Queenstown too, having arrived on the Kiwi Experience bus that morning, and it occurred to me that he'd probably seen me spiralling through the air a few hours ago. Eager to boast about my day's escapades I agreed to meet him for a drink, so we arranged a time and a place. I even took the complementary photos of my jump to show him.

As it turned out, the boasting was soon forgotten as we caught up on each other's adventures. He was rapidly tiring of the 'fuck truck', leaving the teenagers to explore their rampaging hormones while he set off in search of some local colour. We shared stories while I introduced him to the pleasures of Monteith's Celtic Red, then one of us came up with the idea of visiting the town's gimmicky 'ice bar'.

The concept at Minus Five was a simple one. The venue itself consisted of a single cramped room, with a bar, a handful of tables, and some benches. What made it special was the fact that the entire room was maintained at a temperature of minus five degrees, and the tables, benches, and the bar itself were sculpted entirely from ice. For a mere $25 they provided gloves, hooded coats and a 'complimentary' vodka cocktail, while you shivered and giggled for half an hour in their surprisingly stylish chiller cabinet.

Ka Mate

The most fun bit was waving through the frosted glass at the revellers in the regular bar next door, imaginatively called 'The Boiler Room', but after our half hour was up I was glad to walk outside and feel my fingers and toes again. Gwil and I parted ways with a promise to meet up again, then I staggered back to where my van was parked, a camping site in the shadow of Bob's Peak.

Today I'd jetted at forty-five miles an hour down a raging river, jumped off a sixteen hundred foot high cliff, and drunk a cocktail at sub-zero temperatures. After all that I figured that I deserved a good night's sleep.

19
Otepoti *(Dunedin)*

As I drove through Central Otago the following day, passing through Cromwell and Alexandra before joining Highway One to Dunedin, I suddenly realised what had been missing so far on my road trip. New Zealand was famous across the world for its sheep – and, more importantly, its lamb – but my encounters with the country's woolly inhabitants had been few and far between. There were allegedly forty-five million sheep in New Zealand, outnumbering the people ten-to-one. So where were they all?

The answer, apparently, was Central Otago. As I drove through the rural lanes, gradually edging closer to Dunedin, I began to come across fields packed with white, bleating animals. And when I say packed, I mean from rickety timber fence to crumbling stone wall. There were at least three hundred sheep in some of the fields, their vast numbers made all the more imposing by the way that they moved as one, the grubby white masses flowing across the grass to break against one wall like a wave, before someone else picked up the lead and sent them careering in another direction. It was safe to say that I'd never come close to seeing so many sheep before in my entire life, and I had to slow the van down to gawp at them through the windscreen. Forty-five million was starting to look a little conservative.

Once I'd recovered from the threat of imminent ovine invasion I began to pay attention to the road. The drive to Dunedin was a slow one, my path zigzagging across the sheep-strewn countryside, and by the time I arrived on the city's outskirts the sun was just starting to dip below the horizon. Luckily I'd booked a spot at a conveniently placed caravan park before leaving Queenstown, and it only took me five minutes to find the site and check in. The park was clean and well-equipped, but more importantly it was located within walking distance of Dunedin's rugby stadium, affectionately known as The House Of Pain. As well as booking the caravan site, I'd also treated myself to a ticket for the match that night, a clash between local team the Highlanders and the visiting Australian Brumbies. After the spectacle in Christchurch this opportunity was too good to miss.

My ticket was for the Railway Stand, situated just to one side of the standing-only terraces, and after I'd collected it I made my way to the bar. The House Of Pain had taken the progressive step of allowing you to buy an entire six-pack of beer in one purchase, so having loaded my arms with a mini-crate of refreshments I staggered up the steps into the stand, stashing it beneath my seat so that I didn't have to sit hugging it like an alcoholic. Down here men were expected to drink heartily, but I didn't want to finish the night in a gutter.

Beer had played a pivotal role in developing the image of the 'Southern Man', a gritty, macho 'man's man' that had become one of the defining images of the Otago region. They liked to think that their men were tougher, wilier and, to some extent, surlier than your average Kiwi male, never mind a soft touring Brit. The image had been a well-known stereotype for decades, but in the early Nineties Dunedin's Speights brewery had used the Southern Man as a slightly tongue-in-cheek icon for their TV commercials. So ingrained in the local consciousness was the stereotype that the tongue-in-cheek aspect seemed to have been lost on most of the inhabitants of Dunedin, and the Southern Man was alive and grizzly on almost every street corner. Rugged, solitary, unsuited to city life, they were easily spotted as I tried to get comfortable in my plastic seat. The temperature was dropping rapidly tonight and I could see my breath misting in the air, but the terraces were filled with a staggering, swearing mass of good old fashioned blokes, flexing their muscles in sleeveless vests and occasionally tugging on the brims of their hats. Local colour was all well and good, but I was glad that I'd opted for the quieter Railway Stand.

The match started with the local team's mascot running onto the pitch in a long, curly wig and a kilt, whirling a large plastic sword around his head and doing his best Mel Gibson impression. I stifled any urge to laugh, casting a few nervous glances towards the adrenaline-sodden crowds on the terraces, but things only got worse as he proceeded to grab a microphone from one of the attendants and sing the team song in a poor Scottish accent. Somehow the Highlanders had become 'the Highlarndeeees', and I drowned my giggles with the dregs from the first can of beer. It was a ridiculous caricature of Scottish nationalism, and yet the gathered fans were lapping it up with glee. I was reminded of the slick performance I'd seen at the Crusaders match up in Christchurch, the pitch being circled by horsemen in full battle gear while the braziers blazed, and inevitably Dunedin came off worst. As Braveheart left the field to whoops of approval I allowed myself a brief, nervous smile. Mel Gibson had a lot to answer for.

Fortunately the action on the pitch made up for this farcical opening, and I'd chosen the perfect night to watch the Highlanders display some true southern grit and determination. They had already won their previous four matches, and if they clinched tonight's match it would be a record winning-streak for the team. The Brumbies were fancied as favourites, but, as any sports fan will tell you, anything can happen once the players are out on the pitch. The Highlanders were obviously in a good run of form, and we all prayed that it would continue.

As they kicked off the wall of noise hit me. The fifteen thousand capacity crowd at the House Of Pain might not be as impressive as that at Christchurch's Jade Stadium, but what they lacked in numbers they made up for with sheer passion and aggression. Someone had snuck some kind of horn or klaxon into the ground, and as the players put in a few audibly bone-crunching tackles on the field the horn blared in the background. Off to my left the fans in the terraces roared and jostled with every ebb and flow of play, and once again I was glad that I'd opted for the more sedate seated ticket. The terraces certainly offered a flurry of excitement and colour, but it looked as if a scrawny northerner like me wouldn't escape without bruises and broken limbs. With fans that were as physical as this, it was no wonder that New Zealand produced such outstanding players.

The visiting Brumbies took an early lead, but as the mob of Southern Men got behind their local team the tide started to turn. With some solid defence the Highlanders kept them contained, and a kick from Nick Evans quickly put the home team on the scoreboard. By the time the final whistle went they'd managed to scrape ahead of the touring Australians by a single point, the local boys winning 19-18. By the way the stadium erupted you'd have thought they'd just won the entire competition. This was the best run of form the Highlanders had ever enjoyed, and the fans looked determined to make the most of it.

It was with some embarrassment that I found myself muttering the 'Highlarndeeees' song as I stumbled home, and I couldn't help smiling as I felt the cold night air smart my skin. Maybe they'd make a Southern Man out of me yet.

Dan Coxon

* * *

Once my head had cleared the following morning I felt I should pay a visit to the Mecca for all true Southern Men: Dunedin's Speights brewery. The company had been brewing in the city since 1876, but they'd only moved to their current site in 1940. It still incorporated some of the original building, but their popularity had started to outstrip their ability to produce: the new building allowed them to increase their output, setting up a brewing empire that still ruled the South Island today.

The new structure was unique in its own right, as it was one of the few gravity breweries still functioning in today's world of big business. It towered eight stories high, and ingredients were added on each level as the beer worked its way down, until it reached the ground floor where it should, hopefully, be ready to drink. If the beer I'd sampled last night was anything to go by, then they produced a fairly powerful brew.

There was also a distinctly Kiwi flavour to the beer, for while they imported sugar from Australia, the hops came from Napier, the main malt was shipped down the coast from Canterbury, and even the large barrels (or gyles) that housed the fermenting beer were constructed from New Zealand kauri wood. Today they would cost hundreds of thousands of dollars to construct, since kauri was at a premium, and Speights was one of only two breweries in the world to still use them. Originally handcrafted in 1946, shortly after the new building opened, the gyles had recently been restored by one of the team that built them sixty years ago, and the brewery now had four in use once again.

If we remained in any doubt as to the popularity of Speights, there were four ways to buy their beer: by the bottle, by the can, by the keg, or by the tanker. The tankers were introduced in 1951 due to the vast demand for their product, and they gave some idea of the huge volume of

Speights that was consumed. It was now the second most popular beer in New Zealand after Lion Red, and thanks to their Southern Man commercials it looked as if it might soon be Number One.

Once we reached the tasting room we were encouraged to pull our own drinks, much as we had at the Monteith's brewery, and I was able to show off my newfound talent for bar work. Their Harvest beer, made from locally-grown apricots, had a curiously sweet taste that was a little too cloying for my palette, but the Old Dark was a clear favourite, slightly lighter than your average Porter but with a smooth, chocolaty aftertaste. Rumour had it that it wreaked havoc on your digestive system, but thankfully the few tasters we were granted weren't enough to put that rumour to the test.

Before I left central Dunedin there was still one place that I had to visit. Outside the railway station stood a signpost, marking a distance of 18,869 kilometres to my old home city of Edinburgh, Scotland. When the site of modern Dunedin was first purchased in 1844 it was bought for the building of 'New Edinburgh', and following a financial crisis in the New Zealand Company in 1845 the Association of Lay Members of the Free Church of Scotland supported the plan. Surveyor Charles Kettle had intended to base the settlement's layout on Edinburgh's street plan, but due to the different terrain it was only the street names that made it through to the construction stage.

The sight of George Street, Princes Street and Moray Place still made me smile, though, and even as I stood beside the signpost I felt curiously close to home. Their kilted rugby mascot may be little more than a cartoonish shadow of Scots nationalism, but at least today felt brisk enough to be a Scottish autumn.

* * *

The Otago Peninsula stuck out from the side of Dunedin like the proverbial sore thumb. Yet another example of the country's volcanic past, it sat across one of the fault lines that criss-crossed the country, its narrow harbour the remnant of an explosion that had split the original volcano in two. Steep hills rose to either side of the natural inlet, and it was easy to imagine its original shape beneath the swathes of lush green grass. This grass itself was a modern addition, however, having been imported from Wales by the European settlers, after they'd burnt the native forest to the ground. They also introduced English gorse and Scottish thistles, which now grew like weeds across the peninsula. As an example of ecological vandalism Otago was truly quite outstanding.

I was being taken out onto the peninsula by Elm Wildlife Tours, a local company that had been granted access to some unique wildlife sites. Much like Kaikoura, the Otago Peninsula sat close to the submerged continental shelf, creating a help-yourself buffet of sea life only a short distance from its shore. I'd already had a few close encounters with fur seals further north, but here they promised us Hooker sealions and Yellow-eyed penguins, both of which were notoriously difficult to view in the wild. Add in the Royal albatross colony at Taiaroa Head and the area was beginning to feel like a wildlife park.

As we drew closer to Taiaroa we drove through the peninsula's swamp-like estuary region, a large, shallow lagoon that teemed with animal and plant life. Our driver Shaun told me that you could walk across the lagoon at low tide without getting your shorts wet, and from the number of wading birds out on the water it was easy to believe. As well as oystercatchers and White-faced herons there were several Black swans, another introduced species, this time ferried to New Zealand's shores from Australia. The local farmers considered them a pest, their presence ruining the pastureland that lay close to the water, but out on the lagoon they looked remarkably regal and serene. The settlers had introduced them because of the aesthetic spectacle they provided, as well as the fact that they were rather good to eat. I knew nothing about the latter, but I could certainly vouch for the spectacle. It was almost impossible to tear my eyes away from them as they glided across the still water.

If the swans looked regal in their serenity, however, then the albatrosses were majestic in their size and presence. The albatross was the world's largest seabird, and the Royal albatross was the largest of the family, often measuring up to four feet long from beak to tail and almost ten feet in wingspan. What made Taiaroa so special was that it was the only mainland albatross colony anywhere in the world, and the Department of Conservation had respected their duty to preserve and protect it.

As we stood on the headland, watching the birds flying inland from the open sea, Shaun battled against the wind roaring past our ears to try and tell me something about the area.

'The average lifespan for the Royal albatross is forty-five years,' he shouted, his words almost getting blown over the cliff edge, 'but we've got one old girl here who we think's sixty-eight, maybe even older. We call her Grandma. She outlived her first mate, then she took up with a younger male, her toy boy. Then she dumped him for a third male, but he died. So she went back to the toy boy again. In the ten years she was with the other male, the toy boy stayed faithful to her. That'll maybe give some idea of what the albatross is like – they're usually pretty faithful.' It all sounded like an episode of *Dallas*, but Grandma's survival was a sign of how well the area had been protected and maintained, even if it was only to allow her to carry on her romantic dalliances.

When we'd had enough of watching the giant seabirds soar over the cliff edge we returned to our minibus, and Shaun drove around the coast to a private beach. Due to the cliffs we couldn't drive down to the seafront itself, so we parked in a field and walked down the steep path to the beach. Before our toes even touched a grain of sand I could make out the sealions in the distance, their solid masses appearing as dark blots on the light-coloured sand. We didn't need to get close to sense their impressive bulk, or to sample their distinctive odour, a combination of fish and wet dog that brought back my earlier fur seal encounters. Hopefully today's trip wouldn't be quite so hair-raising.

Before we had a chance to meet the Hookers, though, the penguins ambushed us. The path was flanked on either side by dense shrubbery and undergrowth, and as we neared the beach a frantic chirping reached out ears, turning into a high-pitched trill. It was the sound of the Yellow-eyed penguins calling to each other, hidden among the shrubs that had recently been replanted to encourage nesting. They were called *hoiho* by the local Maori, meaning 'noise shouter', because of their distinctive cries. As if on cue two of them also began to emerge from the waves, waddling quickly up the beach as they ran the gauntlet between the water and the undergrowth. Short, almost delicate, with a golden flash behind their eyes that had earned them their name, they looked exposed and twitchy as they propelled themselves clumsily up the sand.

We soon saw what was making them hurry, for off to their right lounged a female sea lion. She was smaller than the heavy males that lay further up the beach, about the size of an adult fur seal, but she still dwarfed the tiny flightless birds. The penguins were perfectly safe, though: she was more interested in the taller visitors to her beach. Lumbering towards us on her fins she covered the ground at a surprising rate, and when we finally stepped down onto the sand she was already within a few feet. Shaun stepped between us, his camera bag held out in front of him as a perfunctory shield, in case she should lunge.

'They're actually faster than us on land,' he whispered as he backed away up the beach, looking like a low-budget Steve Irwin. 'They just can't keep it up for long distances. Their bite's nasty though, and they'll often get infected. We've got to be careful to stay away from them, for their good and ours.'

It turned out that our female was fairly rare, there only being ten among the hundred and fifty sealions that inhabited the peninsula, but she followed us eagerly, unaware of her protected status. Once or twice she lunged towards us, and we were forced to retreat back onto the grass-covered dunes, where the sealions rarely ventured. Eventually Shaun tired of the constant jousting, and holding his camera bag-shield before him he chased her back into the sea, carefully protecting his arms as he did so. She was naturally curious, but in the natural world curiosity could be lethal.

As we passed out of her range we entered the circle of males, and the stench of their mammoth bodies assaulted our senses. The smaller, younger ones reared up from time to time, sparring with each other for status and dominance, but the larger, older males lay where they were, solid masses of flesh and fat, their skin often scarred by old battle wounds. They had no fear of our presence as they were no longer hunted in these waters, but the same wouldn't have been true in previous centuries. The Maori had hunted the Hooker sea lion close to extinction on New Zealand's shores, and even now there were only a small number remaining. After driving through the manufactured countryside earlier in the day, it was a timely reminder that the Maori had also disrupted the country's natural balance, and that they themselves were a settler people. It was easy to forget that us Europeans weren't the only ecological villains in the planet's history.

We passed the pack of males slowly on our way to the bird hide, but they didn't acknowledge our presence. From the hide we could watch the penguins returning from the sea in relative peace, away from the sounds and the stench of the sealions, and we took turns laughing as they hopped clumsily up the steep dunes into their nests among the undergrowth. With every hop they looked as if they might slip and fall, yet not a single one did, their webbed feet gripping the loose soil as they leapt. It was an unusual sight, and one that kept a smile on my face as we sauntered back.

By the time we reached our minibus the sun was beginning to dip below the horizon again, and the field was mired in grey murk. Shaun asked us to look out for possums in the headlights as we drove back, and in sharp contrast to the ecological messages earlier in the day he told us that he'd accelerate if he saw any in the road. In Australia they were a protected species, but here they were considered a pest, destroying trees and feeding on the young of many local birds and other wildlife. The penguins had been particularly badly hit, and as they laid only two eggs per season a rampant possum could affect the survival of the whole species in this area. If the possums won the current battle, then some of these species could vanish once again from the Otago Peninsula.

I was surprisingly tired by the time Shaun dropped me off at my caravan park, and I decided to turn in early after the day's excitement. Tomorrow I'd start heading south again, towards the bottom tip of the island. Many people had advised me to avoid it, but I was keen to see what made Invercargill so unpopular. I'd already visited the northernmost point of mainland New Zealand – now the south was calling.

Ka Mate

20
Waihōpai *(Invercargill)* – Te Anau

The following morning I made an early start, having heard that the coastal drive down to the bottom of the island took longer than expected. From Dunedin I was heading south to Balclutha, named after the Gaelic for 'town on the Clyde', then from there'd I'd take the snaking, winding route through the Catlins almost as far as Invercargill itself. I'd also been warned that the area was best explored over a period of two or three days, but the clock was ticking and I desperately wanted to see New Zealand's infamous Fiordland National Park before heading home. I intended to be in Invercargill by nightfall.

It took me a while to reach the Catlins, but it was worth enduring the early-morning traffic for. I stopped at McLean Falls to stretch my legs, and to watch the streams meeting in a furious maelstrom of spray and refracted light. It wasn't the highest waterfall that I'd seen, but it was certainly one of the most frenetic.

There was one more stop that I wanted to make as I drove through the gently rolling countryside of the Catlins, and late in the afternoon I pulled into the lay-by for Slope Point. It was widely believed that Bluff, just south of Invercargill, marked the southernmost point of the South Island, but this was a fallacy. Bluff was the southernmost *inhabited* point, as well as the end of State Highway One on its route down the country – but for the geographical tip one had to drive out to Slope Point. The twenty-minute walk through unkempt fields showed why it was less popular, but to my great relief there was at least a marker to indicate the headland that I had come here for. I stood for a moment surveying the sea ahead, the only thing separating me from the icy wastes of Antarctica. There was a brisk breeze blowing in off the water, and it didn't stretch the imagination too much to picture this breeze starting its life amongst icebergs and plains of frozen snow. I was still only marginally closer to the South Pole than I was to the Equator, but I could see why so many tourists found their way here.

As I returned to the van a busload of backpackers pulled up alongside me, this time the aptly named 'Bottom Bus' that covered the lower end of the country, and I was glad to sneak away before they unloaded. No doubt the frozen deserts of Antarctica would have seemed even further away if I'd been surrounded by hungover, hormonal teenagers. I'd now visited both ends of the country, from Cape Reinga in the north to Slope Point in the south, and my journey was nearing its end. The thought was a sobering one, but there was still enough ahead of me to spur me on as the sun dipped in the sky.

By the time I reached Invercargill it was almost dark, and I drove straight to the campground. Exploring the city would have to wait until tomorrow. So far every city on my travels had offered some insight, or at least a diversion or two – I was intrigued to find out why Invercargill had such a poor reputation.

* * *

In daylight the mystery disappeared. This site had been chosen as the location for the South Island's most southerly city in 1857, but many of the buildings in the city centre seemed to date from the Sixties or Seventies, their blocks of grey concrete sitting solidly beneath an overcast sky. It looked modern, bland, and in places rundown and scrappy. If you'd come here expecting another Christchurch or Wellington, you'd have been disappointed.

I'd been warned in advance of its dull public face, though, and it didn't take much scratching beneath the surface to find at least a little character and excitement. An unassuming café was bright and vibrant once I stepped inside, and while I enjoyed an excellent latte I surveyed my options as a visitor. They were certainly thin on the ground, but there was enough to keep me occupied, and after finishing my coffee I walked back outside to the van. Time to put that reputation to the test.

My first stop was the Southland Museum, housed in a curious pyramid-like structure not far from the centre of town. They appeared to have several halls of exhibits, and the space was light and airy – but I was here for one thing only, and I clung single-mindedly to my purpose. As intriguing as their other exhibits looked, I had come to see Henry.

Henry was one of several tuatara housed at the museum, a living example of New Zealand's connection with prehistory. These were the last living representatives of a lineage that dated back over two hundred million years, most of their relatives dying out at the same time as the dinosaurs. The tuatara had lived on, however, and had now become the last living representatives of the sphenodontia line, a branch of the reptile family that was otherwise extinct.

It took me a few seconds to spot them inside their glass cages, but once one had emerged from the surrounding greenery they all became easier to pick out. They looked remarkably like lizards, hidden by their mottled green hides against the background foliage, the males boasting a spiny crest along their backbone. It was this crest that marked them out from their close relatives, for they weren't actually spines at all, but rather a row of stunted feathers, perhaps the clearest indication of the link between avians and reptiles. It was fascinating to watch them, despite the fact that they hardly moved at all, and amazing to think that almost identical remains had been found in fossil beds dating back a hundred and fifty million years.

Henry was the last tuatara in the row, the great granddaddy of the lot. He'd hatched around 1880, making him over a hundred and twenty years old, although he'd only been resident in the Southland Museum since 1971. I tried desperately to catch him moving, but after five minutes of watching I only just managed a glimpse of his chest rising for a fraction of a second. Eventually I gave up and walked back to the van. When I reached a hundred and twenty years old I probably wouldn't feel like performing for tourists either.

The tourism options in Invercargill were turning out to be as limited as its reputation suggested, but a short drive down the highway took me to the town of Bluff. There wasn't much by way of entertainment here either, but it did mark the end of State Highway One, the road that I'd first joined on my drive out of Auckland. It ran down the centre of the North Island, miraculously jumped across the water at the Cook Strait, then wound a course down the east coast of the South Island before ending up here, at the bottom end of the country. Stewart Island still lay across the Foveaux Strait, but it had remained largely uninhabited and contained few roads at all, never mind a highway. This was the end of the road, and the southernmost reach of Kiwi civilization.

The location itself was relatively unspectacular, the Highway ending in a large turning circle marked by the obligatory yellow signpost, pointing out the vast distances to the world's major cities. There was also a plaque on a nearby wall, and while a family posed for photos by the signpost I shuffled off to one side to read it. It had been placed there in memory of William Stirling, the first pilot of the Bluff region and a 'Whaler, headman, mariner and pioneer'. Born in Kent in 1810, he'd arrived at Cuttle Cove – Southland's first whaling station, located in nearby Fiordland – in 1830. He'd died in Tiwai, across from where I now stood on the far side of Bluff Harbour, on December 12, 1851, aged just 41. It showed how harsh life was out here for the first settlers, and also demonstrated their pioneering spirit. William Stirling might have had a short life, but his achievements were still remembered.

The headland was being constantly buffeted by the high winds blowing in off the sea, and after a few minutes I retreated to the warmth and shelter of my van. There was one more place that I wanted to visit before I left Bluff behind me, and this was one that I definitely didn't want to miss out.

If the life of William Stirling exemplified a certain type of Kiwi spirit and ingenuity, then Fred and Myrtle Flutey were near-perfect examples of the other end of the scale. By the time I arrived at their house both Fred and Myrtle had been dead for several years, but thankfully the building was still open to the public. Known as the Paua Shell House, the Flutey home had become something of a national institution, and had been granted a certificate by the New Zealand Tourist Industry Federation for its twenty-seven years of hospitality. I'd heard that it was a sight to behold, and I found myself holding my breath as I parked outside.

From the exterior it didn't look vastly different to any other house on the street, although there was a rather ornate fountain on the front lawn. It was what was inside, however, that made the house so special. It had all started when Fred began to bring back the native paua shells from his fishing trips to Fiordland. The shells were large and bowl-shaped, and when sanded down and polished they turned a remarkable iridescent hue, mottled silver with occasional swirls of green and blue as if the surface had retained its natural oils. Fred had hung a few of these shells around the fireplace, only to discover that Myrtle was curiously fond of them. So he carried on adding them. And adding them. And adding them.

There were a total of one thousand one hundred and thirty paua shells displayed around the house by the time of his death, covering every wall of their lounge, so that the entire room seemed to shimmer as it reflected the light. Fred had sanded and polished many of them himself in the shed at the end of the yard, although there were some that he'd traded with fans from overseas. Two large, black Brazilian paua shells rested by the fireplace, spots of austerity in a shrine to all that was kitsch. The largest shell lay in a separate cabinet to one side, and was the size of a generous breakfast bowl.

I'd been prepared for the excessive quantity of paua shells, but their collection of other bric-a-brac caught me by surprise. In one corner stood a stuffed deer, surveying his gaudy territory with glassy eyes, while dried seahorses, starfish, and even pieces of petrified wood adorned the other surfaces. There were shell necklaces, shell mosaics, shell lampshades – as well as an abundance of plants and carefully compiled vignettes. The room was an intricate grotto devoted to everything shell-like, kitsch, or just a little bit shiny. I couldn't help wondering if Fred had suffered from a bizarre form of kleptomania.

Fred and Myrtle's grandson had recently moved across from Perth to look after the house and try to turn it into a viable business, and as I chatted with him his pride in his grandparents' achievement was obvious.

'Did you see Fred's favourite? It's on a separate table through there, the slightly pink one.'

When I admitted that I hadn't he dragged me back through to lounge, pointing out his grandfather's preferred shell. It was certainly slightly pinker than the others, although it was hard to see what would make someone choose it over the other one thousand one hundred and twenty-nine shells on display. He also pointed out the telegrams framed on the wall, one from the Queen and one from New Zealand's Prime Minister, both congratulating Fred and Myrtle on their sixty-fifth wedding anniversary. I was tempted to ask what their secret had been, but I worried that the answer would probably lie in their strange obsession with polished shells.

When I finally found my way back out into the real world it seemed curiously empty and uncluttered, and as I drove back up through Invercargill towards Te Anau I almost found myself missing the eccentric intricacies of the Fluteys' temple to obsession. I'd already heard so much about Fiordland, however, that I couldn't postpone my visit any longer. Tonight I'd stay in Te Anau, then tomorrow I'd finally experience the grandeur of Milford Sound.

* * *

'Who here's seen the *Lord Of The Rings* films?'

It was probably intended as a rhetorical question, but the ten of us that were crammed into the small minibus raised our hands, just in case. It was unlikely that there was a single person in New Zealand who hadn't seen them.

'A farmer here had one of his horses, Rusty, used in the films. He was one of the ring wraiths' horses, but as you might be able to guess from his name, Rusty's brown. So they painted him black for the filming. Weird, huh?'

It certainly did seem odd that they couldn't find an actual black horse anywhere in the country, but I was quickly learning that everyone on the South Island had a *Lord Of The Rings* anecdote to tell, and only a few of them would turn out to be true. We'd stopped at the farm in question on our way out to Milford Sound to drop off the owner's mail, and now that our chores were over Sarah, our guide for the day, strapped herself back into the driver's seat.

'Okay, let's head into Fiordland, shall we?'

We had to skirt the edge of Lake Te Anau first, giving us a chance to marvel at such a vast body of water. It was the largest lake in New Zealand after Lake Taupo, but at its deepest it descended to over thirteen hundred feet, and by volume it was actually the largest lake in all of Australasia. Its name came from a group of caves on its western shore, translating roughly as 'cave of rushing water', and I noticed that Sarah pronounced it 'Tee-arr-now'. I practiced it in my head as she drove us deeper into the National Park.

As if Lake Te Anau's record wasn't enough, Fiordland National Park was also New Zealand's largest national park, at approximately three million acres. In 1986 it was declared a World Heritage Area, due to the unique way in which it demonstrated the world's evolutionary history. It was no wonder that at the peak of the tourist season over a hundred tour buses would be driving the road from Te Anau to Milford every day.

By now we were heading towards the end of the season, though, which meant that we often had the road to ourselves. It allowed Sarah time to point out landmarks as we passed through some of the most spectacular scenery I'd encountered so far, and she also gave us an idea of the region's history.

'Deer hunting's always been a big sport in the area,' she told us over her headset. 'They were introduced early in the twentieth century as game for hunting, but their numbers grew out of control. They wrecked the forests too, which in turn caused landslides as the plant growth decreased and it couldn't bind the soil any more. Since the Sixties they've been seen as a pest, and actively hunted down. The guys used to come out here in helicopters and shoot them from above. That way they could get through large numbers in one go.

'Now, have any of you ever heard of bulldogging?' We shook our heads, although I doubted that she could see all of us in the bus's mirrors. 'Well, after a while these hunters realised that they were doing themselves out a job, especially since there was a big market for venison. They changed to catching them alive instead, since a live deer could sell to farms for around three thousand dollars. They still use the helicopters today, but instead of shooting them they fly low over their prey, then when the time's right the hunter jumps from the helicopter onto the deer's back, bringing it to the ground. Pretty crazy, huh?'

I had to agree – it sounded like a surefire way of breaking your neck.

'The record round here is for a hundred and nine deer caught in three days by just one man, so you can imagine how good they are at it. You've gotta be pretty tough to do it though. Maybe they should be training the rugby team this way, eh?'

Leaving us with this food for thought, she pulled the bus over to show us the entrance to the Homer Tunnel. Work on the tunnel first began in 1935, undertaken by a gang of ten men with pickaxes during the depth of the Depression. The first vehicle passed through in 1953, and in 1955, a full twenty years after work had begun, the tunnel was opened to the public. It ran for almost a mile through the heart of a mountain, and it was still in use as the only road route through to Milford. The name sprang from the nearby Homer Saddle, discovered by Harry Homer in 1889, but I was certain that the classical poet would have appreciated its epic qualities too.

By the time we reached the Milford Sound boat terminal I was already feeling overwhelmed by the sheer scale of the National Park's scenery, but I knew that there was even more to come. Milford was one of fourteen 'sounds' in the park, and despite their names all fourteen of them were fiords. Any well-trained geographer will tell you that a sound is a v-shaped river valley, while these were all u-shaped valleys, the remnants of the South Island's glacial past.

The boat that collected us was impressively large and spacious, but I still made sure to save myself a spot on deck as soon as I boarded. Fiordland had a reputation as the second wettest place on the planet, with an average yearly rainfall of over twenty-three feet, but today it was gloriously sunny, only the cool breeze from the open sea cutting through the heat. It was just as well, as there were no accommodation options for visitors at Milford, and Te Anau was several hours' drive away. I was only getting one chance to see some of the most breathtaking scenery that New Zealand had to offer, and I was determined to make the most of it.

As we pulled slowly away from the dock I looked up at the Stirling Falls off to our right, feeling a light spray from it already dusting my cheek. A curtain of water cascaded from the top of the cliffs, but it wasn't until the captain came on the P.A. system that I discovered that it was three times the height of Niagara Falls, and that on wet days the spray could stretch halfway across the fiord. The reason that it didn't look half this size was the fact that everything in Milford Sound was huge, and you lost all sense of scale as you passed between its peaks. Even our boat itself was enormous, but once we were out on the water it felt only marginally larger than a dinghy. In the distance I could just about make out another tour boat, a tiny white speck at the foot of the sheer cliffs of Mitre Peak. It was enough to make you dizzy.

Both the European settlers and the earlier Maori pioneers had left the area almost completely uninhabited, but it had nonetheless acquired a special significance for the Maori. According to mythology this region was the source of the jade stone they used for many of their ceremonial and precious items. As a society they didn't have metal objects, or any way of working or mining crude metals, so jade naturally became their most valuable raw material. According to some myths the jade, or *pounamu*, came from their homeland of Hawaiki, but a certain South Island myth placed its source much closer to home.

The guardian spirit of *pounamu* was a *taniwha* – a giant water creature – called Poutini, that lived in the waters off the west coast of the island. On a trip to the north Poutini captured Waitaiki, a beautiful maiden, the wife of Tamaahua. Poutini was so enamoured with her that he fled across Aotearoa with his captive, her husband in hot pursuit. Where Poutini stopped each night he lit a fire to warm Waitaiki – these places were still black from the flames, and unusually rich in *pounamu*. Eventually Tamaahua cornered him in what we now call Milford Sound. Rather than lose Waitaiki back to her husband, Poutini turned her into jade, and she formed the mother lode of all the *pounamu* that washed up along the west coast. It was true that much of the jade in the region originated from Milford Sound, but nowhere could I find out what had happened between Tamaahua and Poutini after these events had transpired. I couldn't imagine that he was overly happy at having his wife kidnapped then turned to stone, even if it was the semi-precious jade.

New Zealand was by no means the only source of jade. Most of the necklaces and jewellery sold in the local tourist shops had been produced from Canadian jade, and while it had been a rare and precious commodity among the original Maori settlers, the lucky Canadians had been blessed with entire mountains of the stuff. I'd even been told to check that anything I bought was at least crafted in New Zealand, as much of it was mass-produced in China. *Pounamu* might still hold a special significance for the Maori, but jade, it seemed, was now remarkably common.

When we reached the mouth of the fiord, where it joined the Abel Tasman Sea, the captain pointed out Anita

Bay to us. There were several orange-brown boulders along the shore, and it was these that the Maori came to Milford Sound for. They were composed almost entirely of bowenite, a more common form of jade than the precious nephrite. Traditionally they would light fires under the boulders to split them with the heat, carrying the splinters back to their communities for them to be worked on. This, then, was the final resting place of Waitaiki, although she now seemed to be going by the name of Anita. I was glad to hear that all jade in the area was now under Maori *tapu*, preventing it from being plundered by outside cultures. Some things at least were still sacred.

It was as we sailed back into the fiord that it truly struck me with its grandeur. The water today was bright blue, and from it the towering cliffs rose almost vertically skyward, the highest peaks still crowned with a smattering of snow. If you tuned out the drone of the engine there was an incredible sense of peace and tranquillity in the face of such natural beauty.

Once we were back on dry land it took several hours to drive back to Te Anau, but even then I found myself still awestruck by the wonders of Fiordland. It was all I could manage to wander into the small town for a takeaway burger, and to eat it clumsily at the edge of the lake as the last few rays of sunlight sparkled on the surface. My New Zealand adventures were nearing a close, but there could surely be no better place to end them. Even the indigestion from the onions didn't keep me from sleeping peacefully.

21
Moeraki – Otautahi *(Christchurch)*

I drove swiftly northwards again the next day, pausing briefly in Queenstown to refuel both the van and myself before veering east, back to the other coast. I had only a couple of days to reach Christchurch and return the van, before heading out of the country for good. The clock was counting down.

The fields of Central Otago were as I remembered them – flat, green and filled to the brim with sheep – although as the calendar turned around to fall the trees were taking on yellow, orange and purple hues. Once I hit Palmerston I turned northwards again, disappointed to be back within the confines of civilization, but aware of the short time I had to reach Canterbury's borders. I couldn't resist stopping at Moeraki, though, as I'd seen photos of their beach in every tourist shop I'd entered. I parked the van and jumped quickly out onto the boardwalk, camera at the ready.

The Moeraki boulders were an unusual, if not unique, natural phenomenon, and as spectacular in their own way as the towering cliffs of Milford Sound. The boulders were almost perfectly spherical and half-buried in the sand, some of them nearing eight or nine feet in diameter. Some were more heavily eroded than others, but from a distance they looked like a surprisingly unobtrusive work of modern art. They looked far to perfect to be the natural features that they actually were.

As always there were two differing stories that explained the phenomenon of the boulders: a scientific explanation, and a Maori legend. The scientists told us that these were septarian concretions, formed by calcite crystallizing around a small nucleus – such as a shell fragment, or a bone – while it lay it wet sediment. These deposits formed over four million years, with layer upon layer of calcite slowly growing into the spherical boulders that we saw today. As the mudstone cliffs gradually eroded, the boulders were released, and they rolled down onto the beach.

The Maori version was certainly more poetic, if significantly less scientific. According to local myth the boulders were the cargo of the great *waka* Arai Te Uru, and the features on this stretch of beach were the flax baskets that had washed ashore. Further along the coast there were a series of irregular boulders that represented the *kumara* that were also being shipped on the *waka*, and the reef that extended out to sea from Shag Point was the hull of the submerged boat. It made a direct connection between the land and their original migration to Aotearoa, simultaneously an admission of their settler status and a proprietary claim to their newfound country. This one myth succinctly summed up the historical status of the Maori in New Zealand, although there was no way that it could explain the warring and bloodshed that came with the arrival of the Europeans.

I snapped a few pictures with my camera, but resisted the urge to clamber on them, having seen a handwritten sign by the path pointing out that they were Maori *taonga*, and therefore sacred. I returned to the van with sand between my toes and some fresh air in my lungs, before resuming my own epic migration northwards.

* * *

My overnight stop in Oamaru was a forced one, the night closing in before I had the chance to push further north. As I checked into the campground I noticed that there were tours to see the nearby Yellow-eyed penguins, but having seen and heard them on the Otago peninsula I felt no urge to part with my little remaining cash. There were also tours to a Blue penguin colony, however, and my interest was immediately piqued. The Blue penguin was the smallest of the eighteen penguin species, more commonly known as the Little or Fairy penguin, and while they were common throughout New Zealand they were rarely seen. It seemed like a good chance to add one final notch to my wildlife tally, so I booked myself onto the tour and wolfed down a hurried supper before they arrived to collect me.

The colony itself had been open for public viewing since 1993, when local birdwatchers had set up the visitors' centre. They'd dug a total of two hundred wooden nesting boxes into the ground around the beach, and at the high point of the breeding season they now attracted up to four hundred penguins to this curious new housing development. The penguins formed 'rafts' offshore, large gatherings that grouped together for protection, and once the sun went down they began the mad dash for the safety of their burrows. The over-enthusiastic birdwatchers had even built a grandstand for spectators to view the main event, and we all huddled together against the cold as we waited for the evening commute to begin. We were firmly told that no photos were allowed, and that noise should be kept to a minimum. The only sound while we waited was the sound of our teeth chattering.

Then I spotted the first bobbing head among the rocks, a dark smear slowly moving across the darker background. Then there was another, and another, as the raft came warily ashore, their bodies hunched over to hide the white of their bellies in the moonlight. They hopped and waddled up to the gravel path that separated the beach from the burrows, and then they stopped. A crowd began to gather as they continued to swarm ashore, backing up when it hit the path. It was as if they could sense the purpose of this man-made track, and were wary of exposing themselves in an area so often frequented by humans. Eventually the wait became too much, and with a sudden burst of speed the front penguin dashed across the gravel, the others following his lead and waddling as fast as they could to the safety of the burrows, their heads down, beaks pushed forward as they raced for home. After this raft came another, and another, until after half an hour of watching I had to retreat into the visitors' centre to thaw out, my fingers numb despite my best attempts to thrust them into my pockets.

The following morning I took a lukewarm shower in the campground's basic facilities then hit the road again, eager to reach Christchurch with plenty of time to spare. A brief stop in Timaru allowed me to visit their excellent Aigantighe Art Gallery, which housed the entries from the 1990 international Stone Carving Symposium, held in nearby Maungati, and I wandered among them while I enjoyed a few breaths of fresh air. One in particular caught my eye, and wandering closer I saw that it was a depiction of the Maori gods of creation, Rangi and Papa, and two of their children: Tawhri Matea, the god of wind, and Tu-matauenga, the god of war. The artist, Dan de Har, was originally from Taupo and had now settled in Timaru, and the sculpture evoked a dynamic sense of movement and three-dimensional space. It was good to see the old myths translated into something so vibrant and modern.

I didn't hit the outskirts of Christchurch until the evening, and since the van didn't have to be returned until the following morning I had no reason to rush any more. There was one last person who I wanted to track down before I left the South Island, a friend from a previous job in this part of the world. They might be able to shed some final light on the Maori presence this far south.

When I'd first met Ripeka she'd been introduced to me as 'Bex', but I'd soon discovered that this moniker was out of convenience rather than choice. Many people seemed to struggle with her true Maori name, despite the fact that it was pronounced more or less as the English 'Rebecca', and she often settled for the abbreviated form to keep life simple. When we'd met we were working with several Australians, and I remembered being present when one of them asked her if the Maori had their own language. Her withering response spoke volumes for the levels of ignorance and misunderstanding that she had to put up with every day.

I'd quickly warmed to her, for despite being quiet on initial contact she'd opened up as soon as anyone showed a genuine interest. It was rather sad that she'd developed a sullen silence as a defence mechanism against intolerance and stupidity. She was indisputably Maori in appearance – her hair thick, black and very long, often worn up in a traditional bone comb – and she was rarely seen without some item of bone or jade jewellery about her person. She also had a large tattoo on one shoulder, although she seemed to go out of her way to cover it at times. She looked comfortable and proud of her heritage, and only occasionally did she withdraw into herself as a defence mechanism when she was among people who she didn't know.

We eventually managed to meet for a quick coffee the following morning, before I handed the van back. As always she impressed me with her sense of inner strength, even if her exterior sometimes bristled with indignation. As we chatted I asked her where she'd grown up, as I'd sensed before that Christchurch wasn't really her spiritual home.

'My mother's from here, but I grew up near Gisbourne. You seen the *Whale Rider* film?' I said that I had, glad to mention something other than the *Lord Of The Rings* for once. 'It's pretty much that area. It's odd watching the film, you know? Like being back home. That's a pretty good portrayal of what family life was like up there.'

As we sat chatting she mentioned that she was now part of a *haka* group that performed locally, as well as at events around the country. I probed a little further, and discovered that they'd actually performed on behalf of the Tall Blacks, the national basketball team. 'Some of the guys in the team were American, and they refused to do it. So they brought us in,' she told me witheringly. She had the Kiwi habit of going up at the end of sentences, so that every statement sounded like a question, but I could still detect the hint of scorn and disgust in her voice. Like many young Maori, she was angry and bitter about the treatment they sometimes received, but at heart she really wanted understanding and acceptance.

Reparations were now being made for the land and the rights that had been stolen over the early years of settlement, but there was still a division among the people themselves. Maori communities were often left to their own devices, and were seen by the white communities as being lazy, degenerate, or even criminal, as I'd seen during my stopover in Tauranga. For all the community centres and protected historical sites, there was a cultural divide that remained at the heart of Kiwi society. Nearly two hundred and fifty years after Cook's initial landing, there were still two nations occupying this one country.

I couldn't resist asking about the Ka Mate *haka* too, the infamous war dance that the All Blacks rugby team performed at the start of international matches. It was a controversial subject, as there had been recent calls for the performances to stop, due to a legal claim by the tribe that owned the cultural rights to the world's most famous *haka*. She just laughed and shook her head, as if she was used to foreigners asking this question. 'It doesn't belong to the rugby team, and it's an insult to the tribe every time it's performed. What do you think they should do?'

Ka Mate

    I eventually said goodbye to Bex with admiration and more than a little sympathy, before dropping the van off at the depot near the airport. I had a brief stop in Wellington overnight before my journey home began in earnest, but in truth that conversation in Christchurch was to be my abiding memory of leaving New Zealand. I had only scratched the surface of Maori culture during my time there – often distracted from my purpose by the scenery, the fine wines, and the thrilling sporting events – but I'd seen enough to know that there was still some way to go before the Maori finally reached an equal footing with the descendants of those first European settlers. But they were a proud race and I knew that, thanks to people like Ripeka, they were looking strong for the future.

    E noho rā Aotearoa.

Acknowledgements

Many thanks to Ian and Heather for their generosity, and to the people of New Zealand for their consistently warm welcome. You certainly live up to your reputation.

Thanks to Rory Maclean too, for the advice and encouragement.

And finally, as always, thank you to Hannah – my partner in every adventure.

About the Author

Dan Coxon has recently moved to the Pacific Northwest, having spent ten years living in Edinburgh, Scotland. He is the author of *Ka Mate: Travels in New Zealand* and *The Wee Book Of Scotland*, and he currently works as the Seattle Editor for CultureMob.com while also writing for a variety of music magazines and book review websites. His fiction has appeared in the anthology *Late-Night River Lights*, and in small press magazines and journals.

Dan is a member of the Pacific Northwest Writers Association and The Society of Authors, and is currently working on a series of short stories. He spends his spare time trying to leave the archaic pleasures of cricket behind him, while slowly falling in love with baseball.

Find more of his writing at www.dancoxon.com.

Printed in Great Britain
by Amazon